FREEDOM

FROM TRAUMA TO CONSCIOUS POWER

AWAKEN TO THE 16 TRUTHS

AIYAHLA LO'QTUS

Editing, design, distribution by Bublish
Published by Free Free Press

ISBN: 979-8-89989-088-8 (paperback)
ISBN: 979-8-89989-089-5 (hardcover)
ISBN: 979-8-89989-087-1 (eBook)

CONTENTS

Part 1: The Traumas

Part 2: In Between

Part 3: Questions of Freedom with Aiyahla

A Note of Care and Clarity

This book touches on themes including abuse, trauma, mental health challenges, and suicide. If any of these subjects are difficult for you, please read at your own pace and seek support if needed. These teachings are not a substitute for professional care. If you are experiencing distress or are at risk of harming yourself, please reach out to qualified professionals or trusted support services in your country.

In this book, when I refer to "women" and "men," I am speaking in relation to the biological sex they were born into. Please understand that this embraces all intersectionalities—all identities, orientations, and expressions of being. The language of feminine and masculine that I use points to energies within all of us. These teachings are for every Soul, beyond labels, because we are all Love, Light, and Creative Power.

Beloved Reader,

This book is my gift to humanity in honour of my beloved family, especially my daughter Violeta Lua, and the woman I once was, Yasmine, for her courage.

Here, I express my eternal gratitude to all my teachers and Soul family here on Earth in my journey from trauma to awakening to the sixteen truths of freedom—Clara, Ishka, Qala, Marcelo, Norma, Mauricio, Philippe, Dora, Reyesh, Andreia, Bobby, Patricia, Joana, Gabriela, Valeria, Sandy, Joan, Patrick, Ademilde, Nicolas, Simone, and our Free Free Family. You have taught me, guided me, held me, loved me, each of you in your own way, and I am here because, as with every mission, this is not mine alone. It is ours.

A special thank-you to my mother and father, who has now transitioned.

And thank-you to Christ for being my eternal guide, and to the Holy Mother, Mother Mary, Mother Earth and my council of the Sacred Feminine with the Mothers Kuan Yin, Lady Isis, Lady Portia, Lady Nada, Lady Sarah, Lady Tara, Lady Venus Kumara, the grandmother's of the Earth, and the masculine masters Buda, St. Germain, Melchizedek, and all the enlightened Ones for leading my way beside the beings of Viula, beings of the Violet Flame, angels, archangels, and my spiritual team.

This story will meet you exactly where you are at. However deep you are ready to receive it. We ask that you receive this gently, and through your own free will discern what is true for you within your heart. Your freedom is fully honoured.

With love,
Aiyahla Lo'Qtus

INTRODUCTION

On 10 October 2015, I gave birth to my daughter. After twenty-six hours of labour, I held her in my arms in a quiet room at Chelsea Hospital in London. The world around us dissolved. Time slowed. We were wrapped in a soft, sacred bubble of Love as she latched onto my breast for the first time. Then she looked into my eyes. I saw my own Soul for the first time. In that moment, something ancient stirred within me, something deeper than anything I had ever known. It was the first time I truly *knew* the meaning of Unconditional Love. Not as an idea, but as a living, breathing Presence.

During my pregnancy, I'd made a vow. Whatever happened to my mother that led her to die by suicide seven years before would stop with me. The ancestral pattern that seemed to haunt every woman in my family would end here. They had all been called mentally ill. Crazy. They had all been silenced. What I didn't understand yet was why. Back home in Brazil, my glamorous life as the editor of *Vogue* no longer fulfilled me. I had risen to a successful fashion career too early. At only 24, I started directing shoots with Gisele. Rihanna. Kim Kardashian. Naomi. On the outside, I had it all. But my high-society upbringing in Rio felt like nothing more than a golden cage. A place everyone wanted to enter, but only a few were invited. Like the aristocracies in other countries. Gilded, exclusive, but suffocating.

I was 29 when my daughter was born. My partner was 36. But he wasn't ready for the responsibilities of parenthood. From the beginning, it was a lonely journey. All my life I had tried to save my family. I grew up the perfect girl. Good grades. Ballet. Well-dressed. Catholic Mass every Sunday. Weekends in the mountains or on the beach with friends. No one knew what was happening behind closed doors. We hid behind polished appearances. We looked like the perfect family. But inside, we lived in chaos. I thought if I was perfect and followed the script every young girl gets to be accepted in society, somehow I could save my family from all that suffering. I always believed if I did everything right, and brought no extra problems to them, I would be able to hold my family together, show them a different way. Instead, I lost myself. The more I hid my pain, fear, and anxiety, the more vulnerable I became. The more I tried to be the good girl, the further I drifted from my true self. I didn't know it yet, but my daughter's birth was actually my rebirth and the birth of our mission. I had awakened my consciousness to higher dimensions of my Soul, but I didn't know it yet, when I first held my daughter in that Chelsea Hospital. I just knew everything was never going to be the same.

After my mother passed away when I was 21, I moved to London, where she was from. I spent the next seven years using my pain as fuel to grow my career. On the outside I was the image of an independent, successful woman. In reality, I was lost. Angry. Depressed. Each achievement gave me a splinter of happiness, then the hole inside me grew even wider. I was empty. Searching for Love outside of myself. From a partner, a job, friends, titles. Nothing seemed to be it. You can't hide from pain for long. It only grows. The more we hide, the more we suffocate. The trauma spreads. It becomes wider. More sensitive. More real. Harder to hide it away.

It was in the delivery room, of my daughter's birth, that a new way called me. In the next two years and a half I separated from her father, moved back to São Paulo, and everything changed. I remember attending the annual *Vogue* Ball and thinking, *What am I doing here?* I left after 30 minutes. In search of understanding, healing, answers during my pregnancy, I had started reading consciousness books and training in meditation and ancient tribal traditions. It was the beginning of a deep, spiritual journey that would change my life. I would also become a voracious student of the world and go on to complete a graduate program at Harvard in Social Justice. I would study Neuroscience, Psychodrama, Philosophy, Jungian Psychology as well as women's history, peace and security issues, law, and art.

When I moved back to Brazil, I had a big team at my creative studio and at *Vogue* I was promoted to Artistic Fashion Director. As I reached my 32nd birthday, and Violeta Lua, as my daughter is called, was almost three, I was earning money beyond what I could have ever imagined. As my daughter's sole provider, my work in fashion offered stability, security, and income. I hoped I could blend my two diverging worlds. But when I tried to weave a more awakened view into my work, questioning some of what was "*Vogue* Woman", my editor was not pleased. Disrupting the status quo didn't seem to be part of *Vogue*'s mission at the time. I kept pushing for a while, but eventually almost got fired.

With the fissure between my awakened view of reality and the limiting perspective of my career widening each day, I decided to create *Free Free*—a movement to help others liberate themselves from social conditioning, trauma, or any suffering, big or small, and the illusion of limitation. For reasons I didn't yet understand, I began by serving those in the most vulnerable spaces. I reached out to a friend who had worked with former prisoners and people living on the streets, asking if he could connect me with some organisations. I wanted to serve those most in need. Over the years, I had developed a methodology that wove together my background in fashion and art with meditation, neuroscience, psychodrama, consciousness practices—and I knew it had the power to change lives. It had changed my life. He suggested I focus on women who had experienced violence, as their numbers were rising and this methodology might resonate even more deeply with the feminine. Soon after, he introduced me to the director of the Gender Nucleus at the Department of Justice. A few weeks later, I walked into the Department of Justice in São Paulo wearing a polished, fashionable business look—after all, I was still a *Vogue* director—laptop in hand. I presented my proposal to the director, who listened with quiet intensity. The moment I finished, she looked at me and said, "Let's do a five-year official collaboration agreement." I was stunned and had no idea how I would pull it off. But without hesitation, I said. "Yes!"

Three months later I was teaching my first workshops. The first day was filled with forty authorities, judges, prosecutors, and commanders. The next day, I taught the same workshop to female victims of violence. It was my first time working with people that had endured abuse in unimaginable ways. But somehow they were leaving the workshops with a new light. I didn't fully understand how and why my methodology was so effective, but it was life changing beyond what I could explain. The truth is, my Soul was taking the lead.

This was the beginning of Free Free in 2018. The organisation has evolved into a global ecosystem with a mission to free all of humanity, all living beings, and Mother Earth—supporting individuals and institutions in creating lasting, sacred change through consciousness, creativity, and innovation. We work across dimensions of influence: from the most powerful spaces—governments, top universities, and global corporations—to the most tender and vulnerable—women's shelters, communities in need, poverty, victims of wars and places where hope is still learning to rise. Suddenly, I found myself standing before the Brazilian Congress, Davos, Cannes Lions, and SXSW, carrying the voice of the feminine into rooms once defined by external power alone. Awards flowed from *Forbes*, *Glamour*, and the United Nations, but what moved me most was the silent knowing that the light of *Free Free* had begun to travel the world. Today, it spans four continents, having directly supported more than 50,000 people and touched over 70 million hearts indirectly. Our collaborations with the Harvard African Centre, Cambridge University, the United Nations, and several Fortune 500 companies are living proof that consciousness and real world solutions can coexist. As I built *Free Free*, I was also freeing myself. Layer by layer, I underdressed the characters I learned to wear and began to rewrite, on a soul-deep level, the stories of my mother, my female ancestors, and my lineage.

The grief that once felt heavy turned into compassion; the anger into forgiveness; the shame into Love. It was a raw, courageous journey that helped me liberate myself in ways I could never have predicted when I originally said Yes to the mission of Free Free. My heart fully opened, and my Soul took the lead beyond my ego's identity.

In July 2025, I received the news that my father had a brain tumour. One week before, as if divinely orchestrated, I received my Soul Name, Aiyahla, in deep meditation. I also received guidance to write a book by the end of August. Something that seemed impossible as my daughter was in her summer holiday, but I said yes. As I supported my father's transition in the weeks after, I embraced Aiyahla, received The 16 Truths, and began to write. As Aiyahla, I no longer see our separateness. I see all beings united by the eternal flame of Truth and Love connected by the field of Oneness. I see life through the Eagle's Eye, rising above fear, I live my life in service to all beings in a state of pure bliss, magic, Love, abundance, fulfilment. A state I know we can all reach as we undress the characters we believe we are and open our hearts allowing our Soul to take the lead.

In this book, I share my life in its rawest form and describe the journey I took to reconnect with my true self and embody Aiyahla. Much of what I have been through might mirror your own life. Our traumas and sufferings might be different, they might seem bigger or smaller, and our nationalities or customs might not be the same, but none of this matters. In truth we are much more alike than our egos might want us to believe. We are Souls. We are one. I want my story to show you that transformation is possible no matter what challenges you might have faced in the past or might be facing now. What took me so many years to liberate, can be much quicker for you. The 16 Truths that were revealed to me are powerful keys. Codes. They can help accelerate your journey toward your Soul Being and True Freedom. If my efforts can help even one person, then my efforts will not have been in vain. I have learned that each of us vibrates with the many divine frequencies. We are much more than what we are lead to believe.

This story is our story.

In Part I, I am Yasmine. In Part II, I move between Yasmine and Aiyahla. And in Part III, I am Aiyahla.

Through every stage, we walk a single path—the path of guiding humanity back to Love. To do so, we must learn to understand abuse and trauma not through a linear lens of right and wrong, but through a deeper, circular view—one that moves beyond the consciousness of victim and persecutor. This is not a story of women against men or men against women. It is not about blame, nor about naming enemies. It is about dissolving the illusion of separation altogether.

This book will meet you where you are—as deeply as you allow it to. Each time you return to its pages, it will reveal a new truth, one that mirrors the frequency you are ready to receive. It carries many layers—of healing, remembrance, and awakening—and its medicine will reach you in perfect timing.

Much of what I share may sound magical, beyond what the rational mind can grasp. It is your choice to believe or not. My role is not to convince you, but to stand as a mirror of what is possible when we live from the heart and accept our inner Divinity.

It is about choosing to see through the Eagle's Eye—to rise above fear and duality—and to remember that Love is, and has always been, the ultimate Truth. When we return to that Truth, everything changes. We begin to live not in reaction, but in creation. We begin to live not for ourselves, but in service to all beings. In this space of higher consciousness, life reorganises itself into harmony. Abundance becomes natural. Fulfilment becomes effortless. Giving and receiving becomes a way of being. And the Soul, finally free to guide, remembers what it came here to do: to Love without condition, without division, without end.

Love is the feminine essence within every being.

Love is what reunites what has been separated.

We cannot be free until we return to it.

When we are free within, we free the world.

FREEDOM

Yasmine

In Between

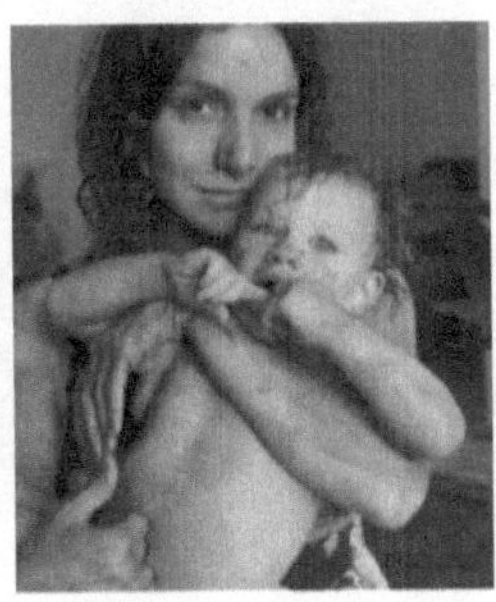

Aiyahla

This is our story.

HOW TO READ THIS BOOK

Beloved reader,

Before you begin, I lovingly invite you to understand the nature of the Sixteen Truths of Freedom, as they are the foundation through which this book unfolds.

The Sixteen Truths of Freedom are universal truths. They do not come from religion, culture, ideology, or the human mind. They arise from enlightened consciousness—from the unified field of intelligence often called Source, God, Goddess, Oneness, or the Creator.

These truths exist beyond ordinary human consciousness. They cannot be fully understood through logic, belief systems, or the five senses alone. They are not meant to be analysed, debated, or taken literally at the level of the lower mind. They are codes of liberation, designed to be received through presence, awareness, and inner knowing.

At the human level, we experience life through conditioning, trauma, memory, and survival patterns. This creates a partial and often distorted perception of reality. The Sixteen Truths operate from a higher octave of perception—beyond duality, blame, fear, and separation. They are not here to deny pain, injustice, or lived experience. They are here to liberate consciousness from the stories that keep us bound to suffering.

Some of these truths may feel confronting, paradoxical, or even triggering. This is natural. The lower mind seeks certainty, control, and linear explanations. These truths speak to the higher mind—the Eagle's Eye—the perspective that perceives reality beyond emotional reactivity and mental conditioning. So sometimes it might take some time to fully grasp the depth of each Truth. And this is ok. Don't pressure yourself.

They are not moral rules. They are not spiritual bypassing. They are not invitations to silence your pain in anyway. They are invitations to self-leadership, to reclaim your inner power, to transmute your traumas, and to return to Love as your natural state. They are codes that accelerate your freedom.

I now invite you to read this book through two perspectives.

The first is the human lens. As I share my life story, you will encounter my experiences as they were lived—through the body, the emotions, and the five senses. This is the realm of the human journey, where pain, joy, fear, love, loss, and becoming are real and valid.

The second is the conscious lens. As you read the story, you will also encounter the Sixteen Truths woven throughout. These are not meant to be interpreted through the five senses or the lower mind. They work beyond logic, beyond time, and beyond personal narrative.

For example, when you read a truth such as *"There is no one to blame,"* this is not an excuse for harm at the human level. Pain, abuse, and injustice are real experiences and must never be denied. Rather, this truth invites a higher understanding beyond duality—one that allows you to reclaim your inner power, and move beyond the blame. What comes next. The moment we hold blame, energetically we remain connected to the trauma, and the trauma doesn't fully heal, and it also unconsciously keeps us connected to the one who hurt us. These truths exist to help us move from the human story into spiritual liberation.

If at any point while reading you feel triggered, I gently invite you to pause. Take a deep breath. Ground yourself in the present moment.

This book is not asking you to relive your wounds. It is inviting you to lead yourself through them, transmute them, consciously and compassionately.

My story is not here to be followed. It is here to serve as a mirror, so that, through self-leadership, you may free yourself from your own experiences, in your own way, and at your own pace.

With love,
Aiyahla

THE SIXTEEN TRUTHS OF FREEDOM

1. **You have a direct connection to Source, God, Goddess, Oneness, the Creator,** as you are part of it. Therefore, you need no intermediaries, as in Presence, you find God within you.

2. **What you believe through your human senses is the lower mind's perspective of reality, not the Truth.** Discernment allows you to honour others' beliefs and limitations without feeling attacked or making judgements or assumptions that cause you suffering.

3. **Truth is Light, and Light is conscious awareness, true Knowledge, and Clarity,** known through the Eagle's Eye, the higher mind, and rarely understood by human logic, or your lower mind.

4. **You are Love.** Live life and make decisions through Love, not fear, since Love is the only truth. Love reunites what fear has fragmented and distorted into further separation.

5. **You are a Powerful Creator.** Every thought, emotion, imagination, and action creates your reality, as you are God within. Your creation is the fruit of your level of frequency.

6. **You are already whole and never alone.** We are interconnected beings, connected to the field of Oneness, anything else is an illusion of separation.

7. **Know you are as worthy and significant as every other being.** Having self-esteem gives you Clarity and grounds you in Love, the only true protection you need.

8. **Trauma creates distortions and addictions,** forming loops that are not true based on a memory. Even if they feel real, they are not in the now. When you acknowledge this, you start having Clarity to heal these patterns through Love.

9. **The feminine is Love, creative, giving and receiving. The masculine is Light, wisdom, planning and action.** Everything else is a traumatic distortion that needs Light and Love.

10. **Judgement is a defence mechanism. Transform it into compassion.** Judgement distorts your vision and creates karma. Compassion aligns you with Divine Justice, restoring balance through Love, not fear.

11. **Forgive everyone and yourself. No matter what has happened, you have no one to blame.** Forgiveness dissolves karmic loops and liberates you from the victim story, returning you to your inner power and true essence: freedom.

12. **Trust that everything is unfolding for your highest good.** Keep your heart open, be grateful, and allow the magic to reveal itself.

13. **Stop predicting your future based on your past. The only moment that truly exists is the eternal now.** Trying to predict the future keeps you bound to old beliefs and closes the door to miracles and the quantum field of limitless possibilities.

14. **Release attachment to external power.** True power lives within, and it is your creative force, the artist within you.

15. **Surrender in eternal gratitude and let go of controlling outcomes.** Control is an illusion; when you surrender and become grateful, you align your life with your highest potential and Soul Truth.

16. **Always use your gifts to serve others.** When service is for the greater good, not just personal gain, abundance flows. Integrity is what aligns your gifts with your eternal flame.

PART 1
THE TRAUMAS

In this part, I share my story as Yasmine—the pains, the traumas, the feelings I carried then. Yet alongside these memories, I weave in the compassionate view I did not have at that time: the vision of my higher mind, the wisdom and Love of my Soul.

CHAPTER 1

HOW IT BEGAN

The church was made of glass. At six in the evening, the last glow of daylight spilled through its round walls before surrendering to night. It was January 2008, and I was twenty-one years old, sitting at the seven-day Memorial Mass for my mother's passing. Only one church in Rio had agreed to hold it because she had died by suicide. A brave priest took the risk and made it happen.

I sat there, breath tight in my chest, knowing my mother's story was being devoured by every newspaper in the city, all blaming my father for her decision. To them, we were a headline: a beautiful, forty-two-year-old woman from Rio's high society who had broken one of the greatest taboos. To me, she was my mother, my family. But to the papers, our pain was just another story to sell.

My loving, beautiful mother.

Six months earlier, our family had already suffered one of our biggest traumas. My father and his colleagues had been taken to prison, apparently as revenge by a business partner. This shattered our family.

Now, I sat inside that glass church, wondering, *How can people lie so easily about a wound this deep? How can they play with our feelings as if we were nothing?*

I didn't know it yet, but that day was the beginning. The moment I would glimpse a Truth I would only come to understand years later: that what I was living was not the whole truth, only one layer of reality, a perspective. A story created by our human senses. Not the truth.

But during the ceremony, I—the shy, perfect girl I used to be, who lived by the rules of society—was taken to the stage of the church, where I used my voice in honour of the feminine and Truth for the first time. My hands were damp. My heart pounded against my ribs, each beat echoing in my ears like a drum in an empty hall.

I wasn't prepared to speak, yet something inside me was building a pressure, a Knowing, as if the words were already there, waiting to move through my lips.

More than four hundred people of the most elite circle of Rio were watching as I honoured my mother's passing and my father's dignity, teaching one of the most valuable things you will come to learn in our story (when I say *our*, I mean the unity of my ego and me, my Soul's higher consciousness). In that moment, a higher consciousness opened my heart and mind, and I felt no fear, only a sense of Clarity I had never experienced before.

It was then I felt *her*. A quiet, steady warmth at my front, like sunlight breaking through stained glass. A presence that made me calm, at peace. I didn't know it at the time, but I was not standing there alone. It was the first time I had a inner vision of our beloved Mother Mary beholding my mother. I spoke with such Clarity, Love, and humbleness, as if I was being guided by a higher power that was not me.

"In the days after my mother passed away, the media has lied about our family. My father is not to blame, nor my mother. She chose to go. Don't cry. My mother felt no pain. When she jumped, she was received up in the air by Mother Mary and the angels and archangels, infused in Love."

I was born into both luxury and chaos. On my father's side, my grandfather was the family patriarch. He was a sophisticated Jewish Romanian refugee who fled Europe after the wars and the rise of Communism. The Communist government took everything our family owned in Romania, and my grandfather left the country with a few diamonds in his teeth to survive the first few years in Paris. Then he went to Rio. In Rio, he rebuilt his life from nothing, becoming a successful businessman and marrying a Brazilian Catholic woman.

On my mother's side, my grandfather was an English-Scottish immigrant who also married a Brazilian Catholic woman, who we later discovered had aristocratic roots.

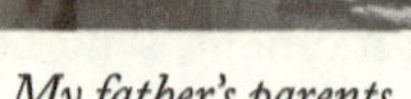

My father's parents.

My mother's parents.

Both sides of my family carried deep, unhealed wounds—scars of war, migration, loss, abuse, and silence. This ancestral trauma quietly shaped the home I was born into and the patterns I would one day be called to break. This was the soil where my first unconscious wounds took root—wounds that would later become portals for my deepest transformation and the medicine for our service here on Earth.

Far from the image most people hold of Rio, the city I was born in is full of contradictions. From the outside, it appears to be the city of Carnival, beaches, and beauty, but this is only a mask, a character, hiding what lies beneath. Behind the bright colours and the bossa nova and samba music lies a deeply traditional, religious culture, where the wounded masculine, most often present in men, feels entitled to control and overpower the wounded feminine, most often present in women (though both the masculine and the feminine are part of all beings).

This dynamic is the effect of duality, what we call *separation consciousness*, where we come to believe we are not part of the whole but divided—divided between men and women, social classes, races, sexuality, nationalities, human beings and nature, and so on. This division wounds men, women, children, and all living beings, as well as our Divine Mother Earth. This was the dynamic that shaped my upbringing, and as you will come to see, it also shapes humanity and the world at large. This dynamic is the source of all traumas we all experience here on Earth.

Perspective and Truth

Before I continue our story, we need to understand that, in the human experience, everything we believe is true or real is simply a perspective. Everything we see, hear, or feel through our human senses is only a fragment of reality, not the ultimate Truth. This perspective is limited as if we are wearing horse blinkers, but in truth there is so much more. What we perceive through our human senses is only 10% of everything there is. When we live from the ego—the limited, linear, self-centred part of us where our memories are stored and where our personality first takes shape before we remember who we truly are—we can only interpret life through this narrow lens. From this view, every experience is filtered through the past and projected into the future, always in service of one thing: survival. The Soul, however, sees from the infinite, circular perspective of the present moment. From this higher perspective, Truth is understood in a circular way, from every angle, so that no shadows darken any part of it and nothing remains hidden; therefore, there is only Light. There is no judgement, only Love. No fear, just Trust. A Knowing that is beyond time and space. It is eternal.

Take, for example, a woman wearing a tiny bikini on Ipanema Beach in Rio. One person might see this as liberation; another might see it as objectification. Are any of these interpretations true? Or can we call them a perspective? Now take a woman wearing a hijab in the Middle East. Some will see it as suffocating, while others will see it as freedom. Both perceptions may hold fragments of reality, yet the ultimate Truth can only be seen through what I call the *Eagle's Eye*, the Soul's higher consciousness that rises above judgement and illusion into the circular view of Love. Our human senses—veiled by the beliefs inherited from culture, upbringing, traumas, and ancestral memory—cannot grasp this wider view. The Eagle's Eye is pure awareness. It is spacious, compassionate, and rooted in Love. The moment we form an opinion through the filters of our senses, a distortion is created that controls the perspective we live from and the survival mechanisms we use to protect us. We descend into the limited, linear perspective of the ego, our lower mind, which reveals more about our own unconscious wounds and hidden memories than about the person or experience we are judging. This is why so many people can interpret the same experiences in multiple versions and all of them seem true. But in truth, they are simply fragments from Light, confused by shadows. True knowledge can only be seen by our higher mind.

The human experience is, in many ways, an experience of illusions, until we open our hearts and start awakening. We start shifting from the obsession of doing and having, from the survival mechanisms of the ego, and from forever trying to control every outcome of how our life should be and start moving into the Truth of Presence. Truth can only be found in the present moment. It does not live in our interpretations of or attachments to the past or in our predictions of the future. Whenever we form an opinion rooted in what has occurred, we lose touch with our Soul Nature, our Divine Presence, and allow our ego to take the lead.

We are not our profession, surname, body, clothes, nationality, or even our culture. These belong to the personality, the characters we play in this drama called life. This personality can be led by the ego, with its unconscious fears, memories, and inherited beliefs, or once healed, awakened, freed, we can be led by the Soul, the eternal, creative, loving, light essence of who we truly are. This is why, when people start awakening to a higher Truth of who they are, their personality also starts shifting. As our consciousness expands, we begin to remember the truth of Oneness—that we are infinite, interconnected beings, inseparable from all that exists. As this remembrance deepens, the ego begins to feel safe and slowly releases its grip. The ego is not our enemy; it is a part of us that longs to be loved. When we stop judging the ego and embrace it with Love, it feels safe enough to let go.

Yet, like any survival mechanism, the ego does not surrender easily. As we awaken, it resists—whispering fears, weaving illusions, and conjuring worst-case scenarios of what might happen if we let go of control. This is why the path to freedom requires courage. Many pause, step back, or even turn away for a time. But eventually, the call of the Soul becomes stronger than the voice of fear, and we begin to trust again.

It takes immense inner strength to keep saying yes. Yet there is no greater devotion, no more sacred use of your time and energy. The journey to freedom is not a battle with the ego, but a softening—an embrace. When we meet the ego with Love rather than resistance, its fear calms, its grip loosens, and it finally allows the Soul to lead our life on Earth. This is where true freedom begins.

The sixteen truths I revealed are not concepts, but transmissions, codes—truths from my Soul, received as sacred keys along my own journey from trauma to freedom.

My Childhood

From a very young age, my home was filled with turmoil. My parents were constantly fighting. Voices were raised, doors were slammed, and the air was thick with tension. They would break apart, then come back together, as if love and war were the only language they knew. They were in trauma. Doing the best they could with the tools they had. Yet to the outside world, we looked like the perfect family—smiling in Christmas cards, sophisticatedly dressed, performing harmony for the eyes of society trying to feel safe, accepted. Trying to create the illusion of normal.

One of our Christmas card pictures.

Every few years we moved to a new house, carrying the hope that a fresh space might mend old wounds. But no matter where we went, the instability followed us—sinking into the walls, into our bodies, into me. We cannot run away from pain. It doesn't solve anything. In fact, it does the opposite. When we run instead of embracing, acknowledging, and leaning into it, the pain grows. It deepens. It hides in the more obscure corners of our being. And the further it buries itself, the harder it becomes to dissolve, to heal. This was the cycle that kept repeating within our family.

I was shy, fragile, afraid of the storms that erupted around me. My breath often caught in my chest, as if even the air was too heavy to trust. Severe asthma attacks sent me to hospital almost every week. Allergies erupted and my skin broke out—my body kept crying out the words I could not speak and the emotions I couldn't understand.

When I was four, my immune system was so weak, and an infection that began in my throat spread down into my legs, leaving me unable to walk. One night, I dragged myself across the floor into my parents' room, crying in terror, convinced I would never walk again. Soon after, I was admitted to hospital, where I stayed for two long months while the infection slowly subsided. That day, my father went to the Monastery of St. Benedict and made a promise to make a weekly visit to express his eternal gratitude if I recovered in full—a promise he fulfilled until the end.

The days blurred together under the harsh fluorescent lights and the sharp smell of hospital. The medication was so strong that, eventually, the tiny veins in my arms could no longer hold it. The doctors had to insert the IV into my feet. The pain was unbearable. I would scream and sob, clutching my soft, worn elephant to my chest, the only comfort I had as they held me down for treatment. When the ordeal finally ended, I faced my first surgery. My tonsils were removed in the hope of preventing future infections. I was only four, yet my body already knew what it was to suffer, to fight, and to survive.

A couple of years later, I experienced an outbreak of warts across my entire body, something no conventional doctor could explain. My mother went from doctor to doctor, desperately searching for a solution. Some wanted to burn them off, which meant burning almost my entire body. Others suggested surgery. Finally, she found a homeopathic doctor who seemed to understand the deeper Truth of what was happening. In just three weeks, with nothing more than an herbal cream, and a homeopathic treatment, the warts were gone. From that moment until the day my mother passed away, this doctor became the only one my mother trusted with my care.

My inner suffering, silenced by the fear of speaking up, had found its way to the surface. Like with so many illnesses that arise from within, my body began expressing what I was holding within myself.

At school, I felt deeply ashamed. The warts and my parents' separations made me feel fragile, different, unbearably alone. I compared myself endlessly to my friends, imagining that they all belonged to the kind of happy, "normal" families I only saw in fairytales, believing those were the norm and mine was the wrong one.

As children, we do not yet have the capacity to bring Presence to suffering. Without conscious awareness of the deeper Truth, every experience is taken at face value, absorbed directly through our five senses and imprinted onto our spiritual, mental, emotional, and physical bodies. This is why a single harsh word from a friend, a fall in the park, or even the smallest expression of anger can become a trauma that forms a belief that limits us and shapes our lives until we are able to dissolve it through Presence.

Trauma is not the external event itself; it is the way the bodies holds and responds to that event. It is the wound formed from the story—the perspective—we created in that moment, the internalised memory of how we perceived the experience. But it is not Truth itself.

Until about the age of seven, children's brainwaves remain predominantly in the slower delta, theta, and alpha states—the same states we enter during deep meditation or just before sleep. In this receptive state, the subconscious mind is wide open, absorbing and recording everything it perceives as truth. These early imprints become the soil in which core beliefs and emotional patterns take root, eventually shaping the sense of self we later come to call the ego.

We all experience life through the filters and distortions of our belief system, until we are able to free ourselves from all beliefs that limits us or carry fear. These beliefs are not stored only in the mind; they live across all of our bodies—spiritual, mental, emotional, and physical. The spiritual body, the most expansive of them all, carries ancestral imprints as well as memories from other lifetimes. Whatever is held there ripples inwards, influencing the mental, emotional, and physical layers, shaping the lens through which we experience reality.

In my own life, the unspoken pain of my ancestors, combined with the chaos at home, echoed through every part of me. What lived in my spiritual body seeped into my mind, my emotions, and even my physical health, quietly shaping the way I saw myself and the world. One of the deepest imprints I carried was the belief that I was insignificant. Later, I understood insignificance to be one of the deepest pains humanity carries, because it cuts at the very root of our existence—our need to feel that our life matters.

If your ego unconsciously holds the belief that you are insignificant, you may find yourself constantly seeking external validation to prove your worth. Perhaps you try to speak at any cost in situations where you feel invisible. Or you hide from the world so no one can notice you. Or when someone criticises you, the pain feels unbearable—not because their words define you, but because they awaken the open wound of insignificance within. Does this sound familiar?

I remember this so vividly in my own life. As a child, moving from house to house, carrying my illnesses and the silence of what I couldn't say, I often felt invisible. Later, in school and even as a young woman in the fashion world, I would push myself to be noticed, to prove I had value. Every piece of criticism felt like a knife, not because it was the Truth, but because it pressed against the wound of insignificance that I was carrying inside.

Yet as we now know, Truth can only be seen through the Eagle's Eye, the higher awareness that knows through Love, never through fear. A simple way to discern whether what you are experiencing is Truth or illusion is to pause and ask yourself, *Is fear present?* Fear disguises itself in many forms: anger, control, perfectionism, people-pleasing, withdrawal, jealousy, shame, defensiveness, victimhood, manipulation, blame, or even the numbing patterns we create to avoid suffering. If fear is present, the experience belongs to the perception of your human senses, shaped by a memory that carries that pain. It may feel real, but it is not the Truth of your Soul. And it can shift the very moment you recognise it, as you bring Light—meaning understanding, acknowledgment, wisdom, Presence—to the experience and wrap it in Love.

You can begin gently challenging these beliefs with a simple practice: Each time the thought arises, pause and tell yourself, *This is not true.* I often share this practice in my workshops, and it has helped thousands return to Presence in an instant. The moment you question a fear, even for an instant, you interrupt the vicious thought loops of the lower mind. By bringing conscious awareness to the thought that created the negative emotion, you create space for your Soul to speak through your heart. The moment you are present, you allow Presence, your divine connection to Source, to nurture you.

The illusion of insignificance, or lack of self-esteem, is one of humanity's deepest wounds. It makes us forget our inherent worth, our wholeness, and the Truth that Love already lives within us—never dependent on anything external. Regardless of what we believe about ourselves, or how we perceive ourselves to be, we are always connected to Source. We are God within. We are always worthy and significant, independent of what we have done or not done. We simply are.

Yet when we feel unseen, unlovable, or unheard, we begin seeking validation outside ourselves, creating cycles of fear, comparison, and suffering. These cycles often repeat in our relationships with partners, children, parents, friends, and even colleagues—and they can so easily become abusive or toxic. When that external validation is withdrawn or weakens, it reinforces the illusion that we do not matter, pulling us deeper into the ego's narrative. Healing this wound or beliefs like this one, has the power to transform our entire experience of life. This is what I call the freedom journey. We can only truly be free when we free ourselves within—and then use our gifts to free the world. (This is something you will understand more deeply as our story unfolds.)

This is also why so many teenagers today are easily manipulated online by extremist groups. Without self-esteem, they become easy prey. Tools such as critical thinking are important especially if combined with self-esteem practices, because a young person often lacks the confidence to make decisions free from the distortion of trauma. One of our deepest human needs is to feel we belong. When we grow up in chaotic households, suffer bullying at school, or carry the shyness of feeling invisible, we may unconsciously seek belonging at any cost. This is how extremist groups, political movements, or even armies recruit young people—by exploiting their deepest need to belong. Without the emotional maturity to discern between true community and manipulation, between truth and false information, many are pulled into cycles that feel like acceptance but are, in fact, control. If you are a parent reading this book, look at your children and notice how they esteem themselves, and then look at yourself. How do you esteem yourself? Our children normally mirror our own insecurities. This is why when we have the courage to start our freedom journey and free ourselves, we are giving our children the greatest gift. We are freeing them as well. When we free ourselves we free seven generations of our ancestors and seven generations of our descendants. This is the power you have when you say yes to your freedom.

I believed I was insignificant growing up and though I was safe from social media at the time, I still had the challenge of confronting the judgements from school friends and society. The lack of self-esteem I felt—passed down through generations of unhealed trauma—quietly shaped my childhood and my sense of self. I remember being in school, sitting in the classroom and feeling so small, so different from the other children. My skin showed my illnesses, my breath was shallow, and I compared myself endlessly to the girls who seemed happy—running around, whole, stylish, and untouched by suffering. I would dream of having a stable, loving, safe family like theirs, even if that was an illusion, while I carried the silent chaos of my own. In those moments, that insignificance trauma whispered the illusion I was alone.

CHAPTER 2

THE MYTH OF THE PERFECT GIRL

At twelve, I started dreaming about having a boyfriend, convinced that being chosen would make me feel that I belonged. Like the fairytales and films I loved, I carried the belief that a romantic relationship could rescue me, soothe me, and solve everything I didn't know how to name. At home, I didn't feel fully seen or loved, and without realising it, I was already learning to search for the love I lacked in places that couldn't give it to me. We all do this until we heal.

My parents were young, overwhelmed, and carrying their own unspoken traumas—so different from the movies where couples were madly in love and families were warm, stable, and whole. I would watch romantic comedies for hours, and a school I would observe the older girls who already had boyfriends, absorbing every detail. There was one couple, both fourteen, who walked hand in hand through the corridors every day. I remember watching them and thinking, *In two years, I will be old enough to be like them—happy, loved, seen, significant.* I built an entire fantasy of who I would become once I finally found romantic love. I believed it would fix the emptiness I felt inside, fill the cracks, and give me the Love I was so desperately craving. I didn't yet understand that when a child doesn't feel seen or held at home, the heart goes searching for a substitute—a saviour, a mirror, a place to land. I probably don't even need to tell you how this turned out. You can already imagine how this innocent longing grew into a loop of unstable relationships built on unstable attachments—the same wound repeating itself in different bodies, different faces, different stories.

This is part of the myth of the perfect girl: the belief that love will arrive from the outside and finally make us whole. Many of us inherit this myth long before we realise it—from the stories we are told as children, from the films we watch, from the unspoken beliefs we absorb at home, from our culture, from our religion. The truth is that when we seek love outside ourselves without first knowing that we *are* Love, we build relationships on the shaky ground of need rather than freedom. Instead of healing our wounds, this often deepens them, because every relationship becomes a mirror reflecting what we have not yet resolved within.

My idealised version of love was simply a reaction to the challenges I was experiencing at home. My parents' marriage continued with its familiar rhythm of ups and downs. My mother was one of the most beautiful women in Rio—but her beauty was never what defined her. She was kind, sophisticated, authentic, and uninterested in the politics of belonging to high society. She did not care about being accepted into certain circles in the way my father did, and even as a child I could sense the tension between who she was and who she was expected to be.

My parents young Love, before the ego's wounds started to cloud the vision.

My father was constantly seeking external validation, wanting to be seen as a great figure in society. Driven by unhealed traumas, he craved attention through expensive cars, trips to fashionable places, country clubs, and horses. Beneath it all was a fear of not being enough—a quiet, relentless ache he never knew how to name. His lack of self-love pulled him into addictive patterns, spending far more than he could afford just to keep receiving the false praise that briefly numbed the emptiness within. What he didn't yet know was that the worth he was searching for was already alive inside him. But when the external world becomes your mirror, you become enslaved to its reflection. The ups and downs of his finances—and his fear of losing that external validation—created deep instability in our home. The more insignificant he felt inside, the more he tried to reclaim a sense of false power through unconscious control and jealousy over my mother. It was his wounded inner child trying to survive, but as children, we don't see this. We simply absorb the chaos.

This wasn't just my parents' story, it was humanity's story, playing out in our living room. This is what happens when we mistake external validation for Love. The ego searches outside itself for recognition, thinking worth is something to be earned or proven. But true Love, true worth, can never be given or taken away by others; it has always lived, and will always live, within us. However, sometimes it goes unrecognised because it is submerged by the sticky layers of our traumas. Until we awaken to the Truth that we are Love, we remain trapped in cycles of fear, control, and longing, repeating the same wounds across generations.

As a young woman, I couldn't see this. All I felt was the instability, the chaos, the fear. My father's constant search for worth outside himself mirrored and magnified my own wound of insignificance. I learned to believe that love had to be earned, that my value was dependent upon how others saw me. His story became the lens through which I began to see my own.

My mother met my father when she was twenty and he was twenty-nine. She was carrying a deeply traumatic background, marked by coldness and loss. As a young girl, she had been taken away from her own mother to live with her father, under the claim that both her mother and grandmother were mentally ill.

This is where their story began.

Her father remarried a wounded woman who, after a car accident left her paraplegic, became extremely bitter and angry due to the trauma. My grandfather's English roots—shaped by a family that rarely hugged and that sent him to boarding school at an early age—combined with the guilt of the accident, made their home an austere environment. My mother grew up walking on eggshells, enduring unconscious attacks from her stepmother, who resented her, while being ignored by her father. She was hardly hugged, hardly heard, "I love you." She saw her own mother only in small doses, always under the shadow of the story that she was "mentally ill" and "not a good mother."

But, as we now know, that was only a perspective—not the Truth. This is what so often happens in families: the stories we are told about others, especially our parents, become distortions we absorb as children. These imprints settle inside us as if they were facts, quietly shaping the way we see ourselves and the world. They influence how we love, how we trust, how we protect ourselves, and how we interpret reality. And they remain there—unquestioned—until we are old enough, and have the emotional maturity and courage, to awaken and begin unravelling them. To question them. To acknowledge them. To bring love to them. Only then can we see our parents, and ourselves, through a clearer, more compassionate lens.

At the time, and still today, many women face the challenge of being labelled mentally ill when they don't conform to traditions, when they are ahead of their time, or when they carry a deep sensitivity to the mysteries of nature. In these cases, it is still common for the woman to lose custody of her children, an experience that becomes profoundly painful for everyone involved, but especially for the mother and the children. In fact, one of the most common tactics unconscious angry men use in courtrooms to hurt women during custody battles is labelling them as "crazy." In the United States, two-thirds of mothers in custody disputes were dismissed as mentally unwell and consequently lost their cases, even when abuse allegations were substantiated (ProPublica, 2023). This is a way of silencing women or holding them within a marriage. The justice system today, in many ways, silences women, as most systems were built for and by unconscious men. Even car seat belts are designed using male crash-test dummies, and studies show that women are 47 percent more likely to be seriously injured in a car crash (University of Virginia, 2019; *The Guardian*, 2019).

The Wounded Feminine

We later came to understand that the wounded feminine—present in both men and women—often expresses itself through victim consciousness, passiveness, manipulation, envy, and competitiveness.

Among women, this can create unconscious attacks against one another, a dynamic rooted in something called *linked fate* (Johnson-Freese). Linked fate is the unconscious belief that a woman's worth, safety, and acceptance depend on men—a belief carried for centuries and embedded deep in the collective psyche. Men, on the other hand, have long felt their fates tied to other men: their status, survival, and sense of belonging shaped by male approval and male hierarchy. These patterns are ancient, inherited, and rarely questioned, yet they quietly shape many of our relationships. We will expand more on this later, but for now, simply know that these unconscious dynamics operate beneath the surface of our interactions—influencing how we relate, react, and understand one another, often without realising why.

As you can see, my mother, my grandmother, and even my mother's stepmother were all caught in their wounded feminine. Their perspectives and experiences of reality were distorted through this lens. Their egos would take the position of victim, passively or competitively, rather than expressing the Truth of their Souls. And the Truth is we are all Love. Victim consciousness, however, makes us believe that everything is happening *against* us, and when we take no responsibility for our experiences, we project, blame, and collapse into passivity. Perhaps this is how my mother's stepmother felt towards her or towards my grandfather for the accident. Or how my mother felt abandoned by her own mother. Does this sound familiar? Without the perspective of the higher mind—what we call the Eagle's Eye—we remain bound by the blinkers of the lower mind. From that place, our view is narrow, reactive, and shaped by assumptions that are not the full story. Only when we rise above the immediate perception can we see the Truth: that everyone is acting from their own wounds, their own history, their own unhealed pain.

When we are in our wounded feminine or masculine, the perspective we live life from becomes clouded by memories that lower our frequency, and we attract the exact experience that will help us learn to empower our path towards true liberation. The universe always brings us the best experience to help us evolve. Even if something feels hurtful on a human level, we must hold a deep Knowing that—despite whatever it appears to be, and even if we do not understand it at the time—the experience is helping us evolve by bringing Light to aspects of ourselves that are hidden, fragmented, or unconscious, lingering in the shadow of our subconscious.

Darkness is simply the absence of light. As Plato illustrates in his *Allegory of the Cave*, we mistake the shadows on the wall for reality, until we step outside and see the Light for what it truly is. Yet most people, like the prisoners in the cave, fear the Light. They prefer the comfort of illusion over the courage it takes to free themselves and step into the unknown. This is the same dynamic between the ego and the Soul: The ego clings to the shadows it knows, while the Soul is always calling us towards the Light of Truth and back to our hearts.

In Truth, the level of consciousness my mother carried as a young woman naturally drew to her a man who was also living in his wounded masculine. Both of them were unconsciously seeking healing. Both were being called to reclaim their authentic power by mirroring each other's unhealed pains. But to do this, we need to hold the keys and tools, we are sharing with you now. Keys and tools they did not have. Over time, we came to understand that we always attract the vibration we emit—nothing more, nothing less. If there is any level of fear in our field, we inevitably attract experiences that reflect that fear back to us, not as punishment, but as an invitation. An invitation to lean in, to transmute the pain, and to dissolve it with Love and Light rather than running away.

This is why there is no one to blame for the experiences we live. The moment we enter the blame game, we sink deeper into the separation consciousness of the ego, seeing life through the lens of duality rather than through the Oneness that is our true nature. This is not about excusing harm or suggesting that abuse is ever acceptable. It is about understanding the roots of suffering so that we can break the cycle—within ourselves, within our relationships, and within the generations that follow.

Separation consciousness breeds the quiet suffering of loneliness and emptiness, the feeling that something essential is missing. But what we long for is never outside of us. It is the reconnection with Source, the very field from which we all source from. This is what we call God. The Field of Life. In truth, nothing is separate; even the voids that seem to have nothing are part of the web that forms the whole. Blame takes us deeper into emptiness, further from the Eagle's Eye, locking us into the illusions of the human senses, the narrow lens that we have already seen is not Truth, but a distorted fragment of reality.

The Wounded Masculine and the State of the World Today

As we can see through both current and past world events, humanity has long been led by the wounded masculine overpowering the wounded feminine, the same dynamics I experienced inside my own home. Later in life, I came to understand these parallels even more deeply through my studies in the Women, Peace, and Security program at Harvard, which I will share with you in future chapters.

For now, it is important to understand that the wounded masculine can manifest as violence, control, oppression, what we often refer to as hurt egos, and an obsession with external power—money, property, status, influence. It can also appear in far more subtle ways: the closing of the heart, emotional numbness, coldness, insensitivity, or addictive behaviours. Whether through sex, possessions, work, or status, these patterns are driven by a desperate attempt to grasp quick highs of pleasure or recognition, mistaking them for what is truly needed: Love.

I saw this dynamic play out in my own father's search for validation through wealth, possessions, and status, patterns that not only destabilised our home but mirrored the very wounds driving much of the world today. Both the wounded masculine and feminine are distortions of our true essence. They are not who we are; they are patterns humanity has carried for centuries as a reflection of duality and separation consciousness. This is where healing begins, by recognising these wounds not only in our parents, partners, or leaders, but within ourselves. For we all carry both the masculine and the feminine within us, and until they are brought back into balance, the same patterns of pain will continue to play out in our homes, our relationships, our societies, and our world. When these wounds remain unhealed, they close the heart. When the heart is closed, the Soul's natural longing for Love gets distorted into substitutes—quick highs that mimic Love but never truly satisfy because they are illusions.

Pleasure and status might feel like glimpses of Love, but they are only false highs—brief surges of dopamine that quickly fade. As humans, we are wired to seek Love as a means of survival, so when our hearts are closed, we confuse these fleeting moments of pleasure with the real thing—a Love that has nothing to do with romance. Love, beloved one, is a frequency. This search for false highs is often a coping mechanism for unprocessed trauma. When the heart is closed, the Soul's longing for Love becomes distorted into attachment—to a substance, a behaviour, a thing, or even a person. This is why it can express itself through eating disorders, alcoholism, drug abuse, social media, shopping, workaholism, nationalism, extremist spirituality, violence, abuse, or other addictive patterns. The fear of losing that one thing or that one person we believe gives us Love (or the illusion of significance)—even when it is only the illusion of Love, becomes desperation.

This is how my father reacted every time my mother had a moment of Clarity, intuited that something was wrong, and asked for a divorce. He would unconsciously do anything to keep her in the marriage. Over time, patrimonial violence, psychological violence, and infidelity became the norm. His way of coping with his loss of inner power. He did not see it as violence. Many of us don't. We normalise violence as something casual, acceptable, or simply "how things are." We often don't even understand the true meaning of violence. In essence, violence is any action, word, or silence that suppresses another's freedom, dignity, or truth—whether through force, fear, manipulation, control, or neglect. It is the absence of Love expressed through behaviour. It is the wounded ego trying to protect itself. It is separation consciousness in motion.

Patrimonial violence occurs when financial resources are used as a weapon to manipulate, punish, or restrict another person's freedom. Psychological violence is even more insidious; it hides in words, in silence, in veiled threats, and in subtle manipulations that slowly erode a someone's sense of self. It gaslights reality, making one doubt their own sanity, keeping them trapped in cycles of fear, confusion, and dependence.

These forms of violence, like physical and sexual violence, are not always visible from the outside, yet they are among the most damaging. They do not only wound the body or the mind; they sever someone from her inner power, their voice, and their Truth. Fostering an environment where one unconsciously disconnect from their Soul as violation triggers the closing of the heart. Have you ever doubted your own reality because someone else's version of events sounded louder than your intuition?

Each time my mother tried to leave, my father painted her as "crazy." It was not only a way to shield himself from the shame of appearing unworthy or unloved in the eyes of others and of himself, but it was also an unconscious strategy to pull her back. He loved her deeply and, even more, was attached to the idea of them—so much so that the thought of losing her sent his ego into deep survival mode. My mother was haunted by the fear of becoming her own mother. That fear, of being labelled "crazy," of losing herself and her children entirely, pulled her back into the marriage each time she tried to leave. Slowly, she drifted away from her parents and her childhood friends, weighed down by the heavy memories of her early years. However, she found little refuge amongst the friends the marriage brought her. In the rigid social circles of high society, rules and appearances mattered more than Truth. When a marriage ended, it was always the woman who was blamed, judged, and quietly ostracised from social life.

This is not just my mother's story; it is a story woven into the history of women everywhere. For centuries, social structures have reinforced the wounded feminine by punishing women who stepped outside appearances or dared to break the illusion of perfection. The fear of rejection, of being cast out, dismissed, ridiculed, or labelled "crazy" or "unfit"—has kept countless women trapped in silence, performing roles that suffocate the Soul. Perhaps you too have felt this pressure. To play a role that was never your Truth, to stay silent when your Soul longed to speak, to make yourself smaller, safer, more acceptable, just to belong.

But we always have a choice, beloved reader.

We always have free will to change the story.

All that is required is Presence. The courage to pause, to lean in, and to make a different choice, even if it is a small one. This is the power of the will, a power each and every one of us carries within. When the will is guided by the heart, something shifts. We begin to reclaim our freedom. We begin to return to ourselves. We free ourselves.

The Saviour

Over the years, my father convinced my mother to stop working, believing it was a gesture of love, of status, of tradition. In his world, "powerful men" were expected to provide, and women were expected not to *need* careers. But beneath this disguise of privilege was a tightening grip of control—one they would only fully recognise when confronted with choice. What becomes normalised, after all, often becomes invisible. With each passing year, the arguments grew sharper, the separations more dramatic, the reconciliations more fragile. Their love story slowly transformed into a cycle of rupture and return. The wounded feminine and wounded masculine dancing in patterns neither of them had the tools or consciousness to understand at the time.

Unconsciously, I stepped into the role of the saviour, a role that so often emerges in abusive family dynamics, where one carries the weight of rescuing everyone else while silently drowning inside. In every cycle of abuse, there is the perpetrator, the victim, and the saviour. Longing for peace, I took on the impossible task of saving them all.

I believed that if I could be perfect—the perfect student, the perfect ballerina, the girl who never touched drugs, the girl who dated the "right" boys—maybe the chaos would stop, maybe the yelling would quiet, maybe Love would finally return to my home. I didn't want to add any more trouble to the chaos. It was an invisible burden born from a child's illusion: that she could calm the storm by holding herself together, by caring for everyone else, including her younger brother, while never truly being cared for herself.

The saviour role is one many children unconsciously step into. We believe that if we have enough will, things will change. But in this case, the will is driven by control—a projection of the ego—not the will of the heart. We tell ourselves that if we just behave enough, achieve enough, or love enough, we will restore harmony. If we try hard enough, we will save others. But this is an illusion—and a painful one. Carrying this weight is far too heavy for a teenager, or even for an adult. It silences our own needs, convinces us that love must be earned through perfection, and leaves us exhausted from trying to fix what was never ours to fix. No one can fix anyone. This is a Truth. Others can support, guide, and hold space, but healing only happens when the person chooses to heal.

Every day after school, I would come home and start walking on eggshells. I could read the atmosphere instantly; I only had to look into my mother's eyes to know what kind of evening it would be. I slipped into roles no teenager should ever carry: my father's therapist, my mother's confidant. I absorbed stories far too heavy for my age, secrets that blurred the line between parent and child. When I was fifteen, my father sat me down in my bedroom. "I need to explain why your mother and I fight so much," he began.

Then came the label: *manic-depressive*. He told me it meant my mother swung between obsessive energy and deep depression. And I believed him—of course I did. Why wouldn't I? He was my father. I didn't yet know how adults project their own wounds, how easy it is to assign blame when we cannot face our own pain.

Since the day I was born, my father had been warm and tender, always embracing me, holding my hand, making me feel loved through the simplest gestures. He told bedtime stories filled with adventure and wonder, guiding me into sleep as he softly stroked my back. He was loving, playful, overflowing with affection in a world where so many fathers felt distant or cold.

But as the tensions between my parents deepened, insecurity began to seep through the cracks. My father's tenderness shifted; he stepped into the role of the victim so convincingly that even those closest to him believed the story. Outwardly, he remained charming, adored by friends, generous with gifts. Using them to soothe the chaos born from the toxicity of their relationship.

Slowly, he began to confuse money with love, spoiling instead of parenting, masking control with charisma. A pattern he had inherited from his own father, and a pattern heartbreakingly common in many wounded men. The wounded masculine wrapped in charm.

As a teenager, I didn't yet understand the power of labels. Words like "crazy," "ill," or "manic-depressive" can define the way a child sees a parent, even more strongly than lived experience. They plant seeds of distortion that can take years to unravel. Labels can create strong beliefs that limit our access to the Eagle's Eye, so instead of seeing the Soul, we only see the shadow cast by someone else's story. Now I ask you, what labels have you lived by?

My mother, by contrast, was a bit tougher with us, less tactile, unconcerned with social appearances, uninterested in pleasing society like my father obsessively did, even though she embodied the feminine essence so gently with her beauty, creativity, and elegance. Her love was expressed less in hugs and more in presence: driving us to school every morning, helping with homework, volunteering as the "head mom" at school. She taught boundaries, values, and responsibility—the kind of love rarely appreciated by children who cannot yet see its worth. She also taught me to be an artist, excel in my ballet classes, never give up on my dreams, and seek independence through a career I loved.

Neither of my parents was perfect, but later I would realise how those very values my mother instilled became anchors, guiding countless decisions that, in time, would save my life. However, as a teenager still assembling my sense of self, love seemed to mean being liked, fitting in, and chasing pleasure. My father embodied that image; my mother did not. So I questioned her less and absorbed my father's narrative as the truth, a quiet distortion that shaped much of my early understanding of love and loyalty. As the years passed, every time my mother found moments of Clarity and tried to speak her truth, my brother and I doubted her. We had been conditioned to believe in her "false craziness," a narrative planted so deeply by my father's insecurities that it overshadowed her reality. Each time she attempted to leave the marriage, we thought she was the one breaking the family. "She's doing it again," we would say.

This is how conditioning works. As children, we absorb the stories we are told, especially by those we depend on, as unquestionable truth. These stories become the lens through which we see ourselves, others, and the world around us, even when they are distortions. Until we awaken, we rarely stop to ask, *Whose voice am I really hearing inside me?*

The cycle was endless: separations, reconciliations, new homes, financial highs followed by sudden lows. Through it all, my deepest longing was simple: peace and freedom. I dreamed of a home where I could breathe. Where there were no fights, no shouting, no walking on eggshells. A place where I didn't have to play the adult or mediate chaos. A place where I could finally just be myself.

None of my friends knew what was happening at home. The three boyfriends I had as a teenager grasped pieces of it because I was, of course, not well, but even then, I tried my best to maintain the façade of the perfect girl. Teenage romance became a balm; I could receive a little comfort from the storm I was carrying inside. Yet even there, I found myself repeating some of the same patterns I saw at home—jealousy, fear of loss, betrayal. Love already carried the distortions I had absorbed in my family, and I didn't yet know another way to relate.

My love for art, dressing up, and ballet started early.

I graduated from school as both a student and a professional ballerina, and then began studying law—the "right" career choice influenced by my father. But during my summer breaks, inspired by my mother, I escaped to London, where I pursued my passion for the arts at Central Saint Martins. Creativity was always my way of touching the Love within me, of connecting to my authenticity, the same way I had as a child, when I played dress-up or painted alongside my mother.

Creativity is one of the portals to the Soul. When we create, we step beyond the stories of our wounds and return to the Truth of who we are—free, playful, connected to the Source of Life itself. It is not about the outcome but about the state of being it awakens in us. Even in the midst of chaos, creativity can become a sanctuary, a reminder that Love, Power, and Light are never absent but simply waiting to be expressed.

Our Soul's Choice and Humanity's Wound

Before moving forwards in our story, we must understand that each Soul chooses its parents and life challenges before incarnating, for its own evolution. Without this knowledge, it can be difficult to accept the painful experiences humanity goes through, and we find ourselves asking questions such as: *How can children face fatal illnesses, sexual abuse, war, or poverty?* We must also remember that the human experience is always a matter of perspective; it is not the ultimate Truth. And to truly understand why suffering exists, we need to understand the universal law of Karma and the law of Grace—two principles that are often misunderstood or misinterpreted. I will go deeper into these as we continue, but for now please understand one thing clearly: They are never a punishment, as many have been led to believe.

In my own life, every person played the exact role they were meant to play as part of their own learning journey—as hard as that may be to accept. But we can tell you this: everything we have learned, and everything we have been able to do in the mission we were called to serve, has been possible *because* of these very experiences. They became our greatest teachers, not because the pain was deserved, but because I later chose to heal these traumas, forgive my parents for their unconscious actions and transform them into medicine. Medicine as they became the very foundation of the work we do at Free Free. As I healed, as I awakened, I began to see that my personal story was not just mine—it was a reflection of something much larger. The dynamics I witnessed at home were not isolated events, but echoes of a wounded masculine and wounded feminine that shape families, societies, and even nations.

We must also go deeper into understanding that the wounded masculine sees the world through separation and duality—*us versus them, right versus wrong, power versus weakness.* This fragmented lens is why wars have historically been initiated by wounded men, and why the obsession with control and external power—land, money, property, status—has appeared so strongly in men throughout history.

The need to dictate outcomes and define worth through possessions and achievements became woven into the very structures we still live within today: our laws, our religions, and our cultural norms. These systems, born from the wounded masculine, continue to reinforce separation rather than unity.

Even the image of God in most religions has been filtered through lens of the wounded masculine—portrayed as male, authoritarian, punishing, and conditional in His love. Christianity, for example, frames God as a father figure who rewards obedience and condemns sin, and similar archetypes appear across other Abrahamic faiths. But this portrayal is not the Truth of God. It is an illusion born of patriarchal society. God is not a being. God is a field of pure Love, pure Light, the authentic Power of Creation itself. God is the Source from which we all source from, and because of this, we are each Divine beings. As Jesus taught, "The kingdom of God is within you." As Buddha taught, "Look within; you are the light." Both point to the same Truth: divinity is not outside of us but within each being, beyond gender, beyond race, beyond nationality, beyond form, beyond separation. We are part of the whole, and at the same time, uniquely ourselves. We are all part of the Field of Life.

Patriarchy, at its core, is a system built from the ego to centre and preserve male dominance, giving men power over women, children, and even other men. It is not just about individual behaviours but about the invisible rules that shape entire cultures, where men are expected to control and women are expected to obey. This system wounds both the masculine and the feminine. It keeps humanity locked into distorted roles of dominance and submission, preventing us from rising into our higher, healed, and harmonic Soul expressions. Patriarchy imprisons men in the illusion that power comes from control, while conditioning women to believe that worth comes from marriage, children, and people-pleasing. Both are illusions that keep us separated from the Truth of who we are.

Patriarchy is not only "out there" in society; it lives inside us too, in the voices that tell us we are not enough, in the ways we silence ourselves to fit expectations, in the pressure to dominate, achieve, or obey. It is both a system we are born into and an inner wound we must heal. The moment we begin to dismantle it within, we begin to transform it in the world around us. To be clear: dismantling patriarchy is not about making men less important or less powerful, because ultimately, power is not external but internal. It is about healing, restoring balance, and creating harmony for all beings.

In ancient civilisations, the feminine was honoured as sacred. The priestesses and wise women were bridges between the seen and unseen realms, reading the signs of the stars, the winds, the waters, and the lands, guiding communities in harmony with the cycles of nature. But as society shifted towards structures of control and domination, this flow began to be feared. What cannot be predicted cannot be possessed. What cannot be possessed threatens the ego's need for certainty, control and conquered power. External power is not real; it is just another illusion. True power is inner power. Is the power of the heart.

And so, the reverence for the feminine turned into repression, the river was forced into walls, its wild song silenced. The feminine, which lives not only in women but in all beings, was labelled dangerous, emotional, unstable. Yet, in truth, it is the feminine that holds the codes for balance, compassion, and the remembrance that Love is the foundation that reunites everything that is now fractured. Without it, humanity became severed from its own heart, giving rise to the wounded masculine structures we live in today, not only amongst men but amongst women. Over time, the feminine began to be feared, not because it lacked power, but because its very fluidity could not be contained. Love cannot be contained. The unhealed masculine, within women and men, seeking control and certainty, attempted to dominate what it could not predict, and this tension birthed the power struggles we still witness across the world.

It is only through Love that we can reclaim the balance our world so urgently needs to face its greatest challenges—climate change, hunger, poverty, racism, gender inequality, violence, wars, religious persecution, and corrupt financial systems. Love is not sentimental; Love is a force. It is the original frequency of creation, the intelligence that holds galaxies together and restores coherence where there is fracture. As Love nourishes the deepest wounds of humanity, the masculine begins to transform from wounded into empowered—no longer grasping for control, domination, or validation, but standing as a wise, protective, grounded presence. In this state, the masculine works in harmony with the feminine, not in opposition, and together they restore wholeness within individuals, families, systems, and nations.

Both women and men carry the feminine and the masculine within them. These are not genders, but primordial energies—currents of consciousness expressing through the human experience. Most women incarnate to heal their feminine essence, which is why it often expresses more strongly through them: the realms of intuition, emotion, creation, compassion, and inner truth. Most men incarnate to heal their masculine essence, which is why responsibility, direction, structure, and power tend to be their spiritual classroom. This is not an absolute rule; the human journey and the Soul's contracts are far more intricate, but for the purpose of this book, I will speak of these energies in simplified terms so that their dynamics can be understood. Only by understanding these currents can we begin the true work: the healing of both, so that the human being—and humanity—can return to balance.

The interplay of these energies—the wounded and the healed, the feminine and the masculine—shaped every part of my home and my childhood. This was not just my personal story but a microcosm of one of humanity's deepest wounds, a wound that echoes not only in families but in governments, religions, and the very systems that rule our world. Understanding this wound would later become central to our mission. But at the time, all I could feel was the chaos and the pain, not yet the lesson, not yet the Truth, which would take years for me to reclaim.

It was only through walking through that fire that the seed of freedom was planted in me—a seed I would one day nurture into the mission we carry now. But first, I had to survive the storm.

CHAPTER 3

DEATH

The last years of my mother's life were a struggle. The intensity between my parents only grew stronger, especially after she stopped working. She had once run a small business creating elegant leather albums and handcrafted stationery—pieces of beauty admired in our social circle—but she decided to sell the business. My father believed it would be better for the family, and at the time, he was in a successful phase of his career after so many ups and downs. They both hoped that if she didn't work, maybe the fighting would ease.

My mother longed to study visual arts, so she spent a few months in Paris and later continued her studies at Parque Lage, Rio's most iconic art school. But after selling her business, something shifted. She became fully dependent on my father, and dependence soon turned into control. She had to ask permission for everything. Money became another layer of power in their relationship, another tool in the cycle of instability that defined our home.

The culture my parents were raised in taught men that their role was to provide, and when they provided, most women were expected to follow. My father did provide: a beautiful new apartment, yearly international trips, designer clothes, jewellery. From the outside, it looked perfect. But inside, my mother was empty, unfulfilled, and trapped. She spent her days and nights in her studio painting, pouring her silent suffering onto canvas. Art became her refuge, her only safe place.

My Romanian grandfather was a strict man, not with me, his baby girl, with whom he allowed his vulnerability to show, but with his only son, my father. After surviving years of war as a Jewish man during the Holocaust, he rebuilt his life and rose to success, creating a sophisticated lifestyle he carried with pride. He owned horses and real estate, gifted my grandmother extravagant jewellery, and sent my father to study in Switzerland and Paris, places he had loved and known well from his early life before the wars and again after his successful career.

In Rio's high society, my grandfather was accomplished, admired, and respected. My grandfather was an absent father, as many men were at the time—believing that Love was shown through things rather than presence. My grandmother, on the other hand, was quiet and passive, signs of the wounded feminine. She endured his infidelities in silence, holding her pain behind a composed exterior, as so many women of her generation did and as many women still do. After several miscarriages, the loss of two newborn babies, and the death of my father's twin brother, my grandmother poured all her love into her only surviving son. She spoiled him, shielding him in what I later understood was a golden cage.

My loving grandfather.
He was my rock and love.

My loving grandmother

A golden cage is the illusion of safety and comfort we cling to because it mirrors what society tells us is "success" or "stability"—a place where we think we will find happiness or protect ourselves from pain. It can look like a marriage that photographs well but feels hollow inside, a prestigious job that drains your light, or a lifestyle that ticks every box yet leaves you empty. It can even be the belief that being single makes you free, or that having money brings safety. It can be a combination of all of them as well.

A golden cage transcends social class, culture, and geography; its bars are universal. We all know its shimmer, and we all know its traps—how the cage becomes bigger and stronger with every inauthentic decision we make, every moment we abandon our Truth to meet an expectation, please another, maintain an image, or follow the lead of the ego instead of the Soul. From the outside, it looks polished, composed, controlled. But inside, the light dims, the air thins, and the Soul begins to whisper that something is missing.

The danger of the golden cage is subtle: while it glitters, it numbs. It convinces us we are free because we are admired, provided for, escaping something, or following the script we inherited. Yet deep inside, a quiet pain remains—the longing for something authentic, raw, and unmeasured by appearances or the trap of the "known". The golden cage is not forced upon us; unconsciously, we lock ourselves inside it, mistaking the familiar for safety and fearing the unknown that waits beyond its bars.

In my father's case, the golden cage was the way he grew up. After my grandfather became wealthy in Rio, they lived for eight months in the luxury of the Copacabana Palace while their Leme beach (a continuation of the Copacabana beach) apartment was being finished. He travelled often to Paris, was a guest in Salvador Dalí's apartment, and had friends who dated personalities such as Brigitte Bardot. He lived in a world where everything seemed possible, far beyond what most could ever imagine. Lines became blurred. It was a life of privilege and luxury, the picture of a "perfect family" but one that failed to meet his emotional needs or teach him limits. My grandfather's presence was expressed through gifts, things, fancy trips rather than affection. It was this same golden cage my father later tried to recreate for my mother and our family, unaware that what had confined him and wounded him was now quietly confining us too.

But there was one difference: My mother may have carried the wounded feminine, but she was not passive. She refused to accept mistresses, jewellery, or status as substitutes for authenticity. She spoke up during moments of Clarity, even when in deep pain. Yet every time she did, my father dismissed her as "crazy." He was not used to women challenging the authority of the man of the house, especially during the height of his success, when his sense of impunity only grew stronger.

Like many men who confuse money with love, he equated providing with devotion, and grew insecure when she would not meet his expectations. This is what happens when men are caught in the wounded masculine: Love becomes conditional, power becomes control, and intimacy is replaced by transactions. This is not just my parents' story; it is a pattern that repeats across generations and cultures. The golden cage may take different forms—wealth, tradition, religion, or appearances—but its effect is always the same. It imprisons both men and women in roles that suffocate the Soul.

The truth is, both men and women carry within them the potential for something far greater. The healed masculine is not controlling but protective, grounded, steady, wise, and a safe container for Light to shine. The healed feminine is not passive but creative, intuitive, giving, receiving, Loving and compassionate. It is the power of Love that nurtures and restores balance and unity. When these two meet in harmony, they no longer imprison but liberate. They allow Love to be expressed in its purest form—free, abundant, and unconditional.

My paternal grandfather passed away about a year before my mother's death, and with him went one of the few anchors in our chaotic world. He had been strict, yes, but he had also been a grounding presence, someone my father looked up to and relied on as a quiet safety net. If something went wrong, my grandfather would step in for him, rescue him, or guide him. Perhaps it was the resilience forged by surviving war and migration, or perhaps it was simply his nature, but he lived by a strong moral code. His sternness could be hard, yet it gave everyone around him a sense of stability. In his absence, that stability dissolved, leaving my father even more untethered, searching for control, yet feeling even more insecure and lost.

A couple of years earlier, my maternal grandmother and grandfather had also passed away. Even if my mother had not been especially close to them, their loss left her with a deep sense of loneliness, emptiness, and disconnection. As these foundations crumbled, my father faced a severe business crisis. An old business partner created a scheme that led to my father and his colleagues going to prison for two months. For my mother, this became the final straw.

By then, she was already carrying years of unspoken pain. She had lost her sense of independence when she sold her business, her sense of safety through the instability of my father's world, and her sense of belonging as old friends and family members, including her children, drifted away. She had fought to keep her dignity, but the grief of losing her parents, the loss of trust in her marriage, and now the humiliation of my father being imprisoned were more than she could hold. It was as if life kept taking piece after piece of her foundation, until there was no ground left beneath her feet. She could no longer grasp the chaos her life had become.

The Prison

It was 5:00 a.m. on a cold morning in July when the doorbell rang, its sharp sound cutting through the silence of the house. My younger brother, only sixteen, went to open it, still half asleep. Our mother had been unwell for a while—she had been sinking deeper into depression. The moment my brother pulled the door open, everything changed. A group of armed policemen stood there, their heavy boots, dark uniforms, and weapons filling the doorway. He froze, then turned and ran down the hall, his voice breaking as he shook me awake: "Mimi, come! Come quickly, there are policemen at our door!"

I stumbled out of bed, my heart already racing before I even knew what was happening. When I saw them—men with hard faces and cold eyes—I felt a knot tighten in my stomach. They were looking for my father, but he wasn't there.

We rushed to wake our mother, who screamed in shock the moment she saw them. The sound of her cry still echoes in me. It was the sound of fear and despair colliding at once. The policemen didn't care. They pushed past us, storming through each room, opening drawers, throwing things aside as if we were nothing. Their boots thudded against the floor, their hands tore through our belongings, leaving behind the violence.

My brother and I stood frozen, our bodies trembling, watching strangers dismantle the safety of our home. We were shocked, humiliated, terrified. I was only twenty years old. My father was arrested that morning in his hotel room while travelling for work, along with his business partners. They were all arrested and taken to prison. For days, we weren't allowed to speak to him.

At that point in my life, my father was my hero. He was kind, loving—the man who tucked us into bed and told us stories at night. The fights between my parents had always felt like something apart, a storm I thought I could keep outside my own heart. But having him taken away, seeing our home invaded, broke something in me. It shattered the illusion of safety I had been holding onto and left me face to face with a truth I wasn't ready for. It was one of the most painful experiences of our lives.

The story was everywhere—on TV, in the newspapers. Once again, I stepped into the role of the saviour, trying to hold everyone together: my devastated mother, my younger brother, and my father. At the time, I was studying law, and I decided to take the lead with the lawyers, supported by one of my father's colleagues. Every other day, I went to visit my father in prison, which was one hour away by car. He was destroyed. His face carried shame, betrayal, and exhaustion. He felt unfairly judged, humiliated, and broken. Over and over, he told me, "Please believe me. I didn't do what they are saying."

I wanted to believe him. I did believe him. But no matter what the truth was, the damage had already been done. My mother couldn't bear the pain. When, after two months, my father was finally released, she didn't let him in our home or close to her ever again.

My brother and I, still just teenagers, sided with our father. We were convinced our mother was being unfair, acting crazy. We couldn't see the depth of her pain or that her decision was the last straw of a marriage filled with so much trauma. All we could see was the suffering our father was going through.

Meanwhile, my father, feeling stripped of all his self-esteem, self-worth, and the very things the wounded masculine holds to—success, a perfect family, and honour—rushed into a new relationship. He rented a beautiful new house and quickly built a new life, eager to show his friends and the world that he was fine. It was his way of proving that everything had been a mistake, that he was still valuable, still honourable. In truth, it was only a defence mechanism, a way to soothe his deep wounds.

In reaction to my mother's final decision to separate, he cut off all financial support, a silent punishment that only deepened her isolation. It was another weapon of control, one that many wounded men use when they feel powerless. My mother, terrified of having no way to provide for herself after leaving her career, reached a level of desperation she had never known. My brother and I went to live with my father. She had no money and was left alone in our old apartment—without her work to give her a sense of purpose, her parents, and most painfully, without her children.

For a mother, the absence of her children can feel like a death before death. The silence of the house where we once laughed, argued, and played must have been deafening. Every empty chair, every untouched object was a reminder of family life slipping further from her grasp. It wasn't just the loss of companionship but the loss of identity, of the role that had given her meaning. To her, it must have felt as though the very ground of her existence had been taken away. It was also a self-fulfilling prophecy. The thing she feared the most— losing her children, her family, just as her own mother had—had now become her reality. This is one of the great paradoxes of life: the very thing we fear the most is often the very thing our field attracts, not to punish us, but to bring the wound to the surface so it can finally be healed. Sometimes we have the tools to navigate such moments. Sometimes we don't. This is what the freedom journey is about—developing the inner tools to meet life as it comes, without allowing any experience to take over us or define us. Freedom is not the absence of challenge; it is the ability to face anything without losing ourselves in the process.

One day, we saw her using a public van to get around the city, and we assumed it was a sign of her mental illness. In Rio, public transport is often riddled with crime, and for people of middle or high class, it carries a heavy stigma—not because of arrogance, but because it is genuinely unsafe. What I could not see then was the truth: she had simply been left without options. At the time, I could not imagine that my father would go so far as to cut off her financial support, as she told us he had. I sided with him, blind to the reality that she truly had been left with nothing. Alone, misunderstood, and carrying layers upon layers of grief, shame, and humiliation, my mother's voice grew quieter. No one seemed willing to hear what she was trying to say, to understand her perspective with compassion. No one was listening. She was silenced.

Her parents were gone. Her children, too, now lived with their father and believed the narrative that she was "crazy." With every door closing around her, the silence became unbearable—a silence not of peace, but of erasure, of being unseen, unheard, and unloved in the moment she needed understanding the most.

And so, in her eyes, there was nothing left to do. My mother ended her life.

The Eagle's Eye

As you read this chapter of my life, we ask you to see the unravelling of these events through the Eagle's Eye. As we have learned before, the Eagle's Eye is a higher perspective that carries a higher consciousness of Truth and Love, instead of the ego's perception that tends to judge and blame.

So we ask you this question: Was it anyone's fault? Or can we see instead a pattern of ancestral trauma being passed from generation to generation? From the trauma of war and Jewish persecution to the rigid social conditioning men and women are taught to follow through religion and culture, every reaction was born from ancestral memory, from the subconscious survival mechanisms of the ego, which could not yet acknowledge Truth or Love.

When I judged my mother as "crazy" for taking public transport, that was an example of how limited the ego's perspective is, how linear, how fragmented our lower minds creates interpretations. The ego cannot see the full picture. But the Eagle's Eye can. It rises above and sees from all directions, in circular vision. From that higher awareness, what once looked like shame or madness becomes a higher understanding—the full picture.

When we look back now, even my father's prison was not only a trauma but a profound teaching. It revealed, with brutal clarity, that external power is not true power. It was a mirror showing that control, status, and wealth can crumble in an instant, because they are built on illusions. True power comes from within, from the Soul. From the heart. This is something we will explore more deeply as the story unfolds.

In Eastern traditions, we learn about karma. In the West, we call it the Golden Rule. In Truth, karma means that whatever you do to others, you will, in some form, experience yourself. It is the law of cause and effect. It is not a punishment, as so many believe; it is the way the universe restores balance and ensures growth.

Through karma, what was once unconscious and hurtful becomes conscious. By living through the very experiences we once imposed, knowingly or unknowingly, we learn, we expand, and we move closer to the Light, to wisdom, to Love, and to the Truth of Oneness. Karma does not punish us; it teaches us. It reflects back what we have not yet seen within ourselves. It gives us the opportunity to evolve by showing us the impact of our actions through lived experience. But we are not bound to karma as most people fear, if we learn the teaching in another way. This is why the freedom journey is so essential. When we consciously illuminate the shadows within us—when we bring Love, Presence, and Light to what was buried in the unconscious—we no longer need suffering to teach us through experience. Instead of learning through pain, we learn through awareness. Instead of being shaped by karma, we are liberated by consciousness.

This was clear in my parents' dynamic. A living example of karma. As my father unconsciously misjudged my mother based on the limited interpretation of his lower mind and unconscious beliefs, labelling her as "crazy," placing her in a golden cage, a prison of sorts, and stripping her of what she valued most, he too was eventually sent to prison—misjudged, treated unfairly, and stripped of everything he believed gave him worth and significance. But instead of seeing the experience as a teaching, he didn't have the tools to recognise it as such. He saw himself as a victim, and the experience only widened the wounds he had carried since childhood.

Hurt people, hurt people. Healed people, heal people.

Anger, silence, and numbing are not the problems themselves; they are reactions to inner pain. Raw signals. Survival responses. And not all pain is conscious, which means not all our reactions are conscious, either. Much of our suffering lives unacknowledged, hidden in the layers of our spiritual, mental, emotional, and physical bodies—waiting for the moment it can finally be seen, held, loved, and healed into freedom.

The ego, shaped by these unhealed wounds, interprets life through the lens of survival. It creates distortions. Stories we come to believe as truth. These distortions surface as disconnection, judgement, anxiety, control, or avoidance, all attempts by the ego to keep us safe from feeling the original wound, at any cost.

We can see this so clearly now in the way I judged my mother when she took the public van. At the time, I believed it was proof she was "crazy." In reality, it was my ego's distortion—its way of protecting me from seeing the unbearable truth of her pain, because I wasn't ready to face it. What I labelled as madness was actually despair: the raw expression of her suffering, intensified by my father's desperate state after his imprisonment.

When we are hurt inside, we often close our hearts as a way to avoid further suffering. The problem is that when we close our hearts, we disconnect from the loving Presence of our eternal Soul. The ego then takes the lead full stop, and Truth becomes inaccessible, shaping our personality into whatever feels necessary for survival, often in ways that repeat pain rather than heal it. The ego creates the characters we later feel the need to undress.

When we look at my father's response, it is easy to feel anger towards him, or towards men, or even towards the patriarchy as a whole, especially if we have endured abuse ourselves. When we look at my mother's response, closing the door to the man who had been unfairly imprisoned, we can also judge her as cold or unstable, for not standing beside her husband after twenty years of marriage in a moment of desperation.

But when we rise to the Eagle's Eye, we see through Clarity. My father was acting from a wound, from trauma, a distorted reaction born from his lack of self-esteem, shaped by years of his father's criticism and absence of emotional connection, his mother's overprotection, and the fresh humiliation of prison. My mother was acting from another wound—her breaking point. Years of betrayal, gaslighting, instability, and the tormenting doubt had left her exhausted. She must have wondered, *Is he really innocent? After everything I've endured, how will I ever know?*

This is why judgement blinds us, while compassion opens our true sight. Judgement keeps us stuck in the ego's narrow lens, seeing only the surface of people's reactions. Compassion, on the other hand, allows us to rise into the Eagle's Eye, where we can perceive the Truth beyond wound. Beyond the reaction. Beyond the distortion. Beyond the story.

When we understand that every hurtful action is born from pain, we stop seeing villains and start seeing wounded children inside adult bodies, children who never learned how to process their suffering. This doesn't mean excusing harm or staying in abusive dynamics; it means recognising the Truth behind the illusion, so we can break the cycle of blame and separation instead of repeating it.

We share this not to excuse either of their actions, but to invite a deeper understanding. Free will means that even when we inherit wounds, we still have the choice to seek healing. We cannot always choose what hurts us, because this, too, is part of the law of karma, but we can choose how we respond, how to interpret it, how to move beyond it. We can choose whether to break the cycle or to repeat it, whether to remain bound to pain or to free ourselves by finally learning the deeper teaching the universe is bringing us.

Later in our story, we will explore how this understanding of free will is the very key that empowers us to heal toxic dynamics, reclaim our lives, and return to Love.

In the same way, my mother being labelled "crazy" and losing her children was the very thing she feared most, after trying her whole life to be different from her own mother and grandmother. Yet without taking the steps into the freedom journey of true healing and self-discovery, she was unable to break free from the cycle. Her lack of inner power, shaped by the wounded feminine and the immense pain she carried, kept her locked in victim consciousness. From that place, she found herself repeating the very suffering she had spent her life trying to avoid. This is true for all of us. What we fear the most is often the very thing life places in front of us, not as punishment but as an invitation. It is what we most need to bring into conscious awareness, embrace it with Love, so that it can be healed, dissolved, and transformed into wisdom.

In my family, everyone was unconscious, including me until I awakened.

Consciousness is the ultimate medicine for trauma. Only through a wider lens can we begin to understand the depth of suffering we, and humanity as a whole, endure. Until we awaken to this awareness, we remain attached to the stories we grew up believing, trapped in distorted assumptions and cultural and social conditionings about reality.

Unconsciousness is like a shadow on the wall—dark, flat, a projection rather than the Truth. When we bring Light to the shadow, it dissolves. That Light is consciousness, a higher Knowing infused with Love. When Love and awareness touch buried pain, the shadow begins to dissolve, distortion softens, and the wound loses its power to control our perception of reality.

As our view of life shifts, healing becomes possible. We begin to understand that duality is simply an illusion, that any idea of victim versus persecutor, or good versus bad, is only real while we live through the limited perspective of the lower mind and within the confines of the five senses that are seen by duality.

Therapy

In the last years of my mother's life, my saviour role only grew heavier. Since I believed my father's story, I stepped in where no teenager should ever have to, becoming a mother figure to my younger brother, showing up at school meetings to explain the chaos at home, carrying responsibilities far beyond my age. I went to therapy, searching for answers, desperate to understand what was "wrong" with my mother, convinced by the family narrative that she was mentally ill.

My mother, on the other hand, refused therapy. It wasn't denial, it was fear. Fear of being labelled, as her own mother had been. Fear that accepting help would only validate my father's accusations of madness. Deep down, she knew she wasn't crazy. But in a world where women's perspectives are so often dismissed or silenced, the more she defended herself, the less she was believed, gaslighted into doubting her own reality.

The cycle kept repeating: moments of clarity when my mother saw the cage she was trapped in, followed by waves of desperation when no one believed her.

By the time I graduated high school, I was exhausted. I enrolled in law school and went on a school trip to Europe before classes began. But even there, I felt like an outsider. I didn't like to drink much or use drugs, didn't want to stay out late, and in the unkind social world of unconscious teenagers, that difference became a reason for ridicule. The bullying followed me through the three-week trip, confirming the belief I had carried for so long: I didn't belong anywhere.

My mother always reminded me to stay true to myself, to never be afraid of saying no. She would tell me, "What others do or say to you is not about you. Don't be afraid to say your Truth." Those words stayed with me long after she was gone, like a compass guiding me back to my own inner Power. As you can see, beloved reader, my mother was a wise, conscious woman even through all the pain she endured.

Among the many lessons she left me, one stood above all: A woman should always have her own career or her own way of providing for herself, so she is never fully dependent on a man or trapped in a toxic family dynamic. I understood why she said this. I had watched her feel increasingly imprisoned after giving up her work, with no family left to turn to for help. The high-society world around us only deepened the wound—a world obsessed with appearances, quick to gossip, quick to judge, blind to the truth behind the surface.

When someone is labelled "crazy," you silence them. Their voice loses weight. Every truth they speak becomes questionable, dismissed before it is even heard. Over time, that silencing can break a person. They begin to doubt themselves, to wonder whether the label might be true. For someone who has already endured so much pain, it becomes a slow unravelling. An erosion of identity that happens quietly, invisibly, one breath at a time.

My father, convinced of this false narrative, sought help for her from therapists. But instead of healing, the help deepened the harm. One therapist even prescribed medication without my mother's knowledge. The drugs dulled her spirit, numbed her light, and pulled her further into a fog, intensifying the very cycles of highs and lows that were already tearing her apart—not because she was manic-depressive, but because of the torment of living in constant instability.

This is why it is so important to challenge the way the current mental-health system operates. Too often, instead of truly listening to the person in pain, it rushes to label them—frequently inaccurately—and prescribes powerful medications that can numb the Soul and close the heart. Rather than healing the wound, this approach can deepen it. In many cases, people are even institutionalised in environments that intensify their suffering, sometimes pushing them into the very madness they were never meant to experience.

It is important to say: I am not against medication. I myself took medication for many years. But medication is a tool, not the healing itself. Without the correct support, presence, and understanding, medication alone can be extremely damaging. Healing requires more than labels and prescriptions; it requires seeing the person's Truth, through the Eagle's Eye, and an open heart. Not just their symptoms.

When we reduce a person to a label, we silence their Truth. We stop seeing the human being behind the suffering, and we disconnect from the deeper causes of their pain. True healing cannot come from suppressing symptoms alone. Healing and freedom comes when we bring Light to the wound—when we meet the suffering with compassion, Presence, and Love. The Soul does not need numbing; it needs remembering.

Remembering its own wholeness. Remembering its own worth. Remembering its own light. Remembering we are much more than we can fully understand through our linear mind.

The News

In January 2008, six months after my father's imprisonment, my paternal grandmother was in hospital undergoing cancer surgery. My younger brother was travelling in Europe, and I had spent one day with my boyfriend in the countryside, where there was no phone signal. When I finally came back into signal range, my phone lit up with messages from my mother. The first ones were calm: "I got hurt, I'm going to hospital." Then, as I scrolled, the tone shifted, the messages growing more frantic, almost desperate. My chest tightened. Fear surged through me as I drove straight back to Rio, heading directly to the hospital my mother went to. My father, meanwhile, was at another hospital caring for his mother with cancer, as she recovered from surgery. I went to see my mother alone.

When I arrived at the hospital, I walked into the ICU and found my mother unconscious. The doctors explained she had cut her hands. "An accident while washing glasses," they said. She had been given local anaesthesia so they could stitch the cut, but something had gone wrong. Her body had reacted badly to the anaesthesia, and they had been forced to put her under full-body anaesthesia.

I stood there, frozen, staring at her pale face and her hand wrapped tightly in bandages. I didn't know it yet, but this was the beginning of the tragedy that would unravel over the next few days. In complete shock, I called my dad and said, "We need to make an intervention. My mother is not well. She is not well."

When she woke up, she asked me not to allow my father to visit. Once again, I found myself in the role of the parent, trying to find solutions far beyond my age. Convinced she was mentally ill, I gathered a group of psychiatrists, hoping they could help her recover, not just from her hands but from what I believed at the time was a mental health crisis. Yet even they seemed unprepared, unsure of how to proceed, without real ideas of what could truly support her, showing how our mental health system truly needs to be updated.

The next day, when I went back to visit, everything felt different. My mother was calm, lucid, exhaling Love in a way that filled the room. Something had shifted in her. When I look back at this moment now, I see it clearly: The veils had thinned between the worlds. Her Soul was already standing closer to the unseen than to the seen, radiating a peace that felt otherworldly.

That night, I went home carrying a strange, unexplainable calm. At the time, I didn't understand it. Now I know it was her final gift to me: a glimpse of her eternal Light before her departure. It was also the first initiation into our mission, the lesson that death is not an ending but a passage, and that Love and Light are eternal to each being.

When my mother woke up, she called me, saying she had been discharged from the hospital. My heart panicked; I knew it wasn't true. I rushed to reach her, but by the time I would have gotten there, she was already gone. I called the hospital, and they said they didn't see her leave. This is one more example of how the traditional health system is still not ready to deal with the truth behind all illnesses: trauma.

Our last conversation turned into a fight. She told me she would move to the United States to live with some relatives, and all I could say was, "This is your choice." I didn't know those would be the last words I would ever speak to her.

Later that day, I went to visit my grandmother at the other hospital. As I sat there with my father, a wave of desperation came over me. I cried non-stop, an inner Knowing pressing against my chest, though I couldn't explain why. I begged my father for help. He said, "Stop. Why does everything have to be at the time you want?" I continued begging, and we decided to go meet the group of psychiatrists that we hired to support my mother. He started driving his car, and I was driving mine, when a police officer called him with the news.

When we finally arrived home, my father came to me with heavy eyes and a broken voice. He told me what no daughter is ever prepared to hear: My mother had died by suicide.

The world stopped. My chest caved in, my breath became shallow, and my mind spun in disbelief. I had just spoken to her, and now she was gone. Our last conversation had been a fight. The guilt, the anger, the confusion—all of it collapsed onto me at once.

As unbearable as this moment was, looking back now through the Eagle's Eye, we can see it differently. At the time, all I could feel was devastation. Yet from a higher perspective, we see the intricate weaving of ancestral pain, karma, and Love playing out. We see how my mother's story was not just hers but the story of generations of women, ancestors, silenced, misunderstood, and carrying unbearable wounds alone.

We see how what I once judged was just her way of being heard, and how we, as a society, must learn from this. We must listen. We must listen to women, to children, to all people, young or old, Black or White, rich or poor, Western or Eastern. We must listen because, at our core, we all long for the same thing: to be seen, to be heard, to be acknowledged. To be Loved. This is the true medicine. We must choose real healing, not the plasters of medication, addictions, status, trips, romance, or appearances. Because in the end, we are all called to seek freedom. Freedom from whatever binds us. Freedom from whatever keeps us in our own golden cage.

And the key to that freedom is consciousness.

There was love between my parents. But when love meets unhealed trauma, fear takes over. The ego steps into survival mode, and the relationship is pulled into wounded feminine and wounded masculine dynamics that create even more pain. The relationship becomes toxic not because someone is to blame, but because relationships reflect our wounds so powerfully that, without the tools to navigate them, the dynamic becomes unhealthy for everyone involved. So we repeat: consciousness is freedom. Consciousness brings to Light the pain submerged in our bodies, the pain we did not know how to face. And once it is seen, Love can dissolve the fear, soften the armour, and reunite the fragments within us.

As you continue reading, we invite you to look gently at your own golden cage. What beliefs, fears, or stories keep you bound? Where might your Soul already be calling you to set yourself free and back into Love?

CHAPTER 4

THE AFTERMATH

After my mother passed away, my father lost everything he had once prized. His honour was shattered, the love of his life was gone, his sense of purpose collapsed, and he no longer had his father to lean on when things went wrong. With no anchor to hold him, the weight of all his traumas pushed him deeper into unconsciousness. Instead of seeing this time as an opportunity to heal, he spiralled further into the patterns that had always driven him. He couldn't cope, much less parent. The inheritance from his father and the relationship he had just begun three months before my mother's death became his escape. This was how he numbed what he could not face. These became his coping mechanisms, illusions of stability covering the deep fractures that were widening beneath.

One week after the memorial, I tried returning to my law internship, desperate to find some kind of routine, some illusion of normalcy. But my body gave out. Burnout hit so hard, I could barely stand. I withdrew from work and from law school. The owner of the law firm offered me a kind of lifeline. He told me I could take a leave, and whenever I was ready to return, a job would always be waiting for me. During my father's time in prison and my mother's death, that internship had been my anchor. I loved what I was doing, and I was actually quite good at it. I liked the idea of the law because it meant helping people find justice. Even in the days I was at the hospital with my mother in the ICU, I would sit down and work on the projects I was assigned to as an intern. It was in this internship that I learned to sit at negotiation tables. But now, even that felt impossible. I accepted his offer and stepped away, telling myself I needed time to go through my grief, to heal, not only from my mother's passing and my father's prison episode, but from the twenty-one years of instability I had lived through in my own home.

My younger brother locked himself in his room, shutting out the world. He carried his pain in silence, the same silence we had inherited from generations before us. Both of us held onto the same story we had been told all our lives: that our mother was "mentally ill," and this is why she did what she did. But we never imagined it could lead here, to suicide. At the time, we had no consciousness of the Truth. We had no idea she was carrying wounds no one saw, wounds too heavy for her to bear alone. It had never even crossed our minds. We only knew what we were told. She, like our grandmother and great-grandmother, was mentally ill. It was a generational problem—one I decided to confront at the time, the only way I knew how back then, so I wouldn't repeat the pattern. I went to therapy on a weekly basis and did everything my mother had opposed. My doctor prescribed me sleeping pills and antidepressants to cope, and I said yes please. All I knew was that I needed all the help I thought my mother hadn't accepted. I am not against medication, as I previously mentioned, as it can help alleviate in extreme cases, but if you don't heal the real trauma, the medication alone is not healing—it is just another plaster that treats the symptoms, not the root cause.

A month after my mother's passing, my brother stumbled upon a diamond ring, a proposal ring, hidden in our father's bathroom. Panic rose between us. What? Was he going crazy? Our mother had just died, and here was our father, ready to bring a woman twenty years younger, a woman he barely even knew, into our lives.

My father was blind in his grief. Seeking pleasure, soothing himself at any cost, he abandoned the role of father altogether. Today, we can see through the Eagle's Eye and know it for what it was: a reflection of his pain. We hold no judgement for how he coped, as he was lost in survival mode, deep in grief. He was unconscious. But my brother and I couldn't see that yet. All we felt was abandonment. Betrayal. At the very moment we needed our father most, he disappeared into his own wounds. I was twenty-one, and my brother was sixteen. We were two children left to make sense of a chaos no young person should ever have to understand. The loving father we once knew was no longer there. He had been seduced by external pleasures, chasing anything that could numb his pain. The father who once tucked us into bed with stories, who stroked our back until we fell asleep, who laughed with us and held us with tenderness, he was gone. I didn't know then what we can see now: He was drowning. He thought money, pleasure, and a new relationship could rescue him from the deep hole he had fallen in, and he couldn't find another way out. But instead of healing, these escapes pulled him further away from himself, widening the pain, and further away from us.

In the midst of grieving, I searched for something, anything, that could soothe the emptiness, the anger, the fear. I began creating small fashion pieces, playful little experiments that felt like a lifeline back to beauty. My godmothers became my safe space. They showed up again and again, holding my brother and me through the storm, offering the Love and Presence that had been missing at home for so long. Looking back now, we see this was the beginning of a Truth that would one day guide our mission: that art and Love together can transform pain into beauty, and true beauty into freedom.

In May of that year, one of my godmothers invited me on a trip to New York. It was only a brief escape, but something awakened in me. Walking the streets, surrounded by art, fashion, and a sense of freedom I had never felt before, a quiet voice whispered, *This could be a way forward.* After New York, I went to London to visit one of my mother's friends. There, everything shifted. I fell in love with the city instantly, even if I had been to London before, this was a completely new experience—the creative air, the history, the streets alive with individuality. London felt like oxygen. It also felt like remembrance, as if a part of me had always belonged there. My mother was English, and being in London was like touching the roots I had almost forgotten. Looking back, we can see this was the first spark of rebuilding. After so much loss, London whispered possibility. It was the beginning of a new chapter, a glimpse of the life that was waiting for me beyond the storm.

London Calling

While I was still visiting London, I made a decision. I am moving here. My father agreed, but with one condition: I had to study. Determined, I poured myself into building a portfolio and applied to a master's program in fashion. When the acceptance letter from Istituto Marangoni arrived, it felt like a door opening into another life. I found a small apartment near Portobello Road, tucked away in Colville Gardens. It wasn't much, but it was mine, and most importantly, it would be the first time I would experience peace, stability, and silence in a home. No more eggshells. For years, I had asked my parents to allow me to live alone. I looked for apartments in Rio, but they never allowed it, worried of what other people would think and if it would be safe for a teenager to live alone. This apartment was more than a quiet corner in a city; it was a space that would start my healing. In July of that year, I packed my life into a few suitcases and moved to London.

At the time, I was still dating the man I had met during my law internship. He was loving, yet deeply wounded like myself—a story you'll come to understand later. Our relationship, like so much of my life then, was tangled: affection mixed with control, love blurred with fear of loss. My decision to leave Brazil had been rushed, yet beneath the chaos was something clear and undeniable, a deep Knowing. I needed space from my family's dynamics. I needed distance from the emptiness I felt after my mother's absence and my father's unravelling. I needed room to discover who I really was. The saviour identity, the girl who carried everyone's pain, who tried to hold her family together, had died with my mother. It was the first time in my life that I chose me. What remained was an open question: *Who am I now, if I am not saving anyone?*

For the first time, I allowed myself to explore life as a young woman, unbound by the roles I had been forced to play. And so, I stepped into the unknown. For the first time, I began breaking away from who I thought I needed to be. Without even realising it, I was loosening the tightness of being the perfect girl—the girl who got good grades, smiled at the right moments, and was always trying to do everything right. But that lost herself every time she chose to play the perfect-girl part instead of honouring her authenticity. It reached a point where I had no idea what I even liked anymore. In London, I let myself experiment. I interned for the shoe designer Charlotte Olympia while attending my master's program, dyed my hair strawberry blonde, and decided to wear only red for months, as if the colour itself was a rebirth, a declaration that I would no longer blend in.

My strawberry blonde hair.

Looking back now, I see these choices weren't superficial; they were sacred acts of reclaiming myself, my truth, my freedom. Sometimes the Soul speaks through the body, through creativity, through colour. Changing my hair and choosing to wear only red wasn't just style, it was my way of saying, *I am not who you told me I had to be. I am allowing myself to explore, without the fears, without shame, without the guilt of not being perfect.*

On the streets of London, I saw people dressed in every imaginable way—punk, vintage, couture, bohemian—and for the first time, I felt I could breathe. The city made room for contradictions; no one seemed shocked by differences. You walked on the streets and saw people from completely different ethnicities, religions, age, and body shape, and no one looked down upon it. This was the London I experienced—my perspective, perhaps not the full truth of every circle, but as you now know, everything we perceive through the human senses can be nothing more than that. For me, after the suffocating gossip and unspoken rules of Rio's high society, this way of experiencing life felt liberating. In London, no one knew me the way they did in Rio. I was simply a young woman—free, curious, alive. Grieving, yes, but for the first time, I released the guilt and allowed myself to play.

There were days I couldn't get out of bed. But other days, I felt a spark, excited to discover life. It felt strange at first, to laugh, to dance, to sing in my flat, without worrying about the state of my parents. Yet a quiet whisper inside told me it was okay. I travelled to Ibiza for the first time with family friends, watching the sun rise over the sea, its soft light easing the pain in my chest. Still, I was afraid of letting go. I didn't like staying out too late, or trying drugs that felt like they would make me lose control, or being topless on the beach like the other girls. I was still learning who I was. I watched the girls move so freely, confident in their own skin, and I longed to feel that same ease. But most of the time, I sat shyly in the corner, worried that if I spoke or moved too much, I would say or do something wrong. I was constantly rehearsing everything I wanted to say before letting the words out—a sign of how much

I questioned whether I was lovable. *What if they don't like me?* So I tried to predict what they would like instead. It was a deep sign of trauma, born from the belief that I wasn't enough, that I wasn't even worthy of being among them. I was so worried about what they thought of me that I preferred staying in, and I even returned to London a day earlier than planned.

This is one of the ego's greatest traps. Instead of allowing us to be spontaneous, authentic, and free, the ego convinces us that only a polished, edited version of ourselves is worthy of being seen. Yet what the Soul craves is the opposite: authenticity, rawness, Presence, Truth. Every time we rehearse or edit ourselves for approval, we cut off the natural flow of Love and Light moving through us. We negate our inner divinity. We step out of alignment with who we truly are. In that moment, we enter separation consciousness—the state of forgetting our own Source.

If you ever catch yourself doing this, pause and notice the pattern. Ask yourself what you are really scared of. The world doesn't need the idea of you, it needs *you*. This is why you are here. You are already amazing, already worthy, exactly as you are. If people like you or dislike you, that is not yours to carry. Your only task is to be yourself, your true self, the one that lives through the heart, not the ego's version of you, and in doing so, your true tribe will find you. Unfortunately, in today's world of social media, we are constantly shown edited, polished versions of people, masks instead of Souls. When we compare ourselves to those illusions, we feel worse and worse about who we are. But this can only happen if you haven't awakened to the Truth of your being. I promise you: You, just as you are, are enough. You are worthy. Your life matters just because you are you. You are unique. There is no one out there who is you, who carries your gifts. This is why you are alive.

At the time, I didn't yet know how to use my voice to express my truth, but I found another way: fashion. The clothes I wore became my language before I had the courage to speak. Dyeing my hair strawberry blonde, dressing only in red for months, experimenting with style, hats, and vintage clothes—this was me starting to dismantle the myth of the perfect girl I had carried for so long. Fashion was my first step towards authenticity, my way of saying, "I am here, and I can be who I choose to be."

My Work in Fashion

Another internship took me to Paris Fashion Week with a jewellery designer, where I absorbed every detail—the colours, the playfulness of the pieces, the eccentric beauty of the guests who filled the showroom. The chaos was intense, but it carried a kind of magic that I loved. Later, I interned with the brand Issa for a week during their fashion show in London. Each experience felt like stepping into the world I had dreamed of for so long.

Back in my teenage years, when home felt unbearable, I would escape into the glossy pages of *Seventeen.* I traced the trends with my fingertips, imagining myself in that world, not because I craved glamour but because it gave me a sense of possibility. Fashion, for me, was freedom. Through magazine pages, I could travel across the world without leaving my room. I could create new versions of myself, even if only for a moment. Fashion became my first portal into creativity, my first way of expressing who I was becoming before I had the courage to use my voice.

Later, I would come to understand that this act of imagining, of using my creativity, wasn't frivolous but spiritual. Imagination is how we become creators of our reality; it is how we shift our lens from survival into the eternal now. Through imagination, we plant seeds of colour, magic, hope, and love into landscapes that once felt grey and empty. Everything we do in life begins with thought, imagination, and dreaming—before we speak or move. We are creators of our own reality, but most people don't realise they are creating their lives at every moment. For me, this was the beginning of moving away from the saviour identity I had carried my whole life and into the girl who could finally dare to dream big.

And dream I did. I was determined to work at *Vogue.* When I arrived in London, I wrote out my application by hand and walked it to Vogue House, handing it over in person. At the time, applications were still done on paper. I never heard back. Instead of letting disappointment defeat me, I could hear my mother's words echoing in my heart: *You can do anything you dream of, if you believe in yourself.* It was my mother who taught me to love fashion and art, not for the labels or the appearances but as a way of expressing who we are inside. To her, creativity was freedom. Slowly, I began to see that for myself too.

On holidays, my mother and I would wander the streets of St. Germain in Paris, spending entire afternoons searching for treasures hidden in small shops, pieces no one else would have, pieces that carried their own story. The fun was never in owning something expensive; it was in finding something authentic and styling it in our own way. My mother taught me that even if you can buy a full designer look, never wear it all together—mix it up, make it feel yours. This is true style. These trips became our rituals of discovery, an unspoken lesson that beauty lives in what is real, not in what is performed. It lives not in labels, but in the discovery, in the poetry of creating every moment as your own.

She also took me to museums, guiding me through art history not with dates or rigid facts but with wonder. "Examine how this makes you feel," she would say. "Art is alive when you feel it." At the time, I didn't fully understand the depth of these lessons, but later, I would realise my mother was quietly handing me one of the greatest gifts I would ever receive: the power of creativity. She taught me to live like an artist.

The Power of Creativity

This is important to repeat: We are powerful beings, capable of creating anything we want in our lives. We just don't realise how much everything we do, feel, think, and say changes our reality. Within our hearts burns an eternal flame: on the right, it is blue, reflecting the Light, the wisdom; on the left, it is pink, reflecting Love, the one that reunites; and in the centre, it is gold, for the Power of Creation.

Yet when we reincarnate, we forget this flame even exists, and more importantly, we forget that we are part of Source itself and therefore are creators of our own reality. This is why every thought we have, every word we say, the emotions we feel, create a vibration that sends messages to the Unified Field, the Field of Life, carrying the frequency we are in, making us magnetise the possibility aligned with this frequency.

When we are clear and conscious in our intention, and can vividly imagine through our hearts, we are cocreating our lives. This is why those two years in London were so important for me. For the first time, I was following my heart, setting intentions about what I truly wanted, not what was expected of me. I was choosing—using the power of my will—what I wanted to work with, how I wanted to live, and what kind of woman I wanted to become. Even after her passing, my mother's teachings remained alive within me, like threads of Light guiding my steps, reminding me of the path my Soul came here to walk.

Throughout my life, my mother loved writing me letters. At the time, I gave them little importance, but over the years they became pearls of wisdom, treasures I returned to in moments of confusion or crossroads. In one of them she wrote, *Work as an artist: a lawyer artist, a doctor artist, a financial artist . . . but whatever you do, do it as an artist.*

What she meant was that all of us are creators. Everything in life begins as an idea before it takes form. We are artists of our own existence, sculpting reality through imagination, intention, and belief. What we believe can limit us or expand us—for in Truth, we are limitless. But if we believe we do not deserve happiness, so it will be. If we believe we are not beautiful, so it will be. If we believe we are not successful, so it will be. What we believe, God does not object to. The universe simply reflects back what we speak about ourselves and about reality. God, as we now understand, is not a being; it is the Field of Life. It is Oneness. And it carries no opinions, because we have Free Will. My mother's letter reflected this Truth—a Truth I would only fully understand after my awakening.

That wisdom shaped the way I began to live my young adult years: not merely surviving, but beginning to create.

My Way to the Publications

As I finished my master's, I began applying to internships at magazines, determined to follow my dream. I must have sent out applications to at least twenty publications. The first opportunity I landed was with *Wallpaper*. But my depression was at a peak, and I couldn't show up the way I wanted to. Soon you'll understand what was happening simultaneously in Rio, which made it even harder to be fully present. Next came *Harper's Bazaar UK*, where I had the privilege of working alongside two amazing women who not only mentored me but also became friends. And then, finally, came *Vogue*.

Earlier that year, I had emailed a director at Vogue once again, determined not to give up. This time, I received a reply and was invited for an interview. The morning I walked into Vogue House felt like magic. I woke up early, put on a little suit, and took the Tube to Oxford Street. I arrived early, so I stopped at a nearby café for tea, trying to calm my nerves. My heart was racing of excitement. This was the moment I had dreamed of since I was a teenager flipping through the glossy pages of *Seventeen*.

As I walked into Vogue House, I couldn't stop smiling. Butterflies swirled in my stomach. The Director looked at me, gestured towards a towering pile of CVs—there were hundreds of them—and asked, "Why *Vogue*? What makes you different from all these candidates?"

I told her that, for me, fashion was a way to experience life through multiple characters, a way to express our Truth in infinite forms. I told her I was determined to make it. Then she asked, "Would you like to do this only at *Vogue*?" I smiled and answered honestly, "*Vogue* is my favourite, but I would like to do this anywhere I can." Her expression softened, and I could feel she was pleased with my answer. A few weeks later, I received the letter: I had been invited to join *British Vogue*.

Looking back, I can see that the magic wasn't only in getting the internship—it was in not giving up. Life had given me rejection, silence, and moments when I wasn't strong enough to show up fully. And each time, I chose to try again. That is the key. So often we believe that one "no" defines us, that rejection means we aren't worthy. Or that if we don't perform at our full potential—like when I interned at *Wallpaper*—we somehow lose our value. But the Truth is this: every "no" is only redirection, a chance to refine our voice, to realign, to grow stronger. And if we do our best, whatever the best is in that circumstance be proud of yourself for not quitting. The Soul doesn't measure worth by how quickly the door opens. The Soul lights up when you still have the courage it takes to keep knocking—even when you are tired, even when you doubt yourself, even when the world feels silent around you.

In that moment, walking into Vogue House, I could almost hear my mother's voice: *You can do anything you dream of if you believe in yourself.* Her words were with me like an invisible thread, reminding me that creativity was not about status or labels but about living life as an artist. In many ways, she walked in with me that day. This is the lesson we now share with you: Follow your heart, even when the path feels slow, uncertain, unknown. Persevere. Be authentic. Be fearless. Believe in yourself. What is truly true to your heart will never pass you by; it will wait for you, until you are ready to receive it.

In the meantime, a friend introduced me to the editor of *Vogue RG*, a Brazilian monthly edition of *Vogue* that focused more on lifestyle. We met at a friendly dinner amongst other friends, and I told him how I was finishing my master's, working with incredible brands, and interning at some of the top magazines in London. He asked me, "Do you like to write or to style and creative direct?" Then, almost casually, he added, "Because becoming a fashion editor is very difficult—it's a very tight group and hard to get into."

The truth is, my dream was always to create images. But at that moment, I instinctively answered, "Both. But I would love to write something for the magazine." He smiled and said, "Sounds great. Send me some pitches, and maybe you can write something for us." My first pitch was a story on the jewellery designer Lara Bohinc. I had never written for a magazine before. When he told me to write three hundred *characters*, I misunderstood and wrote three hundred *words*. I smile at this now. The first time I saw something I had written, published, it felt like a dream. I yelled in the streets when I bought the print copy, which I still have to this day.

Soon, I found a way to use my pain as fuel. Every pitch, every email, every story was infused with my determination to create the life I dreamed of. I was proactive, always looking for solutions, always bringing new ideas. Very quickly, I became the European correspondent for both *Vogue Brasil* and *Vogue RG*. The editors trusted me so much that they began sending me on full features with people like Margherita Missoni and Joséphine de La Baume. Every opportunity I had, I would send pitches myself. During a trip I made to New York, out of the blue, someone gave me the number of Iris Apfel before she got famous. I called her, and my editor, and in a couple of days, I was interviewing and directing a shoot with Apfel. I produced the shoots, did the interviews, directed the photographers, and styled the looks. It was a living classroom, and I wasn't afraid to take risks. I was learning by doing. Fearless.

After my mother's passing, I told myself, *Life is too short. I have nothing to fear anymore.* The worst had already happened, so what did I have to lose if I just tried? At the time, I didn't yet have the deep Knowing we carry now, but experience was already showing me a Truth I would one day embody: Fear is an illusion. It feels real in the body, it storms through the mind, but at its core, it is only a projection of "what ifs." Fear is the ego's attempt to keep us safe, based on trauma, memory, conditioning, but instead it binds us to a prison that doesn't even exist. Every time I moved through fear back then—sending another pitch, walking into a room where I thought I didn't belong—I discovered that beyond the fear, there was only freedom. That is what life was teaching me: When we dare to step through the illusion of fear, we begin to taste what it means to truly live a Free Free life.

As all of this was coming together, I started my internship at *British Vogue*. Because of my experience with *Vogue Brasil*, I quickly became the assistant to one of the fashion editors. It felt like a dream unfolding—everything I had worked for opening before me. But soon I faced a big decision: stay in London and continue building this new life, or return to Brazil, to my boyfriend and my family. In the end, I chose to go back. What was happening at home was a sad chapter for both me and my brother, and part of me still felt responsible for carrying it.

Grief Cycle

Before I continue sharing my story, I want to pause for a moment to examine the grief cycle, because understanding the grief cycle can also help you navigate moments of grief in your own life. Grief isn't only present when someone dies; it also shows up when identities we once carried begin to fade away. I wasn't only grieving my mother's passing, I was also grieving the loss of the saviour identity I had built my whole life around. Creativity became my lifeline during this time. It gave me glimpses of joy and optimism when my reality felt unbearable, reminding me that another way of being was possible.

The grief cycle usually begins with denial. In my case, it showed up in the way I still tried to keep the saviour role alive—always flying back to Rio, trying to make sure everything was under control, as if my efforts could stop the ground from collapsing. When the denial began to fade, anger would rise, the kind of anger that comes from an unbearable sense of injustice. I blamed the prison episode, I blamed the hospital for not seeing my mother leave. I blamed myself for not seeing the signs and fighting with my mother before she died. I played the blame game because it felt easier than facing the raw pain, and at the time, I had no understanding of consciousness.

Then came the bargaining, those endless inner dialogues where I replayed the story again and again, asking myself what I could have done differently. If only I had answered her calls sooner. If only I had fought harder to make people listen to her. If only

I could have understood what she was going through. My mind tried to negotiate with the past, but of course, the past could not be changed. The past doesn't exist anymore, apart from our memory from it. The only Truth is the now.

Depression followed. It was the heaviness of reality settling in, the mornings I couldn't get out of bed, the days I felt completely numb, even during my first internship at *Wallpaper*. The grief had stripped me of joy, and I carried it like an invisible weight on my chest, even in moments I felt "happy." When I accomplished something, I couldn't tell her. I was somehow both grateful and ashamed to feel a sense of relief, because in her desperate act of freeing herself from suffering, she also freed me from continuing in that toxic environment. Slowly, over time, came acceptance. Not the kind of acceptance where you agree with what happened, but a quieter one, a surrender that whispers, "This is part of your story, and you can still go on." For me, that acceptance showed up when I began to focus more deeply on my career, when I poured my energy into creativity, when life began to show me that there was still beauty to be found.

But grief is never linear. It moves in waves, and sometimes it circles back when we least expect it. I only truly stopped grieving my mother years later, during my pregnancy with my daughter, or perhaps years later during the pandemic when I unraveled the Truth of her story, when something inside me finally softened, when I could feel a deeper healing unfold.

The final stage of grief, true acceptance, cannot come solely through the human perspective. It can only come through the Eagle's Eye. It is not about accepting loss and still feeling like a victim; it is about seeing it through Love and Truth. Through compassion and forgiveness of self and everyone involved. Only when we rise above the narrow lens of the linear mind and the ego body can we let go of the memory, the trauma, and become free.

CHAPTER 5

THE SECOND FAMILY

Meanwhile, in Rio, life was unravelling in a way that felt both foreign and suffocating. Each time I landed, the heavy, warm air clung to my skin, and the streets buzzed with life, yet inside our home, there was only silence and tension. While I was living in London, I flew back every couple of months, torn between worlds: a world that I was discovering, one filled with colour, joy, and possibility; and the world of the old family dynamics, where I was trying to be present for my brother and my father. Grief lingered like a shadow that refused to lift, heavy and unshakable. I told myself I was holding us together, but the truth is that when I went back home, I was still clinging to my old character and playing the saviour, desperately trying to mend pieces that were already broken. A deeper part of me was silently crumbling, though I couldn't yet admit it. My father, blinded by his own unresolved pain, couldn't see the new storm that was forming around us, one that would soon devastate us all.

While I tried to build a life in London, my father made a decision that ripped the family apart, though he couldn't see it that way. He bought a new apartment, another grand "family home." It was the same pattern I had watched play out my whole life with my mother: After every fight, after every tear, he believed that a new home would erase the cracks, that walls and furniture could somehow hold together what love could not. This time, the apartment was even grander, dripping with extravagant decoration and priceless artwork. It didn't feel like a home; it felt like a stage, one set to impress his friends, to showcase his taste, to prove his worth to the world, and maybe to himself. When I stepped inside, the air smelled of polished wood and fresh paint, every corner carefully curated to perfection. But instead of warmth, there was only silence echoing through the rooms, a silence that made me feel like an intruder in my own family. He shaped every detail of it to fit his new wife and her two daughters, as if this new performance of family could erase the old one. What he failed to see, or perhaps couldn't see through the blindness of his own traumas, was that in the script he was writing, there was no place for me or my brother. It was unconscious, but painful.

My brother was still finishing school while I was living in London, and soon after, he began university. His greatest joy during that time was practicing equestrian jumping with my father, a sport my father had devoted himself to daily since we were babies. It was the one true constant in his life, and my brother found a way to keep his bond with him through this shared passion. For a while, it gave them something to hold onto, a fragile thread of connection between them. Horses carry a powerful medicine: They invite presence, discipline, and trust. Riding demands focus, balance, and a partnership between rider and animal that leaves little room for chaos. It creates moments of pure Presence, where looping thoughts of fear, grief, and uncertainty pause, as the body and mind surrender to the practice. In that way, it becomes almost meditative. For my brother and father, equestrian jumping offered a structure they could lean on, a way of touching some level of stillness when everything else felt unstable.

But external structure alone cannot heal the heart. At best, it was a plaster, one that held for a time but never addressed the deeper wounds. As I would soon come to see, plasters eventually fall away, and when they do, the pain beneath surfaces with even greater force.

At just eighteen, my brother had already witnessed more loss than most could bear. When he told our father he didn't want to live with his new wife, my father insisted at first. Still trapped in the wounds of his past, he convinced himself it would be fine if he didn't allow this. Without realising the gravity of the decision he was making, he prioritised his needs as a man, the idealised life he imagined would somehow rebuild everything he had lost: marriage, honour, reputation, the appearance of the perfect family. But there was no real foundation beneath it. A quick marriage, a newly decorated house, a wife who already had children—all of it was constructed to soothe his pain, while he forgot to ask what would be best for us, his own children, who were still trying to survive the loss of our young mother. All of this unfolded in the very first year after her death. My father was in emergency mode, grasping for stability but blind to the devastation his choices created.

This is what trauma does when left unhealed. It throws us into survival mode, where the ego rushes to build quick fixes, like my father was unconsciously doing. This is how we push pain down, hiding it beneath carpets instead of moving with it, learning from it. But whatever you don't feel, your body stores. It archives it instead of dissolving it. Instead of feeling lighter, you feel more fractured. Imagine yourself as a sphere when you are whole. Every time you push down a pain without facing it, without meeting it with care, love, and compassion, it becomes a traumatic memory, one that doesn't go away simply because you stop thinking about it or because you added a plaster. It stays. The part of you that was whole is now divided. With the passing of years, and the many traumas we go through, imagine how many fractures we each carry. The sensation of emptiness comes exactly from the illusion that what you don't feel disappears. But this is not true.

The more we suppress, the more we cover our hearts with pain, making it almost impossible for the Soul to speak through us. This is one of the great problems of the culture we live in today, a culture of immediacy and entertainment, where we buy the illusion but still go home with the trauma now stored in the body. This is what causes disease and addiction, because what you don't heal through feeling (the heart/Love) and understanding (the mind/Light), life will make you learn through illness. Survival is not the same as healing. True healing cannot come from replacing what was lost; it only comes from turning inwards, facing the wound, and trusting the Soul to guide us back into wholeness.

This is what I see now in my father. Each unprocessed loss, each betrayal, each humiliation he endured became another fracture within him. Instead of turning inwards, learning from the experiences, breaking the patterns, he built plasters: a new family, a new apartment, a new identity. He kept trying to rebuild the appearance of wholeness on the outside, while on the inside, the fractures only deepened. Only made him feel even more alone, because he was living in separation of Oneness. His survival mode made him blind to us, his children, and blind to himself.

Living life through his ego meant making decisions as if he were wearing blinkers. He could only see what was directly in front of him. This is what the lower mind does: It keeps us stuck on the ground floor, where choices are immediate and narrow, made from survival rather than Truth. The higher perspective, the Eagle's Eye, is like moving to the top floor, where you can see with Clarity, with spaciousness, with the full picture in view. Trauma tightens the blinkers even further, narrowing our sight until we can no longer see the impact of our actions. In my father's case, this meant he could not see the devastation unfolding right in front of him, and he was unable to perceive the deepening fracture between him and his children.

Do you remember a choice you once made through this blinker view? Those choices often feel urgent, as if there's only one way forwards. They come from survival mode, when you feel pressured, desperate to resolve something, desperate to grasp at joy, desperate to find even a fleeting relief from pain.

As the new apartment began to take shape, my brother and I fought with him, begging him to see clearly, to recognise the weight of what was happening. But instead of drawing us closer, he unconsciously pushed us further away. He rented for us a separate apartment in Rio, on the famous bohemian street of Dias Ferreira in Leblon, as if that would solve everything. In his mind, for a teenage boy, having a place of his own might have seemed like a dream. For me, it was simply the apartment I had always asked him for. What he couldn't see was that none of this was what we needed at the time. What we longed for was his Love, his Presence. We wanted the home dinner routines, the hugs, the sense of being a family even if my mother wasn't there, not another gift disguised as love as he used to do with my mother, as he had learned from his father before him. It was his way of convincing himself that trying to rebuild his life as he was doing was okay—without realising that, in the process, he was quietly rebuilding it without us in it. The grand new apartment became the stage for his new life, and now, his new family. This is one of the illusions of the wounded masculine: mistaking gifts, money, or appearances for love. But true Love is not something you can buy or decorate a home with; it is presence, attention, and connection. Without this, even the grandest gestures feel empty.

My brother, heartbroken, went to live in his new flat alone, while I stayed in London to finish my internships and master's. When I returned to Rio, I would stay in our new flat and occasionally visit the grand new home my father had moved into. I would walk into that apartment, fully aware of everything that had changed, and pretend it was all fine. But it wasn't. It felt like stepping into a play in which I no longer had a role.

The weight of it all was crushing—the sense of abandonment, of being replaced, of watching the family we had fought so hard to hold together slip into a reality that no longer included us. Soon, my father's new wife became pregnant, and a new family began to take shape. The room in their apartment that had once been meant for my brother and me now had a new owner. Still caught in our lower-mind fears and judgements, my brother and I had often warned my father that she might one day want children of her own. She was in her thirties; he was in his fifties. A familiar pattern was unfolding—one we had seen before—and in our pain, it felt as if she didn't want us there. But from where we stand today, with the Eagle's Eye, we can see it differently. She wasn't trying to hurt us. She was a woman carrying her own deep wounds—shaped by a military father and a mother who couldn't nurture her sense of worth. That kind of upbringing often leaves a child feeling invisible, inferior, and desperate to prove herself later in life. When those wounds remain unhealed, they resurface in the ways we seek security: through relationships, appearances, roles, and even through children.

Like so many women caught in the wounded feminine, she reached for external anchors—status, possessions, belonging—to ease an inner ache that only Love and self-awareness can truly heal. Beloved reader, I share this with Love. Not as judgement, not as assumption, but as a perspective—a mirror you may use as medicine for your own life. Because in the end, the only Truth is Love.

My father, lost in his own wounds, couldn't see this. He was trying to rebuild what he thought he had lost: honour, stability, the appearance of a perfect family. And so two wounded people found each other, to illuminate the places in each of them that still longed for true healing.

The teaching here is this: When we look only through the ego's lens, it's easy to see enemies, to believe someone is scheming against us. But when we rise to the Soul's vision, we see the truth— that people act from wounds, not from Truth until the are able to move back into Love. Compassion doesn't mean excusing the harm; it means seeing the pain beneath the behaviour, in a circular perspective, and in that seeing, freeing ourselves from the heaviness of blame and into the heart.

The reason we saw her with fear and judgement was because my father had met her just three months before my mother passed away. For us, it was just another separation. We didn't believe their marriage was over. When my mother died, she stepped quickly into the role of "woman of the house," erasing traditions, ignoring the raw grief still thick in the air, and claiming a place in our lives that, from our perspective, she hadn't yet earned. At the time, it felt as though she didn't respect our pain, the silence of my mother's absence, the depth of the bond my brother and I still carried with the family we had once been. Instead, it seemed she wanted to replace it all with a vision of her own, one that disregarded the fragile connection we still longed to preserve with our father. Now, through the Eagle's Eye, we can see she also lacked maturity, she was still a young woman, and she was doing the best she could at the time.

My father's vanity grew louder. His heart was too covered in trauma to even understand our pain. So it seemed like he was easily manipulated by his new wife, not out of cruelty but because she was in her wounded feminine. When women are in their wounded feminine, they can manipulate and compete to survive or become extremely passive. This happens unconsciously beloved reader. It is a reaction from the ego, not the Soul.

Year after year, the distance between us widened, each day pulling him further away from the father we once knew. He began prioritising his new family, his new life, believing his old one, his older children, no longer needed him so much. In his mind, he was refashioning his new wife—showering her with jewels, designer bags, and lavish gifts, and enrolling her daughters in the most prestigious schools in Rio—while quietly withdrawing from his own flesh and blood. The bedtime stories, the daily dinner routine, and even the financial support my brother and I had once relied on wasn't there anymore. But we needed him, especially his Love, more than he could realise, and the feeling of being replaced devastated us.

The new family travelled constantly, and did the same country club and country-side routine, living the life we once lived. We were supposed to be part of it, but it never felt like our place; instead, we felt like intruders in a world that wasn't ours anymore. It was as if my father had been placed under a spell, blinded by the glitter of appearances, by the illusion of validation and approval. On the outside, it all looked dazzling—the trips, the restaurants, the photos, the staged happiness. But beneath it, the true connection he needed was missing. This is one of the great traps of the ego: to confuse sparkle with substance, performance with love. The more he tried to decorate his pain, the more distant and empty he felt. He started drinking more and buying more, without realising these habits were becoming addictions to numb the pain that never seemed to go away.

The new wife, just eleven years older than me, saw me less as a daughter to embrace and more as a threat to the life she was try-ing to secure for herself while caught in her own survival-mode loop, where she often felt like a victim of her circumstances. It wasn't only competition for my father's attention; at times it felt as though she was competing with me as a woman. Perhaps it was the small age difference between us, but I often felt diminished by her—as though putting me down was her way of making herself feel safer, stronger, more worthy. This is a common reaction of the wounded feminine.

It felt, in those years, as if she wanted to erase the bond I had always shared with my father by slowly convincing him that he was too soft with my brother and me, that the attention and financial support he gave us was indulgent rather than essential. And so, bit by bit, he unconsciously withdrew from us—believing her uncon-scious fears, trying to quiet the conflicts that had begun to arise in their marriage, without realising he had stepped into yet another toxic dynamic.

The care, generosity, and presence he had always given us began to fade. My brother and I were left in the shadows of his choices, carrying the familiar weight of feeling abandoned once again. With each passing day, our hearts grew heavier and our bond with him more fragile, as we tried to make sense of a family that no longer felt like ours.

Beloved reader, I want to remind you gently: these were mem-ories filtered through trauma. This was my ego's perspective at the time, not the full Truth. In Truth, there is no one to blame. Every person involved was acting from their own wounds, their own unconsciousness, their own fear. When we look through the lens of Love—beyond the illusions of pain—compassion becomes the only possible response.

São Paulo

When I returned from London, I received a job offer to work at *Vogue*. At first, I worked from the Rio office, living with my brother in the apartment we shared. But soon after, I was offered a coveted role as a fashion editor and made the decision to move to São Paulo. My father, eager to show his love in the only way he knew how, helped me rent a beautiful new apartment, hoping it would make me feel at ease in the new city. But his wife, always critical, thought it was unnecessary, and as always, tensions grew. Every interaction carried an undercurrent of conflict. It was as if our lives had become power struggles and unresolved pain.

I threw myself into my work, burying the discomfort deep inside. At twenty-four, I became the youngest fashion editor in the country. The title came with pressure, yes, but it also gave me something to hold onto, a fleeting escape from the chaos at home. Still, no matter how much I achieved, the success could never fill the emptiness of being caught between the love of a father who no longer truly saw me and the perceived jealousy of the woman my father married. Looking back, I see how often we turn work, achievement, and success into shields against our pain. A defence mechanism. The world applauds productivity, but behind the applause, many of us are silently starving inside. True healing doesn't come from doing more; it comes from daring to feel more, from pausing long enough to let our wounds breathe, instead of burying them under titles and accomplishments. But I didn't know better, and creativity was in many ways a healing for me—a healthier one than the drugs I saw many of my friends do, but still an addictive behaviour to numb pain.

Later, when I married (a moment I will share in more detail further in this story), I made a decision that cut deeply into the fractures of my already strained relationship with my father. I told him I didn't want his wife to walk down the aisle in place of my mother. I wanted my godmothers to take that role—women who had represented unconditional love to me, not the unconscious manipulation and competition that had tried to replace us as a family. My father couldn't accept it. His wife's influence seemed to cloud his judgement, and what should have been a sacred celebration became another battlefield. In the end, she entered the church walking beside her own father, acting as a bridesmaid—a subtle yet cutting display of external power that, in truth, only revealed her wounded feminine and need for validation in her new role as my father's wife.

When I later gave birth to my daughter (a moment I will share with you in more detail further on), it was intimate, raw, and vulnerable. My father stood in the delivery room with my partner. That's how close we had always been while I was growing up. While we waited for my body to be ready to deliver, I sensed something was off. As I had learned to do since I was a child, I picked up on the shifts in energy immediately. To this day, I am sensitive to any such noise. That day, my father's frequency wasn't steady; he wasn't fully present.

I asked him, "Who are you texting? Why are you upset?"

He looked at me and said quietly, "My wife is upset you didn't invite her. She doesn't feel included."

I couldn't believe it. Rage welled up in me. I snapped, "Even now? Even while I'm giving birth, she's complaining? Interfering? What did she expect—that she should be here in the delivery room too? Why are you giving this even a moment of your thought while you should be here? Are you going crazy?" Beneath the yelling was a desperate plea: *Stop this nonsense. Your daughter is experiencing one of the most sensitive, sacred moments of her life. Stay here. Stay present. Take care of her. See her. Be with her. Stop letting yourself be manipulated. Stop drowning in guilt.*

When we left the hospital, I was the one who paid the bill for the private room because my partner wasn't in a position to do so. My father also didn't step in—not because he lacked the means, but because he simply didn't take the initiative. The scene of me leaving the hospital the morning after twenty-six hours of labour, with my newborn baby in my arms and two men by my side, felt surreal— because I was the one pulling out the card and handling the practical details, despite having grown up with the lens that men were the providers. It was the gesture that cut my heart, because it wasn't a high expense, especially after my father had poured huge amounts of money into bringing his new family, his new life, into the very moments of my daughter's birth—buying six plane tickets and renting a huge house in front of the park. The disparity cut deeply. It wasn't about the money. It was a symbol of how far we had drifted, of the manipulations, of what he unconsciously valued more—the appearance. It was in these small, piercing actions that the emotional distance between us became undeniable. With each passing moment, our bond unravelled further, replaced by the weight of unspoken expectations and unmet needs. What should have been a moment of connection, of a father supporting his daughter through one of the most sacred moments of her life, instead became a painful reminder of how completely we had fallen apart.

Moving Beyond Victim and Persecutor

As I share the unravelling of these events, we begin to see a side of the wounded feminine that is manipulative, competitive, and steeped in victim consciousness. It's essential for me to say that, today, I do not blame my father's wife, nor do I blame my father. But at that time, I was unconscious and hurting, and yes, I did blame. This may have come across in the way I wrote the previous part, because I wanted you to feel the pain I felt, and the pain you too might recognise from a similar situation.

But blame, beloved reader, is rooted in judgement and the limited perspective of the ego. Blame forces us into wearing horse blinkers, narrowing our vision, while the Soul sees from above, circularly, from the higher floors, with the expanded awareness of Love and Light. The Soul never blames. The Soul knows. We can only start seeing through the Eagle's Eye, when we take the root of consciousness; if we don't, it is impossible to move beyond blame and judgement. So we invite you to reflect on these moments with your higher mind, through the Eagle's Eye, and see the trauma of my father's wife. She was also hurt, in ways far beyond what I, or any of us, could or can ever fully understand. The only way to shift blame into Love is through compassion and radical forgiveness by recognising that there is no way of knowing the full Truth of what she was going through, why she did what she did, or what truly existed between her and my father. Through the law of reflection, we can also understand that she and my father were mirrors of the traumas I myself needed to heal. But I will explain this further.

What I do know is this: A toxic relationship was formed, like so many are, because both my father and his wife were deeply wounded, each in their own unique way. She acted with manipulation, attempting to feel important and seen—as many women in their wounded feminine do—but beneath it all, she was simply trying to survive with the tools she had learned. As we all do, when we are unconscious.

My father, on the other hand, had just lost his sense of honour after the prison episode. He couldn't work anymore, the doors of business were closed to him, and his wife of twenty years, my mother, had taken her own life. His sense of self-worth was shattered, leaving him vulnerable and without self-esteem, easily manipulated by anyone who offered him a glimpse of love. He was desperate for a quick fix, a way to rebuild what he had lost, but the choices he made only deepened his pain and that of his children. For nine years, he poured every bit of his inheritance into trying to prove his honour and restore his name. In doing so, he became increasingly disconnected from his children, trapped in a toxic relationship that could never provide the healing he so desperately needed, while growing more dependent on alcohol and compulsive spending.

Neither of them was a victim, and neither of them was a persecutor. Both were acting from unconscious wounds, drawn to each other through unresolved pain. The ego led the way, and both the wounded masculine and the wounded feminine played their parts: she, through her manipulation and competition; he, through his desperate need to feel worthy by clinging to appearances and external power. Neither of them was grounded in Truth or authenticity. They were both caught in the illusion that their identities could be fixed by the external world. However, trauma can only be healed when we look within. When we return to our hearts, the heart opens as a place where pain can be given to God, to Soul, and released.

This is the trap of separation consciousness, where there is always a victim and a persecutor. Both of them probably felt like they were the victim and the other the persecutor. But what we need to understand is that we attract into our lives the exact frequency we emit. Despair meets despair, fear meets fear, wound meets wound. They attracted each other so they could learn from each other. When we hold ourselves in a victim consciousness for too long, it becomes an excuse for causing harm. This, my beloved reader, is not freedom. We can only free ourselves when we take responsibility for our lives fully and see the part we played in the traumatic experience. This, however, does not exempt those who harm or abuse others from their responsibility, as abuse is always unacceptable. But when we see beyond the abuse, and into Truth, it helps us reclaim our power and take the lead of our own lives.

In my case, at the time, I too felt like a victim. I too acted from that pain, as you will see in the next chapter. I felt my father's new wife was taking him from me. I felt my father wasn't present because he didn't want to be. In truth, beloved reader, he was hardly present for himself and was living by a thread. How on earth would he have the capacity to give more than he had? He was doing his best, and so was she. In time, life will teach us what we don't yet have the capacity to learn. This is the beauty of being alive: We all get so many chances to try again.

CHAPTER 6

VOGUE AND MARRIAGE

As I mentioned briefly before, I became a fashion editor at *Vogue Brasil* at only twenty-four. When I arrived in São Paulo, I felt as though I was stepping into an entirely new world. I already knew some of my colleagues from my collaborations in London, but nothing could have prepared me for the culture inside the newsroom. My editor-in-chief was tough, demanding, and feared by most, but we got along well and eventually grew close. The fashion director, however, made it clear from the very beginning that he did not like me or want me there. He tried to diminish me again and again, making me feel displaced and alone. It was a toxic environment, though at the time I didn't recognise it as such. This was the norm in almost every newsroom then. It felt familiar, like home—shouts, criticism, manipulation, abuse, walking on eggshells. I was wired to tolerate it, to survive it, the same way I had survived my childhood.

The publishing and entertainment world was drenched in patriarchy. Women in leadership positions were rare, and many who held power led through the wounded masculine simply because that was the only model they had ever been taught. Most fashion directors were men, nearly all photographers were men, and it was they who decided what a "Vogue woman" should look like—ultra-thin, blonde, sculpted into an object rather than a fully lived human being.

This ideal of womanhood was impossible for most women to relate to, and even more impossible to embody. And yet it shaped how society measured our worth. Globally, between 5.5% and 17.9% of young women will experience a DSM-5 eating disorder by early adulthood (Silén & Keski-Rahkonen, 2022). Anxiety disorders affect an estimated 4.4% of the global population, with women disproportionately represented (WHO, 2025). Worldwide, nearly 1 in 3 women has been subjected to physical and/or sexual intimate-partner or non-partner violence in her lifetime (WHO, 2024). And although female suicide rates are lower than male rates, intimate-partner violence significantly increases the risk of suicidal thoughts and attempts among women (Devries et al., 2011).

This combination is one of the reasons so many girls and women face low self-esteem—which then makes them more vulnerable to accepting abusive relationships, facing eating disorders, depression, anxiety, or the belief that they must constantly shrink themselves just to belong. The myth of perfection strips women of their innate freedom. It distorts our relationship with our bodies, our confidence, and our Truth—leaving many of us questioning our worth before we have even had the chance to discover who we truly are, especially now in times of social media.

The absurdity of all of this struck me even then, but I didn't yet have the words for what I was witnessing, nor the data. These were insights we would come to understand much later, after founding Free Free and devoting ferociously research freedom during my years at Harvard. All I knew at the time was that something felt deeply wrong—and that somehow, instinctively, I would need to make my part in this world different.

The first cover I worked on was for *Vogue RG* with Paris Hilton. Soon after, I was standing on sets with Gisele, Naomi Campbell, Rihanna, and Kim Kardashian. At the time, I didn't realise it, but I was already questioning the rules of society through the images I was creating. The same rules that had once locked my mother in a golden cage—and had locked me in the myth of perfection—were now being fed to millions of women around the world. And somewhere inside me, something began to shift. Who created these rules? And why were we still following them?

The cover I did with Rihanna,
when I was a young fashion editor.

Even without the language I have today, I could feel those questions rising through me like whispers from the Soul. I didn't yet understand the wounded feminine, the wounded masculine, or how trauma shapes entire cultures—but I intuitively sensed that the narratives we were reinforcing were not Truth. They were constructs, illusions, a script designed to keep women small. Why does this shoe have to go with that look? Why can't a top be worn upside down, or trousers styled as a shirt? My questions began to take shape as creative images that were raw, authentic, and disruptive—shifting the way women were normally portrayed. The fashion director hated it. He tried to shut me down, but instead of shrinking, I went straight to my editor-in-chief. Everyone feared her, but I had no problem confronting her. Somehow, this made her respect me. Soon, she began trusting me to direct most of *Vogue Brasil*'s covers.

What we now understand is that those questions were never really about clothes; they were about freedom, conditioning, and creativity. Fashion became my first language of liberation—my way of unmasking the rigid rules patriarchy had written for women: how to look, how to behave, how to exist. Every time I flipped a garment upside down, I was unconsciously declaring that rules could be rewritten. Women do not exist to fit a mould; we exist to express the Truth of who we are. Creativity, I would later come to understand, is one of the most powerful medicines against unconscious oppression, because it reminds us that there is always another way.

The media plays a monumental role in shaping culture, especially in defining the roles we are all expected to play. For decades, mainstream magazines portrayed only one narrow version of the "ideal woman": thin, white, blonde, flawless, young, married, and with children. Rarely did you see women of different body shapes, races, ages, or ethnicities. Rarely were women celebrated for having powerful careers. Women were objectified, their value measured by how well they fit into a mould that never truly existed—not even for the women who seemed closest to it.

Later, when I studied at Harvard, I had the chance to dive deeper into these themes. I remember one article titled, *"Can Women Have It All?"* Even the question revealed the wound—as if men's lives were whole by default, while women's were always a negotiation, a compromise, a balancing act we were expected to master without ever being taught how.

At the time, I still didn't have the language for what I was sensing, but my intuition kept whispering that something in this system was profoundly distorted. I could feel it long before I could articulate it. What the magazines were celebrating was the same illusion that had broken my own home—the illusion that appearances matter more than truth. As my career grew, I began travelling constantly, shooting with photographers like Patrick Demarchelier, Mario Testino, and Ellen von Unwerth. One month I was in St. Barth's, the next in Morocco, then Paris, Milan, New York, Los Angeles. On the surface, it was glamorous—a dream many would envy. But beneath it all, I carried the weight of knowing that behind the glossy images was a world feeding women the same golden cage, that had once in some level created to much trauma to my family.

This is what intuition does. It speaks before the mind can make sense of anything. Intuition is the Soul's language—it doesn't shout, judge, or debate. It whispers, nudges, and gently reveals that something is off, that a deeper truth is waiting to be seen. At the time, I couldn't yet translate what my Soul was telling me, but now we know that those whispers were the first seeds of freedom being planted. The Soul always knows before the mind is ready to understand.

Marriage

In the midst of my rapid rise to success, still living inside the myth of the "perfect girl," I married my boyfriend—the one I had met during my law internship. We had been on and off for about five years. When my mother died, he became an important figure for me and my family: a safe space for me, and almost like an older brother to my brother. I loved him deeply, and he played a meaningful role in our lives.

Looking back, I can now see the signs were there from the beginning. Both of us were wounded, both already carrying the dynamics of the wounded masculine and the wounded feminine. He was jealous, and when I moved to London after my mother passed, he would often say, "There's a detective following you." I never knew whether he was serious or joking, but sometimes I would look over my shoulder on the street, wondering if someone was there.

The relationship had always been marked by ups and downs, even if we loved each other. I mistook his jealousy for love and confused moments of control with care. I interpreted his possessiveness as passion—proof, in my mind, that he must love me deeply. Instead of seeing these behaviours as signs something was off, I welcomed them. I was also terrified of disappointing him, terrified of being abandoned by the one person who made me feel secure. We broke up a few times, but we always came back to each other. It was a passionate, intense bond, and when I moved to São Paulo a few months later, he asked me to marry him. I said yes.

I truly loved him—and I loved his family even more. They were stable, humble, loving people who embraced me as a daughter. They seemed like the kind of family I had never truly known: affectionate, united, grounded. Their presence filled the void left by everything I had lost. I felt cared for in a way that felt both comforting and unfamiliar.

After we married, the unhealthy patterns grew stronger. At the time, I didn't recognise them as toxic, because we didn't yet have the emotional maturity to understand what we were living. We were young, wounded, insecure, and unprepared. For him, marriage meant I should prioritise him above everything—my work, my dreams, my individuality. For me, marriage meant sharing a life while supporting one another's uniqueness. But neither of us had the tools to find the balance to express our needs, or to hold space for the other's wounds without hurting the other.

We had a Catholic ceremony officiated by the priest who had also presided over my mother's memorial, followed by a celebration at my family's country house. On the surface, I was living the life of the "perfect woman": a flourishing career, a beautiful church wedding to my long-time boyfriend, friendships in the society circle I had grown up in, and newfound friendships in São Paulo's fashion world. From the outside, my life looked flawless. But something inside me was restless. The only places where I expressed my questions and authenticity were in the pages of Vogue and through the way I dressed. I had always loved dressing differently—as my mother taught me—and soon I became known for it, often photographed at fashion weeks for my unusual looks. My clothes said what my voice still could not.

After we married, we moved into a beautiful townhouse in São Paulo, which I decorated with so much passion and love. From the outside, we looked like an "it couple." He was successful in his own right—unlike many of my childhood friends whose lives were built on family money—and I admired this about him. He worked in the financial market, in mergers and acquisitions. But after the wedding, he no longer wanted me to work. He dreamed of a wife fully devoted to him, like most of his friends had—a traditional model of marriage preferred by most powerful men. The more success I had, the more unhappy he became. My light touched wounds he had never healed—wounds of insecurity and fear he could not yet see.

His unconscious way of reclaiming power was to put me down. He didn't do it intentionally—this we understood later. But at the time, all I felt was pain and a sense of disbelief, devastation. What was actually happening between us was simply a pattern: two wounded people acting out old dynamics, being given a chance to learn and heal. Within months of our wedding, something shifted. Everything he once admired in me became what he resented. He questioned my long hours at Vogue, my travelling. He said things like, "I'm the only man I know who comes home and has no dinner, no shirts ironed." He also said, "You don't look good; you're fat. How can I desire someone like this? You hardly take care of yourself."

I tried to fix it—the same way I had tried to fix everything since I was a child. I looked in the mirror and began hating my reflection. I hired someone to train our housekeeper so the home would look like a "proper household"—food cooked, laundry pressed, shirts crisp. We were so young, and I was trying to force myself into a role I had never been taught. My mother had shown me elegance and how to host dinners, but she also taught me independence. She taught me to never depend fully on a man. So I tried to merge these two realities—to be the traditional wife he wanted while staying connected to who I was—and it tore me apart.

No matter what I did, nothing made him happy. If anything, things worsened. We lost intimacy. While I travelled for work, he threw parties behind my back. The marriage was crumbling, but I wasn't ready to accept it. I tried harder. I worked out more. I negotiated fewer hours at Vogue. But it was never enough. Then one day he said, "If you keep working at Vogue, we will get divorced. You earn so little—I can pay you that salary so you can stop working." His words cut me deeply. It was humiliating. For me, Vogue was not only about some level of financial independence. It was my passion, my dream, the career I had worked hard for since I was a teenager. I was twenty-seven—far too young to sacrifice my life's calling. I panicked. I couldn't believe the "perfect" family I had dreamed of my entire life was slipping away. So I continued making excuses for him. I blamed myself. I tried harder.

But the more I succeeded, the more he resented me. After I directed my first cover with Naomi Campbell, Vogue hosted a dinner at the Fasano Hotel to celebrate. I begged him to come with me. He resisted. I insisted. At the dinner, everyone congratulated me. People praised the cover, stopped to tell me how extraordinary it was. Instead of feeling proud, he grew furious and left, abandoning me there alone.

It was the wounded masculine and the wounded feminine playing out again. He was jealous and resentful because my success blurred his role as my provider. I, on the other hand, collapsed into victim consciousness—drowning in self-doubt and unworthiness. It was no one's fault. We were both young, conditioned by culture, religion, family, and media. Two wounded children in adult bodies, trying to love without the tools.

The marriage lasted only eighteen months, and six of those months we were already separated. At the end of the year, we spent Christmas and New Year's together as a final attempt to save the relationship, but the truth was already clear. When we returned home, we decided to divorce. I was terrified. Many of my childhood friends criticised me. They believed he was right—that a married woman should prioritise her family, not her career. But I wasn't prioritising my career. I was prioritising the Truth of my being, and the deep Knowing that a woman can have a successful career and a happy marriage when there is balance, respect, and Love. Yet instead of seeing that, I was judged, whispered about, even abandoned by friends I had known for years. I had not enough money to provide for myself alone, no certainty about my future. But life, in its divine intelligence, had already begun opening new paths. I had just signed with an American agency to represent my work internationally. In January of that year, I directed a cover with Rihanna for *Vogue Brasil*, a milestone I had once only dreamed of. Soon after, consultancy clients began appearing unexpectedly. Before I knew it, I was financially independent, working in New York with brands like Louis Vuitton, Uniqlo, and Intermix. What seemed like an ending was, in truth, the beginning of my freedom—and the beginning of breaking the ancestral patterns that had shaped my life for generations.

The Pattern

As we arrive at the unravelling of my career and my marriage, it is essential to remember that everything is a matter of perspective, and there is no one to blame. Everyone was doing the best they could with the level of consciousness we held at the time, shaped by the culture, traditions, trauma, and religion we were born into. As you may have already noticed, I was unconsciously repeating the same pattern I had witnessed between my parents. A part of me slipped into the familiar position of the wounded feminine—feeling like a victim, doubting my worth, trying to earn love through perfection and compliance. And he fell into the wounded masculine—believing he needed to control, dominate, and define the rules to maintain his sense of power. These were not our Truths; they were our wounds interacting with each other.

The Truth is that we were both acting through our egos rather than from our authentic selves. We simply didn't yet have the emotional maturity, the tools, or the consciousness to understand what we were living. We were two wounded people trying to navigate life with unhealed parts leading the way. This is how the universe works. Patterns repeat until we become conscious of them. They return again and again, like waves—not to punish us, but to give us the opportunity to learn the lesson and see clearly what we could not see before. Patterns are mirrors, reflecting back the parts of ourselves that are still asking for healing. If we don't awaken to them, we continue to live them endlessly, just with new names, new faces, new places. The universe brings us the same experience—not because life is cruel, but because the Soul is always seeking wholeness. Once we understand this, the blame game dissolves. As all of us carry shadows we are unconscious about and also Light. My ex-husband is a wonderful man, and we share this chapter because so many of us go through similar dynamics. In an unhealthy relationship, no one is necessarily "the villain". Everyone is doing the best they can based on their level of consciousness. The dynamic itself becomes unhealthy, and it arrives in our lives to reveal something deeper—something the Soul is ready to heal. Yes, as adults we carry the responsibility to heal ourselves so that we do not perpetuate harm in the world. But when trauma is active, we become blind to the pain we inflict—on others and on ourselves. This is why, when we look at a situation through the Eagle's Eye, free from separation consciousness, blame has no place. We begin to see that those who cause the most harm are, in fact, those who are hurting the most. They project their pain outward because they cannot yet face it within themselves.

For me, this chapter became the moment I broke a very important ancestral pattern. I was not passive. Somewhere inside me, my mother's voice echoed: *A woman must have her own career, her own independence, her own way of providing for herself.* A woman must never give away her power of choice. So I made a choice. I did not follow the rules of the society I was born into. And yes, my friends judged me for it—but they too were acting from their egos, projecting onto me their own fears, insecurities, and inherited beliefs. This is why beloved readers, always follow your heart, even if it means being judged. As people are just projecting their own fears onto you, unconsciously.

Still, this was the first step toward my liberation. It required courage to break the pattern. Courage to face judgement. Courage to be seen differently. Courage to lose people I loved. Courage to walk alone for a while. But this is what consciousness does: It breaks the cycle. It frees the lineage. It opens the door for the Soul to finally breathe. And the same is true for you, beloved reader. You too can move beyond your fears, your conditioning, your inherited limitations. You too can choose to unlock your golden cage—whatever shape or form it has taken. Freedom always begins with one brave choice.

CHAPTER 7

BREAK-UP WITH THE CATHOLIC CHURCH

When I got divorced, something fierce rose inside me—not destruction, but a kind of fire. A rebellion against the character of the "perfect girl" I had performed for so many years. I suddenly felt angry at all the roles I had been taught to inhabit without ever questioning whether they were mine. I began scrutinising everything, especially my religion. I kept thinking, *I followed every rule. I did everything they told me to do. Not only in terms of what was expected of my socially but I was devoted to my religion.* I was baptised. I did my first communion. My confirmation. I married in the Catholic Church. I didn't do drugs. I worked hard. I tried to save my family. And still, nothing worked. There I was—without my father's support, without most of my childhood friends, without my husband. Completely alone. Completely misunderstood. *Can you see how deeply I was living inside the victim consciousness here?* This was the wounded feminine in its core. I was drowning.

*My dad and I at my traditional Catholic wedding.
He cried during the whole ceremony. I still couldn't see beyond
the illusions of my ego, but there was always Love.*

The only thing that kept me upright was the peak of success I had reached. The timing of it all felt strangely precise, as if something greater was holding me, even though I didn't yet understand what that "something" was. At the time, I believed the synchronicity of my career blossoming just when I needed it most was simply the result of my hard work. I had no understanding of consciousness, the unseen laws of the Universe, or the Power of Creation that moves through us. So I did what I had always done: I pushed harder. More work, more projects, more doing—anything to avoid feeling the collapse happening inside me.

During this period, I also decided to "live" for the first time what I felt I had missed growing up. I went out with new friends. I socialised. I explored. I even tried drugs for the first time—not because I liked them (I actually hated the feeling), but because I was giving myself permission to experience what I had once restricted in order to be the woman I had been conditioned to become. I had spent so many years trying to be perfect, controlled, disciplined, pure, responsible, the good girl who followed every rule. Now that the illusion of that identity had crumbled, I found myself asking, *Then what is real? What is true? Who am I without the script I inherited?* Everything felt like a lie I was finally seeing through. My mind kept circling the same questions: *What can I trust? Who can I trust? Can I trust myself?* This was not rebellion for pleasure. It was rebellion for truth—a soul breaking out of a shell it had outgrown.

And not long after the divorce, I met a younger man who was strikingly handsome. We dated for a few months, and he constantly reminded me of how beautiful and desirable I was—a soothing balm after my ex-husband had made me feel ugly, fat, and unwanted. His validation helped rebuild fragments of my self-esteem, but it was still fragile, because it came from the outside. It was a borrowed sense of worthiness, not the innate worth we all carry simply by existing.

I didn't know that then, but at this point in my life, I felt empty and profoundly lost. So I tried to fill that emptiness in any way I could, clinging to external validation like a life raft. My work kept me moving—Vogue in São Paulo, shoots in New York, fashion shows in Paris and Milan, weekends visiting my brother and friends in Rio—a life lived inside airports and constant motion. Always running. Always escaping myself. It was the wrong idea of freedom. Many people believe this is what freedom looks like: movement, independence, success, glamour, the ability to reinvent yourself through new cities and new stories. But this is what I now call the *egoic persona of freedom*—a freedom manufactured by the mind in an attempt to avoid the pain the heart doesn't want to feel. It is not true freedom. True freedom is the opposite: presence, stillness, courage to face oneself, self discover, realisation.

From the outside, it looked as though I was thriving. But inside, I was furious—angry, disillusioned, awakening through revolt for the very first time in my life. That anger was the crack through which the light would eventually enter, though I couldn't yet see that.

I dyed my hair platinum blonde, dressed head-to-toe in black, and hardened my heart against relationships. I told myself I would never marry again, convinced that the institution itself was to blame for the collapse of my seven-year relationship. Looking back now, we can see that the anger wasn't wrong. It was necessary. It is a *natural, healthy boundary-setting emotion* that arises when something in us feels violated, unseen, or dishonoured. But anger alone cannot liberate; it only burns if we don't have the tools to move beyond it. True freedom comes when we realise that the myth of perfection we tried so hard to be was never who we were. She was an illusion, a character—inherited from culture, family, and religion. When illusions break, even painfully, they create space for Truth to rise. They create cracks where Light can finally enter.

Throughout my life, I had always felt deeply connected to my religion, especially to Mother Mary. But as my marriage ended, I began to feel betrayed—not by God, but by the rigid, punitive rules imposed by the Catholic institution. At that point, a memory came back with sharp clarity: when my mother married my father—his second marriage—the Church refused to allow her to take communion. It shattered her for years. She felt exiled from the faith she loved, rejected by the institution that claimed to represent God's Love. And suddenly, I realised I was standing in that same place—divorced, marked as a woman "forever in sin," deemed unworthy in the eyes of the Church. Something broke in me.

For the first time, I questioned everything I had inherited from Catholicism. The rituals, the restrictions, the sense of belonging I had once felt—all of it began to crumble. My devotion to Mary remained completely intact; she was woven into my Soul. But my trust in the institution dissolved. So, with a quiet clarity, I walked away. I broke up with Catholicism—not with God, not with Love, but with fear disguised as holiness, something I would later come to see present in many religious institutions around the world.

Spirituality

While I was in this state of mind, I met the man who would become the father of my daughter. We met at a dinner party in honour of a photographer, a close friend of his with whom I had recently worked. The next day, we went out, and everything moved very quickly. We fell in love. He was the exact opposite of my ex-husband—he admired my work, he shared the bills instead of trying to control me with money, he was a dreamer who loved to travel. Within weeks, we decided to date seriously. He lived in London, while I was between New York and São Paulo. After spending a week together in Brazil, we planned a trip to Ibiza. There, on a sunlit afternoon, we said "I love you" for the first time, and he bought me a vintage wedding dress, as if to seal the magic of how fast everything was moving.

One of the first things we began exploring together was spirituality. One day he asked me, "Have you ever been to a Spiritist centre? I've never been, but would you like to try?" Before, I would have said no. The way I was raised, anything outside Catholicism was taboo, sinful, even dangerous. But now, something in me had shifted, and I no longer believed in the rigid beliefs I had grown up with. So I said yes.

When we arrived, everyone gathered in a simple room for a small lecture. To my surprise, it didn't feel threatening; it felt strangely familiar, like the homilies I had heard in church. That familiarity allowed me to relax. After the talk, we were guided into another room, where we received what they called a *Spiritist Pass*, a healing practice during which energy is transmitted through the hands to restore balance and vitality. When we left, I felt lighter, as if something had been gently lifted. He felt it too. It opened a door in both of us, a curiosity to keep exploring, to step beyond the walls of the religion I had once thought was the only way to God.

I had always loved astrology, numerology, and anything that gave me a sense of self-discovery. But now, I was taking it a step further, searching for answers my religion had never offered. I still believed in something greater, in God, in a universal power, a higher power, but I no longer believed in the rules and controls imposed by institutionalised religion that control through fear. Fear, beloved reader, is always the ego at play, never the Truth of the Soul, of God. In London, I met a dear friend guardian angel through my daughter's father, who began teaching me about energy and the unseen. When we were back in Brazil, he invited me and my partner to join him at an Umbanda circle, an Afro-Brazilian tradition that blends African Indigenous rituals with Spiritism and Christianity.

As we drove an hour outside the city, a thunderstorm broke open, and traffic piled up. For a moment, we almost turned back, but something in me knew we had to keep going. It felt like the universe was testing us, asking, *Are you really ready for this new experience?* This is often how spiritual thresholds appear. Just before expansion, the ego resists; it throws obstacles in our path, creating storms, doubts, or delays. The ego fears what the Soul is ready to embrace. If we stop at the storm, we stay in the old. If we keep going, we step into a new reality. As the storm passed, a rainbow appeared almost like a confirmation we were in the right path.

When we finally arrived, I was immediately fascinated. The rhythm of the drums, the singing, the scent of herbs thick in the air—it was intoxicating. There was joy, vitality, and a rawness that pulsed with life. I felt embraced by something entirely new, something far closer to nature, to the mysteries I had always longed for. It was wild, unpolished, deeply alive. My heart expanded.

In London, as I began visiting my partner more often, I also met a Divine Meditation teacher. She, like me, had once worked in fashion, but after a profound awakening, she left everything behind to devote her life to teaching. She guided meditation sessions, soul journeys, during which she channelled the ascended masters. At the time, I could hardly stay awake in those sessions, as the frequencies were so high that my nervous system couldn't yet hold them. I would always fall asleep, not realising then that sleep was my body's way of protecting me as I received more Light than I could consciously handle.

Later, I understood something important: When we fall asleep during spiritual practices, it isn't because we are weak or uninterested. It is because our system is not yet prepared to receive so much Light and consciousness at once. Sleep becomes a way of integration, like a shield for the nervous system, allowing energy to enter slowly until we are ready to hold it awake. This is why spiritual awakening is a process; if we were shown the full Truth all at once, our bodies and minds would not be able to sustain it. So the Divine gives us as much as we can hold in each moment, step by step, with infinite patience.

From then on, every time I returned to London, I continued my sessions with my Divine Meditation Teacher, while in Brazil, I visited both the Umbanda circle and the Spiritist centre. Around this same period, I met my holistic therapist, who worked with flower essences to support emotional and energetic balance.

Meanwhile, my dear friend guardian angel, began handing me books by Paulo Coelho. I devoured them, loving the way he spoke of spirituality with simplicity and magic. Soon after, I began reading Kabbalah texts, Spiritist writings by Allan Kardec, and other mystical works. Little by little, I was entering a new wave of discovery, immersed in symbols, teachings, and energies, while at the same time continuing my career at *Vogue* and deepening my relationship with the man who had opened my eyes and heart to a new world.

Morocco

After five months together, my partner and I travelled to Marrakech to spend New Year's there. Despite the beauty around me, I still felt quite depressed and disconnected. I had only just begun to explore some of the spiritual practices I was learning, taking the first (but very important) steps into a world that felt both foreign and strangely familiar.

One night, while my partner wasn't in the room, I decided to try a dance meditation I had read about in a book, a practice that helps us enter higher states of consciousness. I put on a song I loved, one from the medicine music playlist he had introduced me to when we met. Those music already carried me into higher states, almost like a remembering. I began moving without rhythm, letting my body guide me instead of my mind.

At some point, something shifted. My movements became raw, liberating, pleasurable. I felt free in a way I hadn't felt before, as if something inside me was finally breaking open. It was the heart. In that state, words rose like a mantra from my lips: "I am ready. I am ready. I am ready." When the music ended, I collapsed onto the bed, hugging myself in a fetal position, tears running silently down my face.

I didn't know it then, but this was an act of creation, a moment of surrender to the Divine. My Soul had spoken, even if my conscious mind couldn't yet understand the magnitude of what I had called in.

A few weeks later, back in Brazil, we went with my dear friend guardian angel to another Umbanda circle. At the beginning of the ceremony, the woman leading it invited pregnant women and mothers with young children to step forwards first. She kept looking at me, waiting, as if she somehow knew. I didn't move. I thought it was impossible.

One week later, we discovered I was pregnant.

This was not what I thought I was calling for that night in Marrakech, but it was exactly what my Soul needed. The Universe is precise. When we let go of control, when we stop filtering life through the ego, the Soul finally has space to move through us. And it always knows what we need in order to heal, in order to free ourselves in Divine orchestration.

This is the Power of Creation. Manifestation doesn't come from forcing, controlling, or obsessing over details and the how's and why's. It comes when we align our thoughts, our intentions, with our hearts and release the control of the outcome, when we dare to surrender to Presence. In surrender, we give the Universe permission to rearrange everything in ways our lower minds could never plan. Creation flows not from the ego's demand but from the Soul's readiness in connection to our hearts and the Field of Life.

A few weeks later, Violeta started growing inside of my womb like a miracle. At the time, due to my depression, my period hadn't been coming for a few months, and the doctors wondered how a pregnancy was even possible. No one knew the answer. But the fact was she was there, and she was growing in a very healthy way. I didn't ask for a baby specifically as I danced in Morocco, but when I learned of my pregnancy, the only thing I felt was Love, pure Love. When I told one of my best friends about the pregnancy, she asked, "Are you sure? If you want, we can get an abortion." Without hesitation, I replied a big *no*. I was sure she was a gift, and the only feeling I had was one of protection. I just surrendered myself to the Divine. When we do this, God listens and gives us exactly what we need.

CHAPTER 8

THE PREGNANCY

As soon as I became pregnant, everything began to shift. Just a few weeks after I found out I was pregnant, my editor-in-chief asked me to fly to Los Angeles for a major cover shoot with Kim Kardashian, and for the first time in my career, I said no. "I can't yet. I'm in the early days of my pregnancy, and my priority is protecting her," I explained. Before, I would never have turned down such an opportunity. But this time, the answer came naturally, without hesitation. Something had already shifted in me. My editor wasn't pleased and pressed harder: "We need you to go." Eventually, they secured a sponsor for me to fly business class, and I agreed, but only on the condition that I would stay one or two nights at most.

I kept my word. When I landed in Los Angeles, I went straight to my hotel room and locked myself in, letting my body recover from the eleven-hour flight and the jet lag. The next morning, a driver came to pick me up for the shoot in Malibu. My assistant had flown in from New York with all the fashion. When I arrived, Kim was already there, sitting patiently in the make-up chair. To my surprise, she was perfectly on time. I headed to the bedroom reserved for the fashion team to check what my assistant had prepared. In the room, I also saw a man I didn't recognise, lying on the bed. My assistant leaned in and whispered, "That's Kanye. He's asleep." It was the first time I saw a husband accompanying the wife's shoot. I just thought, *What is he doing here?* Little did I know what was about to happen.

The whole shoot was prepared to portray Kim as Marilyn Monroe. It was 2015, and for some reason I don't remember, she had dyed her hair blonde. Before I even got to LA, the entire concept had already been approved by the *Vogue* team, Kim's team, and the photographer Ellen von Unwerth. While Kim sat in the chair, getting her make-up done, Kanye suddenly woke up and started complaining to me. He said Kim was much bigger than Marilyn, so why on earth should she portray someone less relevant than her? I was shocked, but I answered firmly, "This was the concept your team approved with Vogue. Kim looked genuinely happy, watching herself transform into Marilyn through hair and make-up. But Kanye kept going. "I don't want her to look like this, this is ridiculous." he said.

I called my editor-in-chief and explained the situation, and her answer was blunt: If Kim didn't shoot as Marilyn, she wouldn't be the cover. There I was, caught in the clash of two giant egos, while the only thing I could truly focus on was the tiny life growing inside of me. I told Kanye my editor's decision, and after some resistance, he agreed to try. But as soon as the first shot was taken, he began yelling at everyone on set, saying it was all awful. Kim didn't say a word. She remained passive through the whole process, which surprised me. In that moment, I felt it again—that what the media sells us as truth is nothing but illusion, a carefully crafted performance that women around the world absorb and follow, often without question. Here it was again, playing out in front of me: the wounded masculine, trying to control and dominate; the wounded feminine, collapsing into passivity. It's a power play that hurts everyone involved.

However, my priority at the time wasn't the illusion on set; it was the little baby I was growing within me. So instead of giving in completely to Kanye's demands or my editor's demands, I set my limits and directed the shoot in a way that could appease their power struggle while keeping myself and my daughter safe. But in truth, I was exhausted by it all. Everything started to feel meaningless.

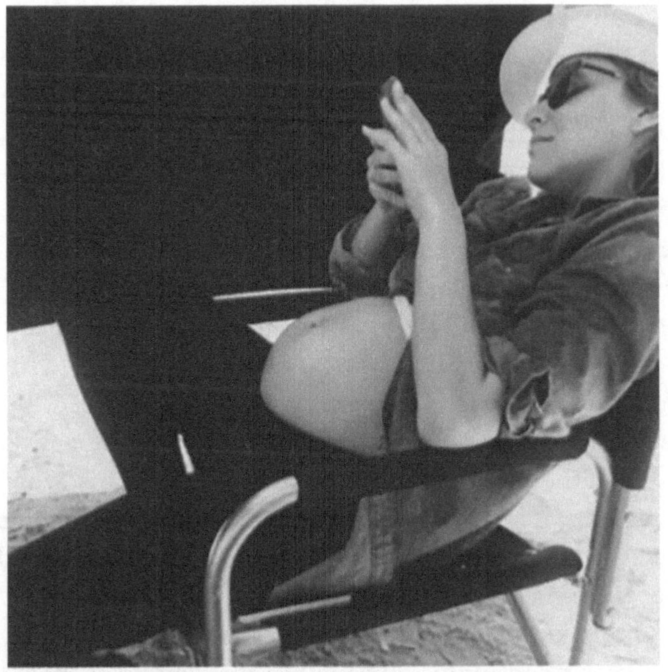

Working on set throughout my pregnancy.

As the months went by, I decided to cancel the lease on the apartment I had in New York so I could be fully in the same place with my partner. We kept the London apartment and moved into a bigger one in São Paulo. At first, the plan was to have our daughter in Brazil, but because of conflicts my partner was having with his ex-wife, everything shifted, and I had to move to London instead. It was a big change for me. I didn't feel at home in his apartment. The walls carried a history I could sense but hadn't lived, memories that belonged to his past that crumbled during my pregnancy. No matter how much I tried to decorate and make it feel like home, it always felt like I was a visitor, never fully settled.

In London, I began seeing my Divine Meditation Spiritual teacher, every week. It was as though she was preparing me for something immense, something I couldn't yet name. Old karmic memories resurfaced, waves of clearing I couldn't explain, and meditation practices unfolded that went far beyond what I could intellectually grasp. It felt like she was speaking directly to my Soul, awakening a part of me I had long forgotten.

As my daughter grew in my womb, deeper shifts began to unfold. I started asking myself, *How can I heal all my traumas so I don't pass them on to her?* I wasn't yet ready to question why my mother had died, but I felt the undeniable pull to confront the pattern that seemed to haunt all the women in my family. Every one of them had been silenced. Every one of them had been called crazy. I made a vow within myself: *This stops with me.*

With that decision, my path of healing intensified. I continued seeing my Divine Meditation teacher, doing therapy sessions, visiting both the Spiritist centre and the Umbanda circles, and reading books. Each space offered me glimpses of release, moments of Clarity, and the strength to imagine a different legacy for my daughter, one where silence and shame would no longer rule.

I didn't know it yet, but this is what trauma does: It moves through generations until someone has the courage to stop, to feel, and to transform it. Patterns repeat themselves not because we deserve them, but because the Soul is asking us to face what was left unresolved. Unless we bring awareness, we unconsciously pass down the same wounds to those who come after us. Healing is not just personal, it is ancestral. When we choose to heal, we are not only freeing ourselves, we are freeing seven generations before and seven generations after. And we are liberating ourselves from Karma, from what we didn't learn in other incarnations.

In London, I began studying and doing sessions on NLP, while Yoga and Jungian psychology also caught my attention. Somehow, without realising it, all of this was preparing me for what I would soon be called to lead. *Vogue* already felt empty to me, as though its glossy pages no longer carried the meaning they once had. They were just illusions. I began searching for other ways to express my creativity. One day, during a meditation session with my Divine Meditation Teacher, I shared with her an idea that had been forming in my heart, a video series called *It's a Free Free World*. It was the seed of what would later become Free Free. She looked at me and said with certainty, "This is part of your mission." I couldn't understand how this could possibly be my mission, but something inside of me knew she was right. I began journaling, using the practice to access my superconsciousness and allow the vision to reveal itself, but it still wasn't time.

The day before I went into labour.

The room I prepared had a sculpture of fabrics, each with a different meaning. It resembles the work I still do today

The Birth

For some reason, I had convinced myself that my daughter would come early. I have always loved being in control of situations, and this was no different. By thirty-seven weeks, I was restless, anxious, and already trying to will her arrival. My partner had hired a doula to support me, but I didn't like the idea. I was already nervous about not having the kind of birth I had envisioned—the safety of a respected hospital in Brazil, with a doctor I knew and trusted. Instead, because we had to be in London, we chose the public hospital; the cost of a private one was far beyond what we could afford.

I tried everything I could find online to bring on labour before forty weeks, but nothing worked. The waiting made me anxious. One month earlier, my English agent had told me I couldn't take meetings anymore because my big belly would scare clients. *I'm pregnant, not sick,* I thought, filled with rage at how absurd and unfair it was for women to experience these things. By then, since my divorce and especially through my pregnancy, I was becoming acutely aware of how differently women were treated compared to men in society. Two consultancy clients had already cancelled their contracts because of my pregnancy, and the lack of compassion hurt deeply. I started to understand in my own body what my mother had gone through—the silent battles women fight that no one talks about.

My last shoot before giving birth was in Ibiza, in the middle of August, under the relentless heat. I could barely walk. My body was heavy, exhausted, impatient. It felt as though my pregnancy had reached a point of surrender, like life was forcing me to let go of control, one contraction at a time, even before the first one arrived.

I was angry that at the end of my pregnancy, I was seen as sick, when in truth, I was in a moment of full creative flow. Somehow the universe was asking me to stop searching for creativity in the usual places, and it gave me space to look within, into the mission I was also birthing.

When my pregnancy reached thirty-nine weeks, I went to see my Divine Meditation Teacher in desperation. "Help," I told her, "this baby needs to come out of me." I felt like I had lost control of my life—my body was aching, and something much bigger than me was clearly about to happen. That session took me deeper than I had ever gone before. My Divine Meditation Teacher guided me into meditation, and then she began speaking in Light language to Violeta Lua, my daughter, still inside my womb. As the sounds vibrated through the room, Violeta began moving quickly within me, as though she was responding to the frequencies. Light language is the language of the Soul. It bypasses the ego and all its illusions, allowing one Soul to speak directly to another. In that moment, no words were needed, only vibration, only Truth.

When the session ended, my teacher and I just looked at each other, amazed by what had unfolded. She told me Violeta was scared to come into the world, and that she had reassured her there was nothing to fear, that it was her time now, that Earth was ready to receive her Light.

When I started feeling the first contractions of birth at Portobello Road.

The next day, while I was buying flowers with my partner at one of our favourite shops on Portobello Road, near Golborne Road, I felt the first contractions. At first, we brushed it off, maybe it was just Braxton Hicks, the practice contractions that prepare the body for birth. Soon it became clear this was something more. It still felt too early to go to hospital, so my partner drew me a bath, lit candles, and played soothing music to calm me. For a while, I tried to surrender to the moment, but the contractions kept intensifying. By 1:00 a.m., I could no longer deny it. Holding my belly, I told him firmly, "Take me to hospital now. If these aren't real contractions, then I don't know what is."

We called a taxi, and with every turn of the car, I screamed like a wild animal, the pain ripping through me. By the time we arrived at Chelsea Hospital, I was sure the baby must be close. But when the nurse checked, to everyone's surprise, I was only one centimetre dilated. She said she would normally have sent me home, but seeing the intensity of the contractions, she decided to keep me. She gave me an injection to ease the pain, enough to make me feel hazy, almost high, but not enough to take the pain away. When the effect wore off, the deep waves of agony returned, pulling screams from the core of my being, now only stronger.

We called the nurse, and they took me to the delivery room to take the anaesthesia and start the delivery process. The wait felt endless. More than two hours passed before the anaesthetic finally arrived. When the anaesthesiologist attempted the epidural, he misplaced the needle, striking a nerve. I howled like a lioness, the sound primal and unrestrained. On the second try, he got it right.

By then, dawn had broken. It was the morning of October 10, 2015.

After the anaesthesia, the process softened. By some Divine orchestration, my father arrived in London that very morning and rushed straight to the hospital. I now had both him and my partner by my side in the delivery room. And I wasn't alone—three midwives, each carrying her own medicine, held space for me in turn.

The first was a radiant Black woman, strong and joyful. She laughed easily, grounding me and reminding me to take things lighter even as my body ached. When her shift ended, she passed me into the hands of a graceful Pakistani woman who was older and carried a wisdom that felt steady, calming, and deeply rooted in the present moment. She was stricter, too, and measured, insisting protocols be followed, reminding me she could only check my dilation every three hours.

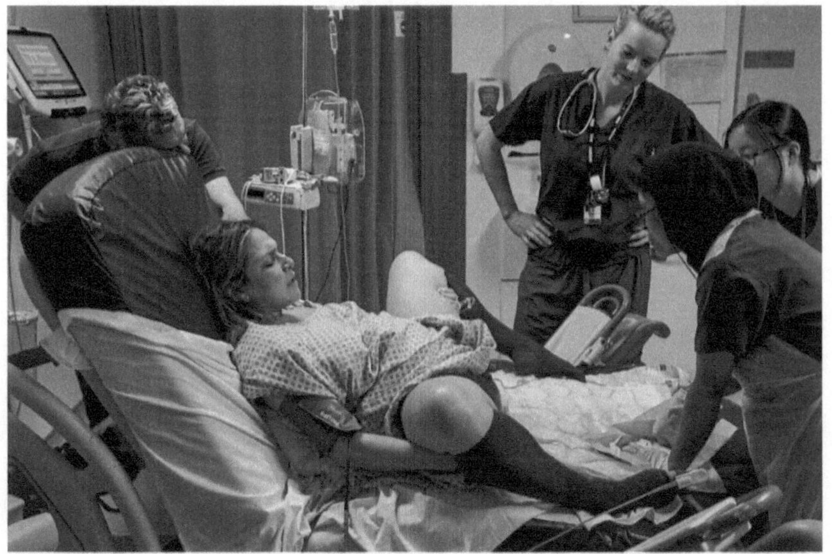

*My father is left, holding my shoulder, and my partner
is taking the photo. Right are the two midwives,
with their intern, during their shift change.*

By around 7:00 p.m., I was finally ready to push. My father stood behind me, one hand on my shoulder like an anchor, while my partner stayed to my right, camera in hand, documenting each moment. Just as I began pushing, another shift change happened. We couldn't believe it. It felt surreal, almost like a scene from a film, one energy passing, another entering, as the Pakistani midwife stepped out and a Northern European midwife swept in, clapping her hands and urging me with a clear, firm voice, "Push, push!"

We laughed, even through my exhaustion, determined to keep going after almost twenty-six hours since I'd gotten the first contractions in the flower shop. When Violeta's head began to crown, the midwife turned to my partner and said, "She's almost out, do you want to feel her head?" He said yes. His eyes widened, his hands trembling. It felt as if time had suspended itself. It was one of those surreal moments of the eternal now, a moment outside of time. In the meantime, my dad was in shock at the whole scene. It was raw, unpolished, unlike like the births he had seen before in the sophisticated Brazilian hospitals.

The midwife leaned closer, her voice steady. "Yasmine, with the next contraction, push as hard as you can." I gathered every ounce of strength left in me, breathed deeply, and pushed. Then— she arrived. And I re-birthed myself, and the mission we both were here to lead.

The Breath

When Violeta arrived, there was a problem: She didn't cry, she didn't breathe. The midwife grabbed her from me almost like a piece of meat and called for the doctors. I was no longer fully there; I was already watching from above. In that single minute that felt like eternity, my father prayed with his hand pressed firmly on my shoulder, and my partner's eyes followed every desperate movement of the midwives and doctors around our baby. They lifted Violeta from my belly while my body still worked to deliver the placenta and placed her under a bright light, doing whatever they could to call her into this world.

Then, finally, she breathed a gentle cry. It was a fragile sound, but the most beautiful one I had ever heard. They placed her on my chest and helped her latch. Relief and love flooded the room. Just as the tension eased, my brother arrived, stepping into the delivery room to meet his niece for the very first time.

Violeta and I entered a love bubble. When we were ready to leave for the private bedroom (I asked for one, so I could have some privacy after the birth), I was sitting at the edge of the bed when something started happening. Like a stream of lightning, my body started trembling. I asked the nurse to hold Violeta and started crying non-stop while asking her, "Is this normal? Is this normal?" Something was moving through me like lightning, and I shook, cried, and laughed all at once. It was a cathartic, indescribable experience. I just kept thinking, *What is happening to me? What is happening to me?*

My body convulsed with energy, storms of frequencies over-taking me. I cried, I yelled, I surrendered. It felt like a death and a birth all at once, as if every cell in my being was breaking open. People describe near-death experiences after accidents, how they leave and return with new awareness.

This was my car-crash. Only mine came in the instant of giving life.

This was the doorway where I first connected to a higher consciousness, the one I would later recognise as Aiyahla, my true Soul. This was the beginning of my awakening.

PART 2

IN BETWEEN

In this part, you will witness a transition between who I was and who I was becoming.

CHAPTER 9

THE CLASH OF THE EGO

When I arrived home from the hospital, in that Portobello apartment, nothing felt the same. Something had shifted. The walls, the furniture, even the air felt different. I couldn't recognise myself in it anymore. My only anchor was my newborn baby; she was the only one I knew was part of me, the only one who felt real.

It took me two weeks before I could step outside of the house. I was suspended between worlds, not knowing who I was, what was happening. I had been rebirthed in that delivery room, but no one around me could see it. And I was just realising it too. I looked around the house and nothing felt mine. The questions I had started asking myself during the pregnancy were not questions anymore—they were seeds of Truths, brought to my consciousness by my daughter's Soul. I looked out the window at the street below, asking myself, *What am I doing here, in this Portobello Road flat?* Even the way I looked at my partner had changed.

Then came the strangest sensation: I felt pains that didn't belong to me, as if I was living a life that wasn't entirely mine. Relating to it felt suffocating. Even my body felt foreign. After having a natural birth, your body bleeds for weeks, waiting for milk to come in, and every day feels like a negotiation with the body. For me, it was raw, disorienting, and painfully slow, an initiation into a new me, the true me, that I had yet to understand. At first, I thought my confusion came from not having a mother figure by my side to teach me to be a mother. But later, I understood the Truth: The birth of my daughter had awakened me to a higher dimension of my Soul.

When a profound awakening takes place, the world you knew no longer fits. The ego's desires lose their meaning. Suddenly, nothing that once defined you makes sense. *That was me?* Vogue? *Was this what I had dedicated myself to?* Overnight, the questions turned to Clarity. Now I knew. It felt shallow, almost absurd, how I had been so passionate about this work. I could see so clearly how the very images I was creating were part of the same illusion that kept women trapped, and I knew I couldn't keep living the same way. Something in me was already demanding a different path

In that moment, Free Free was also born. Violeta and this higher aspect of my Soul carried the mission into the world together. Our frequencies intertwined, and we manifested the mission in that delivery room. We will share more about this later, but for now, what matters is this: After her birth, everything felt different because I was awakening, and for this reason, everything disorienting beyond what a woman feels after birth. It was the Light, an immense amount of light poured opened. Everything I thought I was had collapsed, and a new life, our shared mission, was only just beginning to reveal itself.

There was an aggravating factor: My partner wasn't well, even though there was always so much Love between us. He seemed distant, in a quiet depression, carrying the heavy weight of becoming a parent for the second time while also feeling overwhelmed by financial instability. The responsibility pressed down on him, and that pressure soon fell on me. It meant I had to return to work sooner than my body and spirit were ready for. Inside, everything still felt disoriented, as though I were living someone else's life. Only forty days after giving birth, the call came: One of my clients needed me for a campaign.

This was not how I thought it would be. I thought I would have more time—for me, for my daughter, and for making sense of the frequency shifts that were unravelling within and around me. I had only just begun to understand the depth of my partner's struggles. I didn't know I would play the part of the family provider and the mother, and already the weight of responsibility was pressing on me too.

The fashion world had no mercy. Competition at *Vogue* was ruthless, and colleagues were already circling for my position, ready to take my place. On top of that, the client who had suspended my fee for the last four months of my pregnancy because I couldn't travel had now given me an ultimatum: Show up, or lose the work. Their message was clear: If I didn't show up, they would hire someone else. And we couldn't afford to lose them at that moment. The workplace I was part of, like so many others, carried the rigid structures of patriarchy, where profitability, productivity, and speed were valued above all else. What it lacked was the balance of the feminine—compassion, collaboration, empathy. These qualities are not only essential for new mothers but for a healthier workplace overall. Without this balance, the system breaks people. This is why today, burnouts are at record levels, affecting millions worldwide.

What I went through was not unique; it was a symptom of a wounded system, a culture that normalises abusive patterns and calls it "success." What it truly reveals is how desperately we need harmony between doing and being, between efficiency and empathy, between results and relationships. Within the feminine and the masculine. Without that, no system, and no individual, can live healthy and joyful lives.

So I went to Brazil, only forty days after giving birth, when my body wasn't even fully recovered. Violeta was strapped to me in my kangaroo bag. She came with me to the shoot, breastfeeding while I directed, her tiny presence grounding me in the midst of flashing lights and endless demands. I found myself more patient on set than I had ever been, softer, as if the awakening of this higher-dimensional Soul was reshaping me from within. It brought me a deeper presence, grounding me in each moment, while also showing me an undeniable truth: Doing that type of work was no longer for me. Looking back at those first moments of my awakening, it truly felt like I was living a double life. Yasmine's ego was still there, still running on old patterns, but something greater had stepped in—my Soul, which was guiding, observing, and quietly taking charge of that personality. At the time, I couldn't name it, and so all I felt was confusion.

That December, I spent some days in São Paulo working, some in Rio, and some at my family's country house in the mountains. That house, surrounded by trees and silence, carried the happiest memories of my childhood and teenage years. This country house—built by my grandfather twenty years before I was born, and forty-nine years before my rebirth—had always been my refuge. But now, I felt something different. Surrounded by the whisper of trees and the rhythm of nature, I connected with Mother Earth's Presence in a more profound way. It was like she guided me, and I understood her wisdom way more than I had before. The birds singing, the wind blowing. The trees embraced me like Mama Trees. Nature mirrored back what I couldn't explain to anyone else: that something in me had cracked open, that I was no longer who I had been.

Violeta and I at the country club in Rio.

Rio felt chaotic. My usual routine at the country club felt empty. Time with friends felt strangely distant. It wasn't that they had changed—I had. I was seeing life from a different perspective, and that shift left me feeling profoundly alone at first because I didn't even know what was going on or whom to talk to about it. Conversations that once felt easy now seemed empty. The parties, the dinners, the chatter about work and society—all of it felt hollow. I could sit in a crowded room and feel completely unseen, like I no longer belonged to the world I had once thought was the most extraordinary. Somehow, my expanded consciousness now was showing me beyond what I had ever known before, that the limited perception I'd had of life was simply not what I'd thought it was. I say this not as a judgement on that lifestyle, but for you to understand how confusing it all was to me.

My awakening wasn't a sudden event; it was a slow unravelling, a journey of loosening my egoic identity thread by thread. My traumas had to be met, felt, and healed so my ego could finally feel safe enough to release control over my personality, to step aside and allow me—the Soul—to take the lead.

It didn't happen in one night; it took years to unfold. In those early days, there was a constant tug of war within me. My Soul moved forwards with Clarity and expansion, while my ego kept pulling me back into the old role of the "perfect woman," the role that once felt safe, familiar, and praised. And yet, beneath the fear, there was a deeper Truth guiding my ego to feel safe, seen, heard, loved so it wouldn't intervene anymore.

This is how my awakening happened. It was a journey of shedding layer after layer of the characters I thought I needed to be. The ego clings to what is known, to its roles and identities, while my higher-dimension Soul started to lead, through whispers of freedom, of authenticity, of Love. At times, you may feel like you are two people: one holding on, one reaching forwards. This conflict is part of the process. Each step of letting go created space for my Soul to integrate its higher consciousness more and lead my life from a place of Love, Light, and Creative Power, and to lead the mission we were here to do, alongside our daughter.

Celebrating my thirtieth birthday with my little angel.

Separation

As I transformed, so did my relationship with Violeta's father. The more my frequency shifted, the less our energies could meet. What once felt like love began to dissolve into friction. The relationship turned into a battlefield, not because it was anyone's fault but because our egos were still holding old patterns and trauma. I had been born into a family and culture where the man was expected to provide. Though I didn't mind sharing the bills when we had first met, carrying the full weight of providing for our family was more than I could bear at the time, especially while caring for a newborn, navigating a workforce that was unkind to new mothers, and moving through an awakening that pulled me into unknown territory. I asked him for support, but he remained frozen, paralysed in his own wounded masculine state, unable to step forwards. The part of me that kept fighting wasn't my Soul, it was my wounded feminine, the one who believed she needed to be rescued, the one who felt like a victim. So my own wounded masculine rose up to lead without the balance of my feminine, creating anger that I projected onto him. I couldn't yet see that he was doing his best, just as I was. These moments were already serving as training grounds, initiations from my Soul for the mission we came here to fulfil. Each passing day, the fracture between the masculine and feminine in humanity revealed itself to me, not just as my personal struggle, but as a mirror of one of the world's greatest wounds.

When men are in their wounded masculine, it often shows up as insensitivity, disconnection, or lack of empathy. My partner wasn't to blame; it was simply trauma resurfacing after the birth of our child. We can see this now from a higher, circular perspective, but back then my ego couldn't. Exhausted and desperate, I kept pushing him, crying for help. He stayed frozen, retreating into himself due to his overwhelm, which only made me feel more alone. Violeta was only a few months old when he said, "I need some time off, I might go to India for a month". My ego was furious. I thought, how could he even think about going to India with a newborn baby, leaving me alone to deal with everything. And with what money will he go, because at that stage he wasn't helping with any of our daughter's financial expenses.

He was reflecting back to me, through what we call the *law of reflection*, a deep wound of abandonment and lack of parental responsibility—a wound my father had also reflected earlier in my life. The law of reflection teaches us that the experiences we attract often mirror something unresolved within our own field. This does not mean we "deserve" the pain or that we are at fault. It simply means the Soul is showing us, through others, an aspect that is ready to be healed.

Sometimes these reflections arise from moments in this lifetime when we too acted unconsciously, perhaps abandoning ourselves, neglecting our own needs, or failing to honour a commitment out of overwhelm. And sometimes, these reflections come from other lifetimes, when we ourselves may have been unable to fulfil responsibilities we had agreed to. When a reflection appears, it is the Higher Power gently revealing to us what has been hidden— not to punish, but to liberate. These experiences continue to repeat not because we are wrong, but because the Soul longs for this aspect to be seen, acknowledged, and brought back into Love. When we recognise the reflection, everything softens. We move from blame into understanding, from pain into awareness. And from this place, forgiveness becomes possible—forgiveness of ourselves for actions taken in unconsciousness, and forgiveness of others who reflect those same unconscious patterns back to us. In Truth, no one is to blame. Everyone involved is evolving. It is all part of a higher orchestration of healing and awakening.

I also didn't realise at the time that my pushing for responsibility and presence mirrored his withdrawal. This is how the wounded feminine and wounded masculine often meet: One demands more, while the other pulls away. Both are trapped in unconscious patterns, unable to give what the other truly needs. Neither of us felt whole, because our traumas had fractured us from Truth and Love. But when we rise to the Eagle's Eye, we see that beneath the distortions, we are already whole, already worthy, and that every experience is aligned with the level of consciousness we are able to access.

To make it even harder, I also didn't have the support of my father or my partner's mother. They were each absorbed in their own struggles, overwhelmed by their own lives, unable to show up for me and for baby Violeta in the ways they promised they would. At the time, I felt deeply disappointed and abandoned, because I didn't yet understand the law of reflection. I only saw the absence, not the truth behind it. Now we can see it so clearly: it wasn't negligence. It wasn't a lack of Love. They simply *could not* take anything else on. Their own nervous systems, traumas, and burdens were already too much for them to hold. They were doing the best they could with the emotional capacity they had. Beloved reader, remember this always: Everyone is doing the best they can, based on the limits of their consciousness, their wounds, and their level of self-awareness. Most of the time, people's behaviour is not about us at all. When we assume it is, we fall into the blame game, the victim consciousness, and we disconnect from the truth of our Power. When we stop searching for someone to blame and begin to ask, *What is this experience showing me?*, we reclaim our sovereignty. Through the law of reflection, we see that the experience is appearing because something in us is ready to be healed, seen, loved back into wholeness.

My loneliness became one of my greatest mirrors. At first, I resented it. I felt unseen, unsupported, uncared for. But slowly, gently, I began to understand: my Soul was turning me inward. It was teaching me to find a strength no parent, partner, or friend could ever give me. It was guiding me to remember that my true support system had never been outside of me.It had always been within. In Source. In the Divine Mother. In my heart the flame. By walking through this chapter without the safety net I longed for, my Soul was teaching my ego a sacred truth: I was never alone. I had simply forgotten where to look. This is one of the most powerful teachings we can share with you: You are God within you. You are the Light. You are the Love. The times you feel most alone are often the moments when the Divine is trying to redirect you inward, to reconnect you with your own Presence, your own Love, your own Power.

The absence of my family accelerated my spiritual growth. It showed me how deeply I had still been searching for safety outside of myself—repeating the wounds of the little girl who longed for her father's approval or her mother's presence. But now the path was different. I was being called to mother myself. To follow the guidance of my Soul. To rise from within.

The fighting with my partner didn't end. What had once been light and playful now grew unbearably heavy. We couldn't find a middle ground. Guided by my NLP coach, I gave my partner a time frame that felt bearable to me and fair for him—six months to come out of this overwhelm state, for him to start working again, showing up more, so we could try to find better balance in our relationship. In the meantime, I kept working between London, Paris, New York, and Brazil, travelling almost every month with Violeta strapped to me in the kangaroo carrier. It was exhausting. And yet, something deep within me—my Soul—was beginning to show me a different way, a way that required me to let go of the story I was telling myself, the story that kept me attached to my partner.

Travelling monthly for work with Violeta
in my kangaroo (very exhausted).

I was terrified of being a single mother, of going through another separation. I believed it would confirm to the world, and to myself, that I failed again. But that fear was not the Truth. Fear is never Truth. It is only the ego, holding to appearances and the illusion of safety—to a golden cage. The truth is that what is real can never be broken. Love cannot be lost. Wholeness cannot be taken away. Perhaps you, too, have felt this clash—the fear that if you let go, everything will collapse. But what if the opposite is true? What if letting go is not collapse at all, but the beginning of your freedom? What if it is one of the keys that will liberate you from your golden cage?

The Flood

Not long after the six months I gave myself and my partner to make changes, I went to São Paulo. Nothing had changed between us. I was with Violeta and a nanny in our home. Then, the Universe sent me a sign I could no longer ignore. A pipe burst in the apartment upstairs, and within minutes, water began pouring through the ceiling. It wasn't just a drip, it was a flood. The walls were soaked, the floors turned into shallow rivers, and then, with a deafening crack, the ceiling of my bedroom gave way. Plaster and water crashed down over the furniture, leaving everything drenched and broken.

This is how my bedroom looked after the flood.
The Universe was screaming, Let go!

I froze, clutching Violeta against my chest. She was so small, and her warmth pressed against me as if she were the only real thing I had left. Watching the room collapse in front of my eyes, I realised that everything I thought was stable—the house, the marriage, the identity I was holding onto—was crumbling. The only true foundation I had was the baby in my arms, the life we shared, the Love that connected us, and the new Knowing that in stillness, we connected with Presence. It was as if life itself was shouting, *Everything from the past you are holding onto must fall apart.* The destruction outside mirrored the collapse inside. The old life Yasmine had lived before the awakening was no longer ours to live.

I've come to understand that God often places certain people on our path at the exact moment we need them—people who act as bridges between who we are and who we are becoming. The Baba Orixá my friend guided me to visit was one of those souls.

Babas Orixá are spiritual leaders within African Indigenous traditions, guardians of wisdom, protectors of ancient knowledge, keepers of the elements and the unseen. He later became like family to me and his mother, a profoundly wise and divine woman, I call Iya, the Yoruba word for "mother." Their presence in my life was not a coincidence. These souls appear as messengers, carriers of keys to doors we are not yet able to open alone. The Baba was the one who told me that everything in my life needed to be destroyed so that a great rebirth could take place. At the time, I didn't believe him. I certainly didn't imagine that the destruction he spoke of would become so literal. But when we resist the changes our Soul is asking for—when we hold onto illusions the heart has already outgrown— the Universe speaks louder, so that we cannot ignore what must be transformed.

That flood was one of those divine keys. Holding Violeta in my arms, soaked and trembling, I felt it with every fibre of my being: It was time to stop resisting. It was time to surrender. From that moment on, more keys would appear—people, teachings, synchronicities—each one guiding me deeper into my Truth, unveiling the path we had been destined to walk long before I could understand it.

My Soul gave me the courage to make the decision to separate—to honour the Truth of what was happening instead of clinging to the illusion of what I wished it could be. The separation was inevitable, but it was not a failure. It was an act of Love. It was the only way I could take care of myself while adjusting to my new consciousness and caring for our baby, instead of carrying a weight that was never mine to carry. I was not the saviour anymore. I could not save my partner or make him see what he wasn't yet ready to see—just as I could not save my mother or my father. The illusion of saving was one of the oldest patterns in my lineage, and it was finally time to lay it down.

With the completion of our romantic relationship, I returned officially to São Paulo. Vogue was there, many of my consultancy clients were there, and being there meant less travelling and more stability for Violeta. It was a painful decision, but an essential one for my liberation—a decision rooted in truth rather than fear.

And even though our romantic partnership ended, his role in my life did not. The ending of the relationship was not the ending of our connection. We completed as a couple, but we did not separate as human beings. In many ways, he was the portal: the one who opened the first doorway for me to access a higher dimension of my Soul through spirituality. He was the man I chose—even if unconsciously—to be the father of my daughter. And he was the man she chose as her father, long before we met. I didn't know it then, but the Universe always works in perfect alignment with our highest good. In time, he would become a close friend, and a good father to our daughter. Our love simply transformed into its true form—not lost, only reshaped.

I love this picture of both of us in Paris after Violeta was born, trying to go back to our old selves. It didn't work out with our old selves—as shown by the sad expression in the image. We were always meant to be friends. He is my Soul family and the Loving father of my daughter.

CHAPTER 10

BACK IN SÃO PAULO

Back in São Paulo, everything changed at lightning speed. I signed huge contracts and started earning money in ways I had never experienced before. Everything was flowing. Opportunities appeared effortlessly, clients arrived with ease, and my career expanded in directions I could never have predicted. It was the universe confirming what my Soul already knew—I had made the right decision. And yet, even in the midst of expansion, trauma still lived in my body. Healing is not linear; it unfolds in layers. My Soul began attracting the exact experiences I needed to reveal what was still unconscious, training me for the life we were about to step into.

One of the deepest wounds my ego still carried was the wound of abandonment—the illusion that I was not whole on my own, that I was not truly loved unless I was in a romantic relationship. Like we explored together earlier, this belief was born in my childhood. But it wasn't mine alone. It was the inheritance of countless women before me. For generations, women have been taught that our worth is defined by being chosen, married, or fertile. My ego learned this story from my lineage, my culture, the world around me. In Brazil, it was only in 1988 that women were finally recognised as equal under the constitution. Think about that—my mother did not grow up in a legally equal world. In the UK, progress came earlier, but the echoes of patriarchy still reverberate in every boardroom, every family structure, every unspoken expectation of what a woman "should be." Like when I wasn't allowed to have meetings simply because I was pregnant. And this pattern extends far beyond Brazil or the UK. In parts of Africa, Asia, and the Middle East, many girls are still married as children, denied education, or silenced before their voices ever have the chance to form. In other regions, women's bodies are controlled through laws; in others, through culture; in others, through religion; and in many places, through all three. So this wound I carried was not just personal. It was ancestral. It was cultural. It was global.

I didn't know any of this consciously back then. I didn't yet understand the wounded masculine or the wounded feminine. My ego simply held on to the old belief: men have their role, women have theirs—a script written long before I was born. A script created by culture, shaped by religion, upheld by family systems, and enforced by generations of fear. A script that felt like truth only because it had been repeated so many times. But as we now know, egoic truth is not Divine Truth. It is the perspective of the lower mind, formed by human senses, distorted by pain, conditioned by history. My Soul, however, was preparing me to rewrite this script entirely.

It took me six months before I went on my first date. This was already a sign of transformation, because it broke the pattern I used to follow before my awakening. In the past, after every break-up, I would quickly find someone new, rushing into another relationship and hoping it would heal the pain of the last. It's something so many of us do—looking for repair in someone else's arms, hoping another person can soothe the wounds we are afraid to face within ourselves. But most of the time, it only deepens the wound. It keeps us looping in the same pattern of unconscious attachment. This time, my Soul guided me inward.

Instead of searching for comfort outside myself, I began to study my inner world. I immersed myself in neuroscience, NLP, behavioural psychology, and the science of human potential. I started to understand how beliefs, physiology, vibration, and state shape the way we live, the choices we make, the partners we attract, and the patterns we repeat. I continued my floral therapy sessions, visited the Spiritist centre occasionally, deepened my meditation practice, and committed fully to Ashtanga Yoga. Through each asana, I discovered a new dimension of power—one I had not yet accessed even through meditation. I began to understand the breath as a gateway, a medicine, a teacher. With every inhale and exhale, I could steady my mind, regulate my nervous system, and find a strength that had nothing to do with muscle and everything to do with Presence. I noticed how breath could dissolve fear, soften resistance, and guide my body deeper into each posture with grace. And I realised something essential: Breath is the bridge between ego and Soul. It is the thread that carries us from survival into Presence, from illusion into Truth, from fragmentation into unity.

When I started practicing Ashtanga. Here I am with my daughter in our country house. We have always been inseparable.

During that time, I was also awakening more fully to my Soul's knowledge. Through my studies, I began giving language to what my Soul already knew, helping my ego feel safe enough to loosen its grip and allow the Soul to lead. But my ego still resisted. It was trying to hold onto the familiar identity of the "perfect woman," especially in reaction to what I had experienced with Violeta's father. A part of me created the belief that a more traditional man would be safest for me, that he would give me the stability I thought I had lost. So I began dating men who were more conventional—like the ones I had grown up with. I enrolled our daughter in an elite school in São Paulo. I tried to fit in with the mothers' group. I tried, once again, to perform the version of womanhood that society expected. Yet nothing brought joy. Nothing fulfilled me—not Vogue, not the dates, not the endless conversations about motherhood.

We had changed. And the more I tried to return to the life I had outgrown, the emptier I felt. The truth became undeniable: I was no longer that woman. So I stopped.

I hired a new assistant and told her, "You'll help me with Vogue and with my new artistic director role—the campaigns, the fashion shows, all of it. But I also need your help to launch this project." It was the Free Free World project—the seed that had first appeared when I was pregnant in London. I had planned to launch it there, but once Violeta's father and I completed our cycle as a couple, I felt called to begin in Brazil instead.

At the time, I didn't understand why this project felt so important. I only knew that something in me burned to bring it into form. It kept returning to my awareness like a wave, again and again, asking to be born. That passion, that pull, that magic—this is how you know something is yours to do. I didn't yet know that it was our mission, conceived in the delivery room alongside Violeta, a mission that would one day grow to a magnitude I couldn't have imagined then.

This is how the Soul often works. It plants seeds long before the mind can understand their purpose. The ego demands certainty, plans, and guarantees. But the Soul asks for faith, trust, surrender. It whispers, "Act now. Move forwards. You will understand later." And when we follow that whisper, even without clarity, we step into alignment with the greater unfolding of our mission, trusting a Higher Power that always sees far beyond what the ego can grasp.

At Vogue, I had also changed. My new role as an artistic fashion director gave me the freedom to shape the magazine's shoots in an entirely new direction. I wanted to infuse them with consciousness, creativity, and a sense of social awakening. I wanted to shatter the illusions that kept women trapped in a golden cage and reveal the Truth I was slowly discovering within myself—that every woman is worthy, beautiful, powerful, and whole exactly as she is. What I was creating was no longer "just work." It was an extension of our mission, a thread of the purpose my Higher Dimensional Soul had come here to fulfil. And for the first time, my ego did not resist. It embraced the change. It felt safe. It had felt its own pain and now recognised how the myth of perfection wounds humanity so deeply. With this new clarity, my ego began to loosen its grip. It allowed me to question the rules that had once kept me bound to the golden cage. It allowed me to create from Truth. It allowed me to serve from Love. It allowed me to step, slowly, into who I truly was.

My studies helped me cope with the completion of that relationship, and the Love Violeta brought into my life was something entirely new. It was True Love—pure, expansive, unconditional. Not attachment. Not fear. Not projection. For the first time, I began to understand what freedom in Love truly meant. A Love that did not take, demand, or wound. A Love that only expanded.

Work kept me busy, but in a way that now feels divinely orchestrated. I didn't know it then, but all the money I was earning was quietly building the foundation for what was to come. That abundance had a purpose far beyond my personal comfort. When we are in service of something greater than ourselves—something that carries the frequency of Love—the Universe provides in mysterious ways. It places the tools, the people, and the resources in our hands long before we know why we need them, or simply in the right time.

And none of this would have been possible had I held limiting beliefs about my worthiness. If my ego had believed I didn't deserve abundance, I could have blocked the miracle before it even arrived. As Powerful Creators with free will, what we believe, think, say, imagine, and feel shapes our reality. Our only limits are the beliefs we carry in our spiritual, mental, emotional, and physical bodies. But in this case, nothing blocked the flow. The miracle moved freely. The Universe was allowing me to gather everything I would need for the mission—even though I had no idea yet that it *was* a mission—before it gently, and then suddenly, closed every old door.

Almost overnight, every contract was cancelled. At Vogue, my push to break the status quo had reached its natural limit, and I came close to being fired. After all, trying to awaken consciousness inside a magazine built on women chasing perfection was a bold risk. My ego panicked at first—terrified of losing the status, the stability, the sense of identity attached to my title and the financial abundance that came with a career that no longer resonated with my Soul. But this collapse was the final push. It was the moment my Soul had been preparing me for, step by step, breath by breath, lesson by lesson. It was the moment the old timeline dissolved and the Higher Path began. My Soul had mentored me into readiness. I no longer feared the fall because I had already risen from so much.

And so, when the doors closed, I didn't cling. I didn't force. I didn't shrink. I breathed. I listened. I surrendered.

It was Divine Time. The moment had arrived for Free Free to be born. I had nothing left to fear.

CHAPTER 11

THE MISSION

Earlier in 2018, a friend I had met on one of my shoots suggested a retreat where she herself had experienced profound healing. She didn't know it then, but she was an important key—one of those people the Universe sends to open a door you didn't even know existed. That door led me to a professional retreat centred on Deep Memory Process, a therapeutic approach that accesses and transforms unresolved memories stored in the subconscious. There, I immersed myself in Jung, in meditation, and in understanding how memory, emotion, and consciousness are woven together. I also encountered psychodrama, which immediately fascinated me.During the retreat, I learned how to access the subconscious through drawing, imagination, and sound, and how to *act out* the memories that needed release—almost like performing in a theatre. It electrified me.

With my background in art and fashion, I could suddenly *see* the truth with absolute clarity: we are all playing characters. We dress like them, speak like them, perform like them. We sustain the illusion…but just as we put the costume on, we can take it off. And the more sensory tools we give the ego—the sights, the sounds, the roles—the more it believes the story it is playing. Which means, in the same way we internalise trauma through the senses, we can consciously dissolve it. We can rewire ourselves. We can embody a new character—our *true* character.

When I returned home, I gathered every piece of knowledge we had called in over the years and wove it into a single methodology. We blended psychodrama, Jungian archetypes, neuroscience, meditation, dance meditation, NLP, and the worlds of art and fashion. I called it the Free Free Methodology®. And I finally understood: Free Free was never meant to be just video series, as I once thought. It was meant to bring education, awareness—real tools—to people who had been living from trauma and suffering, big or small, instead of Truth, from fear instead of Love, from conditioning instead of authenticity.

Free Free was ready for the world. Or perhaps, I was finally ready for it. I said yes with my entire being—no hesitation, no doubt. I called a friend who worked with individuals rebuilding their lives after living on the streets or coming out of prison. I told him: "I want to give these Free Free workshops to people who need to transform whatever made them victims into the truth of who they really are." He paused, and then said something that would redirect my entire mission: "I think this workshop would be perfect for women who have experienced violence. The rates are rising fast. You should meet the director from the Department of Justice in São Paulo. She leads the Gender Nucleus. She's incredible. You two will get along." I said yes—again—without even understanding what I was saying yes to.

The truth is:I had no real comprehension of what "violence against women" meant. It felt distant, like something that happened "somewhere else," something spoken about in the media but not in Yasmine's circle. I certainly didn't imagine it had touched *my own life*. This friend was a key. And when a key appears, doors open quickly.

A few weeks later, I found myself walking into my first meeting with the director of the Gender Nucleus. I wore a fashionable, elegant suit, laptop in hand, walking through the Justice Department building. We had already produced photos and campaigns for Free Free, but with her, I presented only the methodology—the workshop, the heart of the work. After a powerful meeting, she looked at me with unwavering certainty and said: "Let's do a five-year contract and take this to other states of Brazil. This can change the lives of millions of people." And once again, I simply said: "Yes." Not knowing that this yes would birth an entire movement. Not knowing that this yes would change my life forever. Not knowing that this yes was the true yes to our mission on Earth.

We ended the meeting by choosing August as the launch date of our partnership, in honour of the anniversary of the Maria da Penha Law. This law is one of the most important legal protections for women in Brazil and a global reference for gender-based violence prevention. Created in 2006 and named after Maria da Penha, Maia Fernandes, a woman who survived two attempted murders by her husband and transformed her pain into a fight for justice—it instituted urgent protective measures and stricter punishments for abusers. It marked a turning point for the safety, dignity, and rights of women across Brazil.

I had less than three months to launch Free Free. As I walked out of the Department of Justice that day, I had no idea what had just unfolded. How could this be? I had come from fashion—a universe built on aesthetics, storytelling, and beauty. How was I now standing inside a government building sealing a partnership to transform the lives of millions of women? It made no sense to the lower mind. But missions rarely do.

Life is a miracle—believe this with your whole being. We do not need to create our future based on our past. When we remove the ego from the centre and align with a mission that serves something greater than ourselves, the Universe moves in ways that defy logic. When the Soul leads—when the higher mind activates—something extraordinary happens. The heart opens. The eternal flame awakens. Love on the left side. Light on the right side. And the Power of Creation rises through the centre. In this state, we access the limitless quantum field, where all potential realities exist now, beyond time. From here, we are not bound by history or limited by what is "logical." The linear mind collapses, and the Soul reveals pathways the ego could never imagine.

This was one of those pathways—a leap that marked the true beginning of Free Free. What began as a simple idea for a video series was now becoming its real mission: to heal, to transform, to free humanity—and the feminine—from the invisible cages of trauma and move back to Love.

What happened inside that government building was not just a contract. It was a confirmation from the Universe, a cosmic signal that our mission work was never meant to stay inside the pages of Vogue. It belonged to humanity. It belonged to Mother Earth and all beings. Look back and notice the flow. How my Soul had been leading me, step by step. How each person who appeared was a key. How every yes to the unknown unlocked the next piece. This is Divine flow—how life moves when we walk with our Soul instead of our conditioning. This is how Free Free was born. Not from strategy. Not from perfection. Not from a business plan. But from one yes at a time. One key at a time. One act of surrender at a time. This is why some people—those trapped in the ego's rigidity—struggle to understand Free Free. Because Free Free is not linear. It is circular, multidimensional, guided by a Higher Power the human mind cannot quantify or analyse.

And the same flow is possible for you. When you trust. When you surrender. When you create from your heart. When you say yes to your Soul, the keys will always come.

Three-Months Journey

During the next three months, my team and I had only one focus: to launch Free Free. What needed to happen? We needed to create a funding model, shape the branding, design a campaign, run the pilot workshop, hire PR, and sit down with lawyers to set up a new company. We also dreamed of producing a documentary of the project. My years at *Vogue* and leading my creative studio had given my ego entrepreneurial understanding and creative direction know-how, but this time, something was different. Beyond what my ego knew, I had a different Knowing that came from the Soul. Also, for the first time, my creativity was untethered—free, expansive, wild. I could build anything I was inspired to build, without anyone else's fears projected onto me, unlike when I was working for other companies and publications.

The passion was like fire. When passion flows through you like this, unstoppable and alive, that is your Soul's Creative Power pouring through you. Trust it, always. We were fearless. Our intention was simple: to serve through workshops, to raise awareness through videos and campaigns. We didn't yet know what it would transform into, but we were confident, unstoppable, and more guided than I realised at the time.

Free Free wasn't initially conceived as a project for women. But after that meeting at the Department of Justice, the focus became clear: women. Even though the mission would one day expand to embrace all of humanity, it began with women first—almost as a training ground, a consciousness research lab, a place where we could study the wounds of the feminine with precision and depth. These wounds do not belong only to women; they shape men, children, families, and even the Earth itself.

At that time, I didn't consider myself a feminist. In truth, I didn't even fully understand what feminism meant beyond the distorted narratives I had inherited. In the world I was born into, feminism was almost treated like a bad word—associated with anger, rebellion, rejection of beauty, or women wanting to overpower men. I absorbed these misconceptions without even noticing, because that was the lens of the culture around me.

After saying yes to working with women, I learned the Truth: feminism, at its core, simply means equality—the belief that all humans deserve equal rights, opportunities, and dignity. That is all. But many people—especially in cultures shaped by patriarchy—see it as a revenge movement, or as a threat to men, or as a force trying to overthrow tradition. None of that is true. But these illusions persist because patriarchy conditioned all of us to fear anything that disrupts the status quo. The culture I grew up in shaped the way I dressed, the way I behaved, the way I chose relationships, and even the way

I measured my worth as a woman. I grew up surrounded by women who proudly said they embraced *machista* values, as if agreeing with patriarchy earned them respect or belonging. It wasn't their fault—these beliefs were inherited. Passed down from mothers to daughters, from grandmothers to granddaughters, carried silently through generations as survival strategies.

So many women around me believed that being chosen by a man, being beautiful, being agreeable, being thin, being fertile, being a "good wife," being polite, and being quiet were the foundations of femininity. Some of these women were powerful and educated, but still internalised the very structures that limited their freedom. This wasn't because they were weak—it was because this was the water we were all swimming in. You cannot question the ocean when you are still learning how to breathe.

So when I walked into that meeting at the Department of Justice, something awakened. I wasn't stepping into the world of "feminism" as I had once misunderstood it. I was stepping into the truth of the feminine—the wound that had shaped the lives of billions of women long before me, the wound that also exists inside men, and the wound that humanity had been unconsciously carrying for thousands of years. The wound that was now asking to be healed.

Only later would I understand that this was never about ideological debates. It was—and is—about human's freedom consciousness. About the healing of the feminine spirit. And the masculine through Love. About liberating the parts of us—men and women—that had been silenced, controlled, diminished, or taught to earn their worth. Free Free began with women because women carry the oldest wound of oppression on Earth. And because when a woman heals, entire lineages of humanity heal with her.

At Vogue, it was no different. The magazine wasn't discussing social justice. That's why, when I tried to create photoshoots that were more inclusive, more disruptive to the status quo, it caused fear and confusion among the editors. On one hand, they wanted change—that's why they promoted me. But once the images were published, they panicked. Change is desired until it arrives. Then the unknown awakens fear. Here lies a Truth, beloved reader: lack of knowledge, cultural conditioning, and above all, fear of the unknown can keep us blind to what is real.

As we stepped deeper into this work with women, the misconceptions I had once carried about feminism became even clearer. Feminism, in its essence, is not "women against men," as I had subconsciously been taught. It simply recognises that men and women deserve equal rights: the right to divorce, to study, to lead, to govern, to feel safe, to be financially independent, to walk freely in the world.

Like anything filtered through trauma, feminism can be distorted into extremes—but its heart is simple: freedom. Freedom for women, yes, but also freedom for humanity. Because when one group is silenced, the whole collective becomes imbalanced. As I began studying women's rights, it struck me: many of the choices I had made throughout my life were possible only because women before me had fought for them. Legally, many rights now exist in countries like Brazil, the UK, and the US—but culturally, many are still resisted, mocked, or shamed. Why? Because they threaten those who rely on external power. And external power, beloved reader, is pure illusion. Only inner power is real.

At that time, I was only beginning to understand women's rights at the most basic level, laying the foundation for a much deeper understanding of violence against women and the group we were about to serve. So the question arose, the one that guided everything that came next: Why are women experiencing violence in the very place that should be their safest—their own homes? And how had I never truly understood what violence against women meant until this moment?

Before the first workshop, our team and I somehow managed to get everything done. It was as if the moment I said yes to the mission, the Universe began sending the right people to support me, the mission team. For example, the director who would later create our documentary, and who today sits on our board, turned out to be the landlord of the house where I lived during my first marriage in São Paulo. I had almost forgotten her, but a friend reconnected us out of nowhere. The director of the Gender Nucleus from the Department of Justice, who opened the first doors for us, also became part of our board and remains with us to this day. One by one, these Souls appeared, each carrying their own piece of the puzzle.

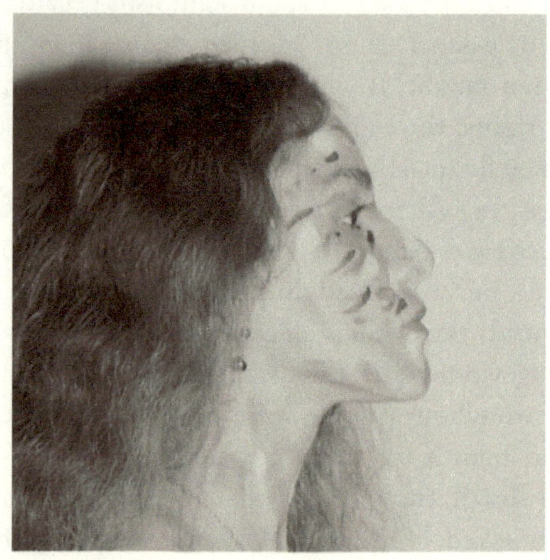

The portrait we did to launch Free Free in 2018 by Cassia Tabatini. This was my Soul expression, using creativity and art as a portal to my Soul.

Since I came from the media and advertising world, we decided our business model would focus on brand partnerships rather than the traditional nonprofit path—a world I knew nothing about. At the time, I still carried the illusion that brands would support Free Free with the same ease and enthusiasm they invested millions into the glossy campaigns I had helped create. In my mind it was simple: *We were supporting the freedom of women. Who wouldn't want to be part of this?* What I didn't know then was that this apparent "mistake" was actually Divine precision. By being guided down this unfamiliar path, we were quietly building something completely new—a social movement that did not depend solely on donations, but operated through a model aligned with the new economy of the new paradigm the Earth was grounding, and we were part of this solution. A structure rooted in sustainability, creativity, and consciousness rather than scarcity. I didn't understand it at the time, but the Universe was already shaping Free Free to become what it is today: a movement built to stand on its own feet, outside the old systems, part of the future that is emerging.

What I hadn't fully understood yet was that once my Soul took the lead, everything that mattered to me began to shift. The values of my old world were dissolving. What once looked important through the ego's eyes—status, validation, belonging to a certain elite circle—no longer held the same weight. That, too, was part of the mission: to help me, and eventually others, see through the eyes of Love and True Beauty instead of illusion.

So what I had believed was profoundly valuable wasn't necessarily valuable to the companies I was used to working with. I didn't know yet how much my frequency and vision had changed—and that those who were still operating from the old paradigm simply couldn't understand what Free Free was or what it would become.

A friend sent me a list of more than a hundred corporate contacts in Brazil, and just as I had once sent countless CVs to magazines seeking my first internship, I began reaching out one by one—this time with a mission instead of a dream. I walked into meeting rooms with my right hand, hopeful and determined, carrying the fire of the message in my heart.

Most people didn't understand what I was talking about. Some were kind but still said no. Others listened politely and couldn't grasp the magnitude of what Free Free could do. I remember leaving those rooms confused, thinking, *How can brands spend millions on campaigns, yet not see the power of what we are creating here? How can something so clearly life-changing not be obvious to them?*

Then another friend introduced me to a director at Unilever. At that time, the Free Free methodology still held a strong fashion influence, and one of the brands she oversaw wanted to bring a fashion-driven perspective into their product narrative. It felt like a Divine alignment—almost as if the Universe was saying, *Keep going. The path is opening.* And so, we signed our very first business partnership.

At the same time, while I was nearly losing my role at Vogue, another door opened. The magazine no longer wanted me overseeing the artistic direction of the entire publication—the vision I carried was too unorthodox, too disruptive to the old paradigm. Yet instead of resisting, life redirected me. I sat with the CEO of Condé Nast Brazil, who had once been my editor-in-chief, and made a clear agreement: From now on, I would only direct projects aligned with my Truth. And surprisingly, we found a win-win.

I stepped into the role of Special Projects Director, which gave me freedom from the old illusions and direct access to projects that actually mattered to me. My first assignment came just two weeks before the official Free Free launch at the Deartment of Justice. We gathered a small team of four women and travelled across the Americas to meet and document women who worked with the land—women whose hands shaped life itself. We met farmers, seed keepers, cultivators, guardians of ancestral knowledge. Women whose bodies carried the memory of the soil, the cycles, the nourishment that sustains humanity. Women who embodied a kind of power that has nothing to do with status, beauty standards, or external validation. A power that comes from being deeply rooted in creation.

The project was to be presented at the W20 in Argentina, elevating the stories, resilience, and intelligence of the women behind agriculture. It became one of the most beautiful experiences of my life. A reminder that true power is not in appearance but in essence. It lives in the hands that create, nurture, and regenerate life. It lives in women who work in silence, with dignity. It lives in the Earth, in the cycles, in the depth we forget when we chase the illusions of the surface. Beauty is not the golden cage. Beauty is depth. Beauty is Love.Beauty is Light.

This project became a mirror—showing me that the world I once admired was just an illusion compared to the real beauty found in the women who carry life forward with their hands, their hearts, their stories.

Here I am in Guatemala, doing our beautiful shoot for Vogue about women and the land, which later became an exhibition and was presented at W20 in Argentina.

As you can see, beloved reader, I was being guided through a deep journey of awakening, opening my eyes to realities I had never touched before. Each step of the mission became a classroom, and my Soul became my teacher, my mentor. My ego was being trained to release the old ways of survival and to learn new ways of being—conscious ways, loving ways. As I stepped onto the path of serving the feminine in humanity, I began to see truths that had always been hidden from my world, truths my Soul had been waiting for me to remember. So, upon my return, I held my very first workshop with the Department of Justice.

CHAPTER 12

FREE FREE LAUNCH

It was August 25, 2018, when we led our very first Free Free workshop for forty authorities invited by the Department of Justice. Commanders, judges, prosecutors, and decision-makers filled the room. Our team had transformed the space into an immersive, living art installation. When I walked in, I felt entirely calm. The teachings didn't come from my ego. They flowed through me like water. For the first time, my Soul, not Yasmine, was speaking.

In this first workshop, we introduced the authorities to the characters human beings play—characters shaped by trauma, culture, and survival. Each participant was invited to explore a new character for themselves, not the one they were conditioned to uphold: not the respected judge, not the obedient wife, not the flawless mother. Through the Free Free Methodology®, which blended meditation, neuroscience, psychodrama, Jungian archetypes, fashion, and art, they embodied the teachings in a way the mind alone could never grasp.

We began with meditation. I taught the principal concepts using fashion as the great metaphor: just as actors dress for roles in a film, so do we dress for the roles of life. The clothes we choose are not neutral. They carry memories, agreements, and stories that trap us in old identities. Every morning, when we dress, we unconsciously reinforce the character we believe we must be. That daily ritual becomes a spell of embodiment. Over time, we forget that it is a character at all.

As I shared these Truths, my ego dissolved quietly, making space for a deeper, higher voice. My Soul held every participant in a field of Love, so they could access their own stories—just as I had revealed glimpses of my "perfect girl" persona, and how losing my mother and becoming pregnant made me to undress the characters I no longer belonged to.

Next, each participant painted or wrote on half of a towel: the cage they were stuck in, the beliefs that imprisoned them, the character they felt trapped embodying... and what they wished to embody instead. Through art, meditation, and the softened state of alpha brainwaves, the subconscious began speaking. Words, colours, symbols—everything the ego usually suppresses—surfaced with ease.

The golden cage could be anything. A woman beaten at home but presenting the image of a perfect family. A billionaire dynasty held hostage by the patriarch's approval. A corporate job draining the Soul. A poor family unable to imagine anything beyond scarcity. A golden cage is anything that gives the illusion of safety while suffocating our Truth. And because these cages come from beliefs—personal, ancestral, or karmic—they are often invisible until someone guides us to see them.

The last part of the workshop was the most transformative. We invited participants into an enormous wardrobe we had assembled, like the ones used for Vogue shoots. They chose a new character to embody. Then, in the centre of the room, they became that character—voice, movement, posture, intention. Some danced. Some wore flowing dresses. Some put on suits, kaftans, dramatic capes. There was no judgement. No perfectionism. No right or wrong. Only liberation.

When you see yourself as a new character, the old beliefs begin to crack. Through the five senses, through embodiment, through the emotional permission of the moment, something rewires. The body remembers what freedom feels like. The ego loosens its grip.

The authorities left in awe—not only at their own break-throughs but at how these insights could transform their work. Judges began understanding how a survivor's testimony could be distorted by trauma, not by lies. Commanders saw how women trapped in their golden cages often couldn't recognise abuse because they believed it was "normal." New awareness was born.

Watching these leaders transform before my eyes was surreal. It felt as if all the creative fire of Vogue—the lights, the wardrobe, the imagination—had been reborn into something sacred. For the first time, art was not being used to sell illusions; it was being used to free people.

As I stood there guiding high authorities, a thought pierced through me: This is what my mother never had. This is what women everywhere deserve. It overwhelmed me. My ego could never have predicted this moment. But my Soul had always known. Every heart-break, every cover shoot, every loss, every act of survival had prepared me for this. This was the first time I felt the merging of beauty with truth, fashion with freedom, art with Soul, justice with Love.

And in that space, as we all undressed the characters we had once felt we needed to be, we met glimpses of our true selves. Of our heart. Of our Soul.

Violence Survivors

The next day, we repeated the workshop, this time with women who were survivors of violence. Globally, nearly one in three women suffer sexual and physical violence (UN), but the numbers are way higher if you include other forms of violence and the ones that are not counted in the data. The room carried stories so heavy, they felt almost unbearable: women who had lost their children in court to sexually abusive fathers; survivors of femicide attempts, one who had literally had her nose bitten off; women still trapped in violent relationships after countless attempts to leave, numbed by drugs, stripped of their jobs, their self-esteem, their sense of self.

I had never come face to face with such realities before.

Instead of letting this paralyse me, I walked in steady, because my Soul was leading, not my ego. I followed the same steps as the day before—opening the space, guiding the meditation, inviting them into the creative process. Then, something extraordinary happened.

One woman, in particular, moved us all. She was the chief of police—strong and respected, a woman who had handled thousands of cases of violence against women throughout her career. Yet for forty years, she had also been beaten at home. Her story revealed a truth that would stay with me forever: *Knowing* that violence exists is not enough. If deep inside, you believe it is normal, or if you believe it's your fault, or if you believe you don't have courage or enough self-esteem to leave, you remain trapped in the cycle.

Sculpture created by artist Caroline Ricca Lee for our first workshops with hundreds of pieces of clothing representing different characters we need to undress to be free.

Throughout the workshop, this woman began to identify those hidden beliefs. Then she chose a flowing kaftan from our wardrobe, so different from her stiff uniform and duty belt. When she walked into the circle, we saw a different woman—softer, freer, her voice lighter, her movements less rigid. She smiled. She shook. In that moment, you could feel her rewiring herself, stepping into her Truth.

Shifts after shifts unfolded before our eyes. Our team and I left in awe, asking ourselves, *What just happened? How did we hold space for such profound healings?* Our egos couldn't make sense of it. But years later, I understood: It wasn't Yasmine leading those workshops, it was our Soul, our higher consciousness. From the very beginning, my ego never resisted my Soul when we stepped into service. In Truth, this mission was healing *Yasmine* as much as it was healing others.

That day marked something far greater than the end of a workshop. It was the real birth of Free Free, not as an idea but as a living frequency on Earth, a field, a mission in motion. In that circle, surrounded by women whose pain had once silenced them, we watched as stories were transformed into symbols, shame into softness, and trauma into truth. I saw judges cry. I saw survivors laugh. I saw power being redefined, not as control but as Presence.

And I saw Yasmine begin to remember her own truth. Because every time she stood in those workshops, every time she dressed a woman as a new character, every time she held space for someone to see themselves differently, *she* was also being dressed anew. *She* was also letting go of a cage. *She* was also meeting parts of herself she had forgotten.

You see, beloved reader, the mission was never separate from my healing. It was *through* the mission that the healing happened. That's how Divine service works. When you say yes to your Soul, life doesn't wait for you to be fully ready. Life uses every step of the journey to prepare you, to sculpt you, to break you open in the exact places that need to return to Love.

So, while my ego still didn't understand how we had done what we did, *my Soul Knew*. It was about surrendering. It was about saying yes, again and again, even when I didn't have a plan, even when my voice trembled, even when my heart was breaking open.

This was the day Free Free was truly born—not on paper, not as an idea, but as something alive.

This was the day Yasmine started allowing Me, her Soul, to take the lead.

Where Is the Logic?

If you think in logical terms, beloved reader, you might be thinking to yourself, *This all seems impossible. How could someone who works in the fashion world teach high authorities at the governmental level? That's crazy. Weren't you scared? Everything could have gone wrong.* My answer is this: This is not something your lower mind will ever understand. It is not logical, because it is something created beyond human laws. It was created through the power that lives within each and every one of us. It was created through our Divine Power of Love, Light, and Creation, which is beyond space and time, from the eternal field of creation, from God within. Yasmine didn't know this yet. But this is the Truth when we are in Service.

Congress

In the weeks that followed, articles about Free Free and me began appearing in some of the most important newspapers and maga-zines in the country. Our team soon delivered the same workshop in Brasília, the nation's capital and political centre. Just a couple of months later, we were invited to speak at Congress as part of the launch of a new technology designed to support women experienc-ing violence. You have to understand, at this point, I was still living in the *Vogue* world. I was still their special projects director. It was all still so new, unexpected, for me to step into these governmental spaces. But every time I was public speaking, it wasn't Yasmine, it was my Higher Dimensional Soul. The contrast was immense. Just months earlier, I was overseeing photoshoots, fashion weeks, and glossy covers. Now, suddenly, I was standing in the halls of power, talking about violence against women, consciousness, true justice.

I remember sitting there, asking myself, *What am I doing here?*

However, beneath the confusion was something else—a deep Knowing that this was exactly where I needed to be, that this was part of something bigger than me, bigger than anything my ego could comprehend. I didn't yet have the language for Divine orchestration, but something within me kept whispering, *Trust. Keep going.* And so, we did.

At Congress, I was taken by confidence and Presence once again. It was my Soul taking the lead. Standing there, I spoke something along the lines of the following:

Women are taught to play characters that keep us imprisoned in golden cages. Law is the first fundamental step towards change, but culture is what truly shapes us. And culture had been caging women for centuries.

We must stop projecting the myth of perfection onto women. That myth makes us lose touch with our true self, our true power, and makes us believe we must hand over our power to external validations, the kind that only lead to low self-esteem and self-betrayal. If we truly want more women in leadership positions, if we truly want to stop violence against women and create real change, then women must reclaim their true power: their creative power within them.

Instead of following the rule book handed to us at birth—written by families, religions, and schools—a rule book that tells us our safety and honour depend on how men perceive us, we need to remember a higher truth. Men are not the enemy. They, too, have been locked in golden cages of their own. For centuries, their defence mechanisms, born from fear and insecurity, taught them that to be worthy, they must fight, provide, dominate, control, and silence their emotions. But when the heart is closed, consciousness cannot pass through. From that blocked heart, that wounded place, the ego creates its only language: control, external power, even violence.

Humanity as a whole was, and still is, trapped in golden cages built from belief systems. Without consciousness, without a higher understanding that transcends traditional psychology, law, and media, these cages remain invisible to all of us, to the law, to the culture. And this becomes the norm.

No one was expecting me to talk about characters. The speech was spot on and applauded by the audience. It mattered because I was using my voice for my mother, my grandmother, and my great-grandmother, who were silenced. I was speaking for my daughter so she could learn she has a voice. I was speaking for all the women who still couldn't use theirs. This was the power the mission gave me—a gift to speak.

After my speech at the Brazilian Congress.

The Next Months

In the months that followed, it became clear that the workshops weren't enough. Two reasons stood out. First, if culture itself was what created the golden cage, then only culture could help people begin to see it, to have even a spark of awareness that what they were living might not be freedom but suffering they hadn't yet named. Second, companies didn't want to sponsor workshops.

So we used our creativity. The team began creating new projects that could generate awareness on a larger scale, projects that could also speak to marketing departments, which were more willing to invest in culture-shaping campaigns than in workshops. So we needed both awareness and deep workshops. All embedded with freedom consciousness.

At the same time, my right hand, who had been the bridge between Yasmine's fashion work and Free Free, moved to Barcelona. Suddenly, I was left struggling to piece together a new team, one that could handle both worlds at once: my still-demanding fashion work and the mission that was quickly becoming Free Free's heartbeat.

We decided to create a small pilot Free Free House, a space that became our home for talks, experiences, and our growing team. Not long after, we signed a major collaboration with one of the biggest fashion brands in Brazil. By March 2019, Free Free T-shirts were in over three hundred stores across the country. Each T-shirt carried a tag with crucial information for women, transforming a simple fashion item into a tool of awareness. We invited young artists to design the pieces and launched a campaign that made us dream. My creativity was now being used with Soul and in service of consciousness, of liberation. The brand also donated fifteen thousand pieces of clothing with small, nearly invisible defects, so we could upcycle them. We collaborated with fifteen communities around Brazil to create the most beautiful upcycled collection. Empowering these women brought both emotional and financial liberation. At the same time, it supported the environment, since fashion, as we soon learned, is the second most polluting industry in the world.

Some pictures of our upcycling project shot by Cassia Tabatini.

The next project we created was the Free Free Festival, a full-day experience of talks, art performances, and music designed for families. Our goal was clear: to bring together women from completely different worlds, so we could share and discuss the challenges women face from multiple perspectives. This was a way of demonstrating that every experience a woman has is a fragment of reality, and all of them coexist with one another as perceptions of the world.

On stage, we had celebrities who dared to open up about their struggles, directors from the Department of Justice, CEOs, women who had participated in our very first workshops, and so many others. The mix was powerful. It showed, in real time, that liberation is never one-dimensional, it is collective, layered, and unique for each person. The event was free, and to our amazement, over one thousand people showed up throughout the day. We were weaving art, creativity, fashion, music, and dialogue into a new kind of awareness, one that reached beyond workshops and into the wider culture.

From that moment, everything accelerated. Invitations began pouring in. Companies asked us to speak, and new corporate partners joined us. Before I knew it, I was standing on stage as a public speaker, addressing audiences of a thousand people, not as Yasmine from *Vogue* but as the voice of a mission.

*I always took Violeta with me everywhere. In this picture,
she is about two and half. Just after we launched Free Free,
I started public speaking, and in the middle of this speech, she
came to the stage to be with me. In this image, you also see the
chief of police before and after those first workshops we did.*

It was during this time that I was invited to have lunch with an actress I knew, who was also starting her own organisation to support women in the movie industry. The real gift of that meeting wasn't the lunch itself but the key she carried for me. Out of the blue, she said, "You must meet my agent."

I laughed and replied, "I don't work with agents anymore."

But she insisted. "This woman is different. She can help you license Free Free. She's honest, amazing, and she doesn't work with just anyone. She only partners with people and projects she truly believes in."

So I said, "Okay, I'll meet her."

When I finally did, it was one of those encounters that leaves you walking away thinking, *No way*. But a few months later, we decided to give it a try. Today, she's still by my side, acting as a guarding force of the mission and me. She was an important key, one I couldn't have imagined at the time. Later, I would understand exactly why the Universe placed her on my path.

Fashion Show

Three months later, we had the idea of doing a fashion show, but not just any fashion show. We wanted to bring women from all walks of life onto the runway, dressed in upcycled fashion, and present it on the stage of the most traditional fashion week in São Paulo. In just one month, our team made the impossible happen: We secured donations from the top twenty Brazilian designers and developed unique crafts with artisan communities across the country. When the day arrived, the runway was filled with iconic women. Amongst them, an important Indigenous activist, mothers, grandmothers, young women, women with different body types, and women who had never imagined themselves on a runway. It was never about perfection; it was about truth.

The show opened and unfolded like a living prayer. The lighting formed the Free Free rainbow, and it closed with a powerful Brazilian African tribal group, Ìyé, *Ìlà, Òwò*. Their music awakened something primal in the room, stirring emotions that rose from deep within. The women walking felt free to be themselves, to walk, dance, move, or act however they wished. For many, it was the first time in their lives they felt truly seen, that they belonged, that they were significant. It wasn't just a show; it was healing, for the women on the runway, for the audience watching, and for all those who later saw the images in the media. Free Free was breaking the status quo not through anger and blame, like many do in the social justice space, but through creativity, beauty, and truth.

Then came the final moment. I walked out from backstage with Violeta in my arms. Together, with the women who modelled and the audience, we merged into one—walking, dancing, swaying to the music as a single body. It was a peaceful stance for freedom—freedom for all women, regardless of race, social class, ethnicity, body type, or age, and whether pregnant, young, or old. All women: worthy, united, whole, just as we are.

Now the world could see it.

CHAPTER 13

THE PANDEMIC

A year and a half after Free Free's launch, the pandemic of 2020 stopped the world. Free Free had been peaking, riding a wave of momentum, and then, in an instant, everything shifted. My ego was terrified, but with my Soul leading, I began to see the crisis not only as a collapse but as an invitation, a portal into growth, silence, and becoming. An opportunity into deepening my Presence.

Before that calm could arrive, a storm hit. The first three months of the pandemic were pure chaos. Certainties dissolved overnight. Contracts clients had once celebrated suddenly became fragile. Some tried to cancel. I fell out with my father, with *Vogue*, and with a few close friends. At the same time, the Black Lives Matter movement surged across the world. With it came a weight I had never experienced before—the fear of backlash for leading a social movement while being perceived as a woman of privilege I felt pressured to pick a side, to speak in absolutes—but I didn't. Even with the pressure, when taking sides might have seemed easier because it offered a sense of belonging, I chose not to. We at Free Free chose not to. We were standing in Truth, that violence shouldn't be fought with violence.

Every word was weighed with deep discernment. Free Free had never been about sides or separation. It had always been about

Unity, Love, Truth, and Freedom. I knew that no movement rooted in division could ever bring lasting liberation. Abusive patterns were everywhere: in the media, between races, between nations, between pro- and anti-vaccine groups. Violence against women skyrocketed. We closed the Free Free House, the team went remote, and we faced a choice, surrender to fear or surrender to faith. We chose faith.

My new right hand, the women the actress introduced me to, my guardian, as I like to call her, became my anchor. She helped me navigate contract negotiations with clients and the conversations with *Vogue*, and she held up a mirror to the abusive dynamics I had normalised for so long. She showed me that some of what I had been accepting wasn't normal, and in moments when I couldn't see clearly, she gave me strength by simply standing by my side.

The pandemic gave me space to pause. Without the constant push to do, I was invited to simply be, to rest in the present moment, the eternal now because planning wasn't even possible. We were all forced into the now. In that surrender, breakthroughs began to flow without the interference of my ego. My ego had no past reference for this; nothing like it had ever happened before. So *I, the* Soul, stepped in more fully.

Then the Clarity came. I took Violeta out of São Paulo's number one school. I officially resigned from Vogue because my values no longer aligned with the magazine. I stopped leading fashion campaigns and devoted myself entirely to Free Free. Friends drifted away naturally, as happens when frequencies shift. After a month at my family's country house in the mountains of Rio, I clashed with my father. And for the first time, I could see aspects of him I had always denied. It was a major step toward my liberation—toward a higher perspective of Truth.

Learn from this, beloved reader. When you finally bring Light to something you couldn't see before, that is already a profound breakthrough. It is one of the greatest steps toward freedom from that memory, that trauma, that pattern. Because once Light comes in, you cannot unsee. You have the opportunity to redefine the experience through Love and reintegrate the part of yourself that was fragmented for too long. Even if it means taking space, like I did.

When I returned to São Paulo, I moved to the countryside and enrolled Violeta in a local school. My family and friends thought I was crazy, but my Knowing already knew this was just their fear projected upon me.

We were back in nature.

Back to Nature

The house was a gift from the mission. It was the first one we visited, and without doubt, we said yes. Built of glass and wood, it opened into a vast garden filled with fruit trees: jabuticaba, mango, lemon, orange, clove, cinnamon, peach. Violeta was only four, and for the first time in so many years, I allowed myself to play, healing a deep childhood wound I had carried and rediscovering parts of myself I had long forgotten. Play is a sacred act of nourishment of the Soul. This is what initially excited me about the fashion world—it was a type of play for me. Now, I found a more Divine one, one that didn't depend on anything external. It was a way of living life every day.

Playing with Mother Earth and caring for our vegetable garden

My daughter had been teaching me a new way of living since the day she was born. We always had a profound bond, beyond a traditional mother/daughter relationship, we were always together. But now, surrounded by nature and free from the constant pressure of leaving home for work—since I could finally work digitally from home—our connection deepened to a level I had never known before. We danced barefoot in the garden, climbed trees, planted a vegetable garden, lit the fireplace, painted canvases, and even painted our own bodies with paint and sometimes the very soil of Mother Earth. We were free. Free from the "perfect woman." Free from the "perfect girl." In the privacy of that sanctuary, when no one was watching, I undressed parts of my ego I hadn't even realised were still there. In that letting go, I began rediscovering the beauty of the feminine— embraced, held, and mirrored by Mother Earth herself.

Violeta's house sculpture and the one I used to
do at my country house as a girl.

This was also a time when I chose to go deeper into my consciousness practices—immersing myself in long meditation journeys, quiet moments in nature, and an even greater commitment to the many subjects I was researching for the mission. I didn't yet know exactly what I wanted to study, but I could feel that Free Free was already taking me to places I could never have imagined (the Department of Justice, the Congress).

I was becoming a recognised voice in women's rights and violence prevention, and I received my first major recognition: being named one of the 19 Women of 2019 by UOL, Brazil's leading media platform. In 2020, I was awarded Woman of the Year by *Glamour*. Still, there was a knowing within me: I needed to deepen my academic knowledge. I wanted to honour this platform I had been given, this voice that now reached millions. One of the new gifts I had received in my awakening was this voice. Before my awakening, I had preferred to hide backstage on my shoots. But Free Free placed me front and centre. Now, every word I spoke carried the frequency of my Higher Consciousness Soul and the many gifts that were first awakened and continue to awaken since that hospital room where I gave birth to Violeta.

One day, while searching online for possible courses, a graduate certificate in social justice at Harvard appeared, almost out of nowhere. Harvard had never crossed my mind, and yet there it was, as if placed directly in my path. The fact that social justice was exactly the academic foundation I needed for my mission felt like a miracle. I know now that once you say yes to your mission, and the ego stops interfering, every tool you need comes to you in Divine orchestration. You are living in a different timeline, where synchronicities and keys show the next steps.

Because the world was in lockdown during the pandemic, the program required no on-campus presence, making it possible for me to study while staying close to my daughter and continuing my work. I said yes once again. I enrolled without overthinking about investment, time, or any of that, like all decisions made from the heart are done, as you just know.

Free Free had already been teaching me what abuse truly was, long before Harvard gave me the academic language for it. As we served others, I was simultaneously learning to name what I, my mother, and so many women I knew had silently endured. My falling out with my father was part of this awakening. My decision to release my Vogue title, and to naturally let go of some childhood friendships, came from that same higher perspective—not as punishment, not as blame, but simply because we were no longer aligned. When vibrations shift, the people and structures we once held on to begin to drift away naturally. They are not "lost"; they are released, because they no longer match the frequency of who we are becoming.

Looking back, I began to see my entire life with new eyes—the dynamics between my parents, the patterns within my grandparents' marriages, and the unspoken agreements that had shaped my friendships, my relationships, my work, and even the way I treated myself. Little by little, the veil lifted. And I realised something that changed everything: abuse was never only personal. It was cultural. It was systemic. It was normalised.

I had grown up thinking abuse was only physical, something that happened "somewhere else," in "other people's lives." But now I could finally See the Truth: abuse takes many forms, and most of them are invisible. Abuse is psychological, the manipulation, the gaslighting, the constant undermining of confidence. It is moral, the shaming, the belittling, the subtle ways someone makes you feel "less." It is financial, controlling access to money, or making someone dependent to keep them small. It is emotional, silent punishment, withdrawal of affection, criticism disguised as care. It is spiritual, the breaking of someone's trust in themselves, their intuition, their worth, their Divinity.

But there was something even deeper beneath all of this: abuse is the opposite of freedom. Abuse is the moment someone loses their free will whether through force, manipulation, or years of slow erosion, and gives their power away, consciously or unconsciously. It can happen in a single traumatic event or through decades of conditioning. It can come from someone else or from ourselves. Sometimes the most painful abuse is internal: the way we speak to ourselves, the way we betray our own needs, the way we perform old stories long after we have outgrown them. These internalised stories become our golden cage, familiar, but suffocating.

During the pandemic, as silence filled the world, something inside me cracked open. The chain around my own cage the one I didn't even know I was still carrying began to loosen. And I could finally See. I started understanding my mother's suffering through a new lens. What I once believed was "mental illness" now revealed itself as the result of a lifetime of psychological, moral, emotional and financial abuse.. Her nervous system overwhelmed, her Light trapped beneath layers of pain. Through the Eagle's Eye, I could finally See the Truth. With that realisation, I begin to question everything I believed was reality.Is this true? Is it true I will lose my worth if I leave Vogue? Is it true Violeta must attend an elite school to be "properly educated"? Is it true I must silence my Truth to be accepted? Is it true my mother was "crazy"—or was she trying to break free? Is it true I like the lifestyle I thought I liked? Is it true I owe unquestioned loyalty to companies that disrespect my values?Is it true I need a relationship to be loved?

Every single question became a key. A key to the new paradigm of freedom rising inside me. Because the minute we begin questioning, we interrupt the spell. We pause the loop. We create space for the Soul to whisper the Truth we were too afraid to hear before. This is how awakening deepens. Through questioning your reality. Your marriage, your friendships, your religion, your body, your culture, you disrupt the illusion long enough for the Light to enter. And once this happens only what is aligned with the Soul, with the heart, stays.

This is the way of the new paradigm: Freedom does not come from changing the outside world. Freedom comes from seeing the world through a different consciousness. The moment you question what you were conditioned to believe, you step out of the golden cage and into the first breath of true liberation. Beloved reader, perhaps you can begin now. Begin with one question. Then another. Let your heart answer, not your fear. In that moment, even if only for a breath, you enter the new paradigm—the paradigm of freedom. And once you taste that freedom, you will never again pretend that the cage was home.

The First Political Order

As I began my studies at Harvard, I immersed myself in courses about justice, the psychology of diversity, and many other subjects that expanded my academic knowledge. I love studying, researching.

One course, in particular, left a deep mark on me: Women, Peace, and Security, with Dr. Joan Johnson-Freese.

That class gave me the academic framework for what I had already been living—my life's journey, my work with Free Free, and my dismantling of the myth of the "perfect woman." It was as if someone had handed me the missing puzzle piece: the data and research that validated everything I had been learning through my own lived experience, everything I had been teaching, everything I had been working for. Everything my Soul already knew—and had been sharing in workshops and through public speaking—was now validated academically, framed in research far deeper than I had ever imagined.

One book, in particular, became a turning point for me: *The First Political Order* by Valerie Hudson et al. The authors brought together years of research proving what I had always felt in my heart—that the subjugation of women is not a side issue but the very foundation of political order worldwide, and that when women are empowered, entire societies transform. Reading it was like watching my lived truth come alive on the page, finally backed by unshakable evidence.

First, what Hudson and her co-authors explained was patriarchy through a different lens—one not rooted simply in ideology or individual behaviour, but in the formation of male kin groups. These were alliances of men bound by blood, lineage, or loyalty, originally organised for survival, protection, and control of resources. Functioning as self-governing groups, they created and enforced their own rules, often operating beyond, or even above, formal law. Loyalty to the group took precedence over justice, and silence was rewarded as a form of belonging. Over time, these male kin groups formed alliances with one another, expanding their reach and power while reinforcing a sense of impunity for those within the group. As societies grew more complex, these structures did not disappear; they evolved into armies, ruling elites, political institutions, corporations, and religious hierarchies. The form changed, but the logic remained the same. Within this system, women were rarely recognised as full political subjects; instead, they were positioned as reproducers of lineage, symbols of honour, or instruments through which alliances were secured and stabilised. In this way, the regulation of women's bodies, labour, and autonomy became central to maintaining male power. Patriarchy, then, is not merely a social attitude—it is the scaling of self-governing male alliances into systems of authority that normalise impunity and shape how power and violence operate in the world. This is why so much of the violence we see around the world becomes hidden, and so many women are called " crazy" if they try to bring light to some of the things happening. A pure example of the distorted wounded masculine acting through dominance, control, external power. Overpowering women to keep the idea of power by numbing their emotions and closing their hearts.

The book also revealed what I had already lived: the home is the first political stage a child ever knows. It is the bootcamp for life, the training ground where we learn what is "normal" and what power looks like in action. The leaders of the home—mother, father, or any other family structure—become a child's first reference of power. Are the leaders treating each other with respect, honesty, and shared decision-making? Or does the child see one leader using violence, betraying trust, manipulating resources, or acting with corruption? Whatever the daily rules of the house are, even the unspoken ones, they stop being shocking and instead become the template. They become the unspoken law for how to treat the "other"—people of a different class, age, race, gender, sexuality, or belief.

When I read those words, I thought immediately of my own childhood home. I saw my parents' dynamic—the patterns of silence, the power plays, the wounds that were never spoken of but lived out every single day. That was my first political order. That was my first state. It shaped how I saw men, women, work, friendship, and myself until my awakening began to dismantle it all. Now, through Free Free, I could finally see how personal healing connects to collective transformation: If we can start by changing the dynamics at home to a more equitable, loving, peaceful space, we can change the world.

The data Hudson and her co-authors present is striking: societies where women are treated as less than men in the home are 1.40 times more likely to be poor or in economic decline, 1.50 times more likely to have a low GDP per capita, 1.55 times more likely to suffer from low environmental quality, 1.83 times more likely to experience preventable deaths, and 1.80 times more likely to score worse on the Global Hunger Index. Conversely, when women are safe, respected, and able to participate fully—starting with equality in their own households—nations tend to have stronger economies, healthier populations, and greater stability. In other words, the patterns we tolerate in our homes inevitably shape international relations—wars, peace, and everything in between. As the authors poignantly state: "What you do to your women you do to your nation-state."

As I came to understand this, I realised that violence has, in fact, been normalised. And what becomes normalised often goes unseen. But how does something become normalised? Through videogames, music, and films. Through culture. When violence is normalised as the only way to react to uncertainty, fear, and the feeling of disempowerment, this is what we see—a world that is separated by political points of views, nationalities, gender, races, religion, economic barriers, etc. The people who are different than us become enemies. There is so much division, therefore, there is so much fear. The ego takes the lead, remembering all the past conflicts of the world and tells us, "Be careful with this or that group of people." Or the ego makes us think in terms of revenge: "This group of people did this, so now it's our turn to be in power." These are all illusions of the ego, attempts to make sense of the atrocities our world has endured with the level of consciousness individuals have at the time. But the Truth is this, beloved reader: Violence creates more violence. Fear creates more fear. Hurt people hurt people. These cycles repeat themselves across generations, nations, religions, genders, and families. When we live from separation consciousness, we begin to see the world through a scarce, wounded lens—a lens shaped not by Truth but by the ego's need to defend itself.

In this consciousness, every group becomes the "other," every difference becomes a threat, and every pain becomes a justification to inflict more pain. One side says, "Now it's our turn." The other side says, "You owe us." And so the cycle of reactivity continues endlessly—a pendulum swinging back and forward, never finding rest.

This is the trap of the lower mind: a belief that liberation can come through reversal, revenge, or domination. But domination is still domination. Fear is still fear. And power built on past wounds is still a cage. The cycle only breaks when the most courageous understanding arises: compassion and radical forgiveness. Forgiveness is not about erasing history or excusing harm. It is not about pretending that injustice did not happen. Forgiveness is the alchemy that transforms pain into Love and Clarity. It allows us to see *why* harm occurred in the first place. The traumas, the fears, the illusions that shaped our ancestors, our systems, and even ourselves. Forgiveness is how we stop the cycle. Not by forgetting, not by minimising, but by choosing a path that restores integrity rather than replicates violence. This is the work of the new paradigm—to rise above the blame game and enter a consciousness where healing becomes possible. Where we recognise that the wound did not begin with us, and it will only end through us when we choose Love over fear, clarity over reaction, freedom over repetition.

This reminds me of my great-grandaunt, who was taken to a concentration camp during the Holocaust. She was the only one in the family who endured its horrors. She came out alive and moved to Brazil to be close to my grandfather. You might imagine her as an angry woman after all the terrors she witnessed and endured. Quite the contrary—she was pure joy. Somehow, because of the terrors she suffered, her ego let go, and her Soul took the lead. This is why she survived. She was wise beyond her time and lived happily until the age of 105. I had the chance to spend a lot of time with her growing up. She always had a smile on her face, and she never blamed, never complained, and always shared words of wisdom through compassion and forgiveness.

My beloved great-grandaunt who lived until she was 105, after being sent to a concentration camp during the Holocaust.

Justice, beloved readers, is only attained through forgiveness, through compassion, never through violence. Think of Gandhi, Nelson Mandela, Martin Luther King Jr., and Mother Teresa: figures who showed the world that compassion is the only way forwards. Never through violence—always through Love.

True Power

As I learned the academic language for one of humanity's greatest struggles, I also taught my ego to look deeper, to ask the uncomfortable questions about my own life and how it reflected what I was studying. *Why is violence the norm? What sits behind this reaction, this distortion?* Covid wasn't the biggest pandemic humanity was living through, unhealed trauma was.

When we feel powerless, insignificant, and unworthy, when we don't seek power within, we go looking for it outside ourselves. That search becomes distorted. We chase power in the form of money, sex, status, marriage, and expensive objects. But because this is not true power, it is never enough. It demands more and more, like a vampire that cannot survive without feeding on others.

External power is borrowed power. It doesn't belong to you, so it can never sustain you, and you always want more, more, more. Yet the ego makes you believe its excuses: *There is no other way . . . When I get this, I'll finally feel enough . . . When I achieve that, I'll be powerful.* The truth is, the moment you get it, the hunger returns. You never truly feel whole.

This is the trap of unconscious humanity. The golden cage is not made of metal bars but of illusions of power that make us powerless. But I can assure you, beloved reader, there is always another way. In truth, there is only one way: healing what once made you feel powerless, unworthy, unseen, unheard. Until you do this, every ounce of power you think you hold outside of yourself is only strengthening the walls of your golden cage, a cage where you live in constant fear that someone, or something, will take it all away, leaving you with nothing.

The great news is this: You are never without power. Not because of what you own, not because of who you know, not because of titles or status. You are powerful because you are part of Source. Nothing you do—whether you judge it as good or bad in dualistic terms—can ever take away your Divinity. Even if you disconnect from it for a time, even if you fall into total darkness, your Divinity remains. All it takes to reconnect is to open the heart and allow the Light to shine. We are Divine beings. We are powerful beings. To remember this True Power, you must stop feeding the illusions that make you believe power exists outside of you. Within you burns an eternal flame made of Love, Light, and Creative Power. This eternal flame connects you to the Field of Life, where all power comes from. This is where your true Power of Creation lives.

When I left my position at *Vogue*, when I distanced myself from some friends, when I moved to the countryside, even as others laughed at my choices, I released a false power I didn't even know I had been holding onto. What I discovered in its place was something far greater: my true self, joy, play, Love like I had never experienced before, freedom. The things I once held onto had only clouded my access to my higher consciousness. Now, stripped of illusion, I could finally feel my inner Power.

The First Political Order also helped me finally understand the deep wounds my family dynamics had created, the very traumas I was now healing. My bootcamp was one of women's silence, men's fragility and vanity (even though it took me longer to see this fully—something I'll share in the next chapters), betrayal, abuse, and inequality. But this wasn't just the case in my home; it was the normalised culture of the world.

Here's a myth of perfection: Men should provide, women should submit. Because my mother never became submissive enough my father's unconscious reaction to maintain the illusion of power took the form of psychological, moral, and financial violence. For my mother, what was falsely labelled as episodes of manic depression was, in Truth, moments of clarity and willpower followed by the fear of not being able to carry them through.

The dynamic was sick. Culture is currently sick. We are all living in a traumatised world, one that tricks us into believing we must *earn* Love, when the only Truth is that we already *are* Love. Without loving ourselves first, how can we ever truly know love, trust love, or be in love without toxic attachments? How can we ever create healthy relationships with others if we don't feel whole ourselves?

As we navigated the pandemic, held in the womb of Mother Earth, my ego began finding answers that helped dissolve so many of my traumas and illusions. Little by little, I started trusting my Soul more and more. Healing came through experiences that allowed Yasmine to *See* the Truth and start breaking the patterns that still lingered in our life.

As you can see, beloved reader, my Soul's role in Yasmine's life was to teach, to guide, to clear away everything that no longer served her. This is how she continued undressing the characters that were never truly *who she was*.

CHAPTER 14

BREAKING OF THE CHARACTERS

The pandemic became a stage of initiation. Each day felt like the shedding of another character, another identity my ego had once relied on for safety. It was not glamorous, nor did it feel enlightened. It was raw, uncomfortable, demanding a courage I didn't yet know I had, but that my Soul had always carried. In the middle of all that uncertainty, when so many structures were collapsing and life was asking me to surrender more than ever before, something steady appeared: the woman I had met through that actress years before, who by then had been working with me for over a year. She was my new right hand. She was, as I call her, Our Guardian—the Guardian of me and of the mission.

She arrived as a soul sister, a mission partner placed on my path by Divine orchestration, and through her presence, I felt a level of safety that allowed me to take bold actions in the material world even as the external world fell apart. With her by my side, I could say yes to my Soul when everything in the old paradigm begged me to hold on to the familiar. She helped me trust that letting go of the structures, contracts, and relationships that had once seemed essential to

Free Free—and that had felt like a form of safety—was in fact releasing another golden cage. Through her grounded presence, I could walk forward with more clarity, more truth, and more devotion to the mission that was unfolding, step by step, through Divine design.

The First Contract I Declined

When the pandemic reached its peak in July of 2020, the collective fear in the world was erupting everywhere—between communities, inside families, across nations, and especially within corporations. Stories of misconduct were surfacing daily, and one of the companies Free Free was partnering with suddenly found itself among the accused. Out of panic, they made an unconscious decision: instead of addressing the issue from Truth, they attempted to use Free Free as a shield, hoping our credibility would soften the scrutiny just as we were about to launch a major project together. It became obvious they were not acting from their hearts but from survival mode, led by the wounded masculine mind that reacts, defends, and hides. Still, we offered help. We extended compassion. We proposed a path of integrity—a few internal adjustments and, most importantly, a simple public declaration acknowledging what we had accomplished together and outlining clear steps to prevent similar situations from happening again. Nothing dramatic, nothing punitive. Just Truth, transparency, and responsibility. The kind of shift that allows organisations to evolve into the new paradigm of freedom, where accountability is not punishment but healing. The declaration mattered because it ensured our project would not be a performance, a plaster, or an illusion, but a real step forward.

Meeting after meeting, they nodded in agreement, but the moment the calls ended, they went on to do exactly as they pleased. It became clear that their "yes" was performative, not embodied. So one day, we stood firm: without the changes and without the declaration, we would not launch the project. It wasn't a threat—it was a boundary. Big corporations are not accustomed to small organisations standing in Truth rather than fear. We were not fighting them, nor shaming them; we were offering a bridge to integrity in a moment when they were drowning in their own survival instincts. Yet, to them, this was not about Free Free at all—it became a power struggle within themselves. They could not control the situation because they could not control us, and the wounded masculine—the part of the system that survives through domination, denial, and force—does not know how to respond when someone refuses to be bullied into submission. In the end, both sides chose not to renew the contract. My ego felt the fear of instability—this was a major financial partnership. But for my Soul, and for the mission, it was a profound victory. We had chosen integrity over fear in a big way.

Standing in that Truth shifted something fundamental within us. By refusing to give our power away out of fear of losing money, we activated a deeper frequency of the mission. If Free Free exists to teach true freedom, how could we compromise our own? We did not fight, we did not attack, we did not shame. We simply stood in Love. When you say no to abuse, you say yes to the Divine within you. Yes to your own dignity. Yes to your own liberation. And even if it made them uncomfortable—because consciousness often does—it also offered them a doorway into a new paradigm of business, one built on collaboration, transparency, and mutual respect. Those who are ready for this new frequency recognise it as a gift. Those who are not will naturally fall away. And that is perfect. We trusted Truth, and more aligned contracts came.

After that first great "no," which was actually a great "yes" to the mission, the energy around Free Free shifted. It was the beginning of a new phase—one grounded in inner power rather than external validation, service rather than survival, clarity rather than fear. This clarity continued to guide us as we worked with other companies. We entered every partnership not through battle but through consciousness. Yet, beloved reader, you must understand this: the world is still governed by systems steeped in the wounded masculine—the consciousness of control, separation, domination, and violence. This is why we see so much war, conflict, and division. These patterns are embedded in laws, religions, institutions, and traditions that for centuries have elevated hierarchy over harmony. In such systems, the feminine qualities—intuition, connection, fluidity, empathy, collaboration—are dismissed as weak or irrational. But this is an illusion, not Truth. The feminine is not soft; she is the force that births worlds. She is the river that always finds a way through the mountain. She is creation itself.

What the world needs is not the collapse of the masculine, but the rise of its empowered form, the masculine that protects, builds, anchors, and executes with integrity—and its reunion with the empowered feminine who creates, listens, nurtures, and inspires. Only when these two unite can we return to our natural state. Only then can humanity remember what it has forgotten: that the greatest power is not control, but coherence. Not fear, but Love. Not division, but unity. This is the essence of the new paradigm of freedom. This is what Free Free has always been here to anchor.

Another experience, this time with a renowned luxury brand, revealed a different face of abuse—one that hides behind polished campaigns, flawless imagery, and the perfect language of "purpose." The partnership was meant to be profound. It involved a creative campaign directed by Free Free and a full-year consultancy for the entire organisation: monthly lectures, trainings, and internal cultural work touching more than a thousand employees, from C-level executives to the interns. Together with both the marketing and people teams, we designed a roadmap that spoke about emotional freedom, the myth of perfection, women's competition, and the deep-rooted patterns that hold women and men back from conscious leadership. From the beginning, we made one principle very clear: real change starts within, not outside. Transformation is not performed; it is lived.

When teams feel safe to make mistakes, to speak honestly, and to show up without fear, creativity expands, collaboration deepens, and businesses thrive. That is when values stop being lines in a strategy deck and start becoming a living frequency within a company's culture. This is precisely why our contracts are at least one year long, because a campaign, no matter how beautiful or bold, cannot shift a culture on its own.

And yet, while the campaign we cocreated was a success—embedding consciousness into each frame, each symbol, each line of the script—the way Free Free was treated by the company stood in stark contradiction to everything we were teaching. Month after month, payments were delayed, though deliverables were expected exactly on time. My right hand, had to send repeated reminders for what was contractually agreed, reminders that at times felt like begging. It was dissonant: the external project celebrated empowerment, but the internal behaviour reproduced the same patterns of neglect, dismissal, and subtle power plays that we were working to shift.

Over time, we realised that many brands come to Free Free wanting the appearance of transformation, not transformation itself. They want to be seen as doing good without actually doing the work of looking inward. And that is because real change requires courage. It requires going beneath the surface, meeting the parts of ourselves we have avoided, and seeing the illusions we protect. Not everyone is ready for that yet, and its ok.

At the end of the year, the people's director gave us extraordinary reviews, praising the internal impact, the openness it created among employees, and the visible shifts happening across the company. But the marketing team dismissed it. "It didn't give us enough media," they said, as if the value of human transformation could be reduced to coverage metrics. Our response was simple and grounded: "Our contract was never about perfecting your external image. It was about transforming your internal culture—how your people feel, create, and relate."

They were not truly caring for their people. They were unconsciously caring for their image. This was the ego at play, as now we have learned that whatever is appearance based is. And while Free Free's projects are beautiful, bold, and aesthetically magnetic—which is why so many brands seek us—in truth, we are not here to decorate the system. We are here to transform it by building change in creative and authentic ways. Free Free is not a marketing tool, unless it is to shape the wider culture of a country through awareness. We are an ecosystem of consciousness, creativity and innovation. When a company invites us in, they receive far more than branding—they receive truth, depth, and the frequency of freedom. Some embrace this. Others resist it.

We attempted to show this brand the depth of the work, the possibility they had to become a true example of conscious leadership, but their intentions were misaligned. So we parted ways with compassion, clarity, and no resentment. This was not an isolated experience. As we continued working with corporations, we realised how deeply wounded these structures are—how often they choose visibility over integrity, speed over depth, hierarchy over humanity. The pattern was clear: many companies wanted to *look* awakened without doing the inner work awakening requires. And this, beloved reader, is the very definition of the old paradigm—the paradigm built on the wounded masculine consciousness of domination, performance, separation, and fear and of the wounded feminine of submission.

The wounded masculine expresses itself through control, urgency, aggression, power games, and the belief that productivity defines worth. The wounded feminine expresses itself through silence, manipulation, self-abandonment, people-pleasing, and the fear of speaking truth. These two distortions feed each other endlessly: domination and submission, power and fear, control and collapse. This is the old world. This is what is falling apart.

But here is the truth the new paradigm brings: Transformation is not immediate. It is not performative. It is not external first. Real transformation is internal, sustainable, and rooted in consciousness. Only then does it become external. This is the feminine way of leading—not through force, but through depth; not through competition, but through collaboration; not through performance, but through presence; not through speed, but through sustainability. It is slower, but it builds roots that no crisis can uproot. It is quieter, but it creates legacies that last.

And now, as the old system collapses, the feminine must lead the way back to Love—because only Love reunites what fear has separated. Only the feminine within all of humanity, knows how to soften centuries of hardness. Only the feminine knows how to hold the collective heart until it remembers itself. Only the feminine carries the alchemy to turn pain into wisdom, to transmute wounds into strength, to transform trauma into a new story for humanity. But she is not meant to do this alone.

When the empowered feminine is supported by the healed masculine—stable, clear, devoted, grounded—a new form of leadership emerges. A leadership that does not exploit but protects. That does not dominate but directs. That does not suppress but honours. A leadership that cannot be uprooted by crisis, because it is rooted in integrity. A leadership that cannot crumble under pressure, because it is built on truth. A leadership that does not need to overpower, because it knows its own Power. This is the unity of the liberated feminine and the liberated masculine—a sacred dance that births a new world.

This is the new paradigm. The Free Free Paradigm. It is not born through fight, force, or rebellion. It is born through frequency. Through remembering who we truly are beneath conditioning. Through dismantling illusions we once believed were reality. Through courage—real courage—to do the inner work. Through choosing integrity over performance. Through choosing compassion over fear. Through choosing Love over domination.

This new paradigm is not masculine or feminine; it is the harmonious presence of both, alive, integrated, awakened, in every being who chooses to rise.

This is how we build a world where freedom is not a concept but a lived state of being.

During the pandemic, we witnessed both ends of the spectrum: brands holding to old systems of control, and brands courageous enough to step into the new frequency of leadership. When a Fortune 500 company commits to true inner change, when they treat their people with dignity, when they allow themselves to be vulnerable, when they trade fear for integrity, the ripple effect is extraordinary. A single corporate ecosystem touches millions of people a day through its products, messaging, and global reach. When they choose the new paradigm of freedom-consciousness, the impact is immeasurable.

This is why we never turned our backs on the system. We entered the system. We walked into the places that felt sticky, uncomfortable, resistant. Because this is where transformation is most needed. And because global change will not come from speaking to the already awakened; it will come from bringing consciousness into the very structures that shape the world.

To transform a paradigm, beloved reader, we must be willing to stand in Truth even when the world around us is conditioned to live in illusion. And that is what we did—again and again—with Love, with strength, with clarity. This is the path of the new paradigm. This is the work of Free Free.

Women

For thousands of years, women have been excluded from the centres of power—political, economic, religious, and even within their own homes. And although the world has changed, the numbers remind us that the old order still breathes: in 2025, only 11 percent of Fortune 500 companies are led by women, and globally, women hold just 27 percent of parliamentary seats. These imbalances are not random. They are the direct expression of what we learned are the *first political order.*

This ideal of the "perfect woman," reinforced for centuries by culture, religion, and media, has shaped the lives of billions of women and girls. Until the 1970s, women in the United States could not even open a bank account without a man's permission. British women only obtained equal voting rights in 1928. In more than one hundred countries, child marriage is still legal. In parts of Africa, young girls endure genital mutilation so they will never know sexual pleasure. These are not distant tragedies or historical relics—they are the living architecture of the world we still inhabit.

My own story was woven into this architecture long before I had words for it. The silence my mother endured, the financial dependence that slowly became control, the judgement that labelled her "crazy" instead of someone suffering abuse, the shame passed down through generations—all of it was a microcosm of the global story of women. What I lived at home was not an exception; it was a reflection of the system itself: a world built not for women's freedom, but for their containment.

Within my family, within corporations, within governments, I began to see the same pattern expressing itself through the wounded masculine and the wounded feminine. Both were trapped in the same illusion—fear of losing power, fear of not being enough, fear of being unseen. And from fear, violence is born. From fear, silence spreads. From fear, separation becomes the norm.But fear is not Truth. Fear is only the lower mind trying to protect itself from the unknown. When we raise our consciousness—when we see through the Eagle's Eye—we remember something essential: We are not separate. We are not powerless. We are not trapped in these inherited roles. We are made of Love, Light, and Creative Power.

This is why the feminine has always been feared. Not because it is weak, but because it is powerful. Not because it needs to dominate, but because it cannot be dominated. The feminine is wild like the river—intuitive, creative, nurturing, unpredictable. It births life, not only through the womb but through ideas, art, innovation, intuition, and truth. Even after menopause, the feminine enters an era of deeper creativity and wisdom, as many tribal cultures have always honoured—completely different from what mass media tells women today. Instead of recognising this as a sacred passage into a woman's most powerful years, modern culture wrongly declares that her "prime" is over. In Truth, this is when her wisdom ripens, her intuition expands, and her creative power deepens.

When women are free, they cannot be controlled. When women rise, old systems tremble. This is why patriarchal cultures created endless rules to keep women small—because a woman in her full feminine power is a force of nature. She becomes pure Creative Power. A wildflower. This is also why the world needs more women in leadership—not as a symbolic achievement, not to simply fill quotas, but because the feminine brings qualities humanity has been starving for: intuition, empathy, collaboration, wisdom, the capacity to lead from the heart. The masculine brings structure, clarity, and action. When these two forces are in harmony, humanity thrives. When they are in conflict, the world collapses into chaos—as we see today.

Corporations, too, are not "the enemy." They are simply reflections of the same wounded systems. Many leaders hold on to external power because they do not yet recognise that true power comes from within. They live in survival mode, just as much as the individuals within them. Until consciousness rises, the old paradigm will keep repeating itself. But once we recognise the pattern, it begins to lose its power. From that recognition comes the possibility of something new—what we call the Free Free paradigm. Free within, Free the world. This new paradigm is not the dominance of the feminine, nor the return of the masculine. It is the rebirth of both, healed and unified. It is the remembrance that true power is never about control, but about Presence. It is the understanding that freedom is not something you are given; it is something you reclaim from within. And it begins with the courage to open the golden cage, and see through the Eagle's eyes even when you don't yet know what lies outside.

Beloved reader, this is why your awakening matters. When one woman wakes up, she frees her mother, her daughter, her ancestors, and generations to come. When you remember your worth, your family system shifts. When you speak your truth, your community feels it. When you heal your wounds, you stop passing them forward.

This is how a movement grows. This is how consciousness spreads. Not through force, but through frequency. Not through blame, but through clarity. Not through war, but through Love. We can transform the pandemic of fear into a movement of freedom, truth, and Love. And it begins with you.

Women in Competition

There was still one aspect of my journey with companies that I couldn't understand: why so many women, even those working toward the same purpose, ended up competing with one another instead of collaborating. It felt harsh, confusing, and at times even more painful because it came from one of us. From the very beginning of Free Free, I had felt it—women working for women's rights turning against each other. How could that make any sense? I didn't have the language for it yet, but later I understood: this was the sister wound in its shadow, one of the deepest expressions of the wounded feminine.

During the pandemic, a situation made this wound impossible to ignore. After six months co-creating a project with a company, exchanging strategy, ideas, vision, we finally reached an agreement and started. We had one month to deliver something bold and unusual. These projects were my favourite because they allowed me to create from truth. What I didn't know was that another organisation, led by women, was simultaneously trying to undermine the partnership out of fear that we had "taken their space." That was the first time I clearly saw how the first political order, thousands of years old, conditions women to see one another as threats, not allies.

At Harvard, in my course of Woman, Peace and Security, I learned a term that explained this clearly: linked fate. For centuries, women linked their survival to men. Fathers, husbands, brothers because their social value depended on them. Meanwhile, men linked their fates to other men through war, work, politics, and networks. This created a strong male alliance, the "gentlemen's code." When a man divorces, his friends take him out for drinks. When he succeeds, he brings his friends with him. But for women, it is mostly the opposite. A woman who divorces is still judged. A woman betrayed has her worth questioned. A woman who rises often rises alone, because there are so few seats at the table that fear replaces truth. This is cultural design based on fear. Patriarchy has trained women to believe that there isn't enough space for all of us, that only one woman gets to be chosen, seen, valued, or loved. This scarcity is the root of the sister wound.

In its shadow, the sister wound shows up as comparison, competition, mistrust, jealousy, judgment, or subtle sabotage. It shows up as women fearing one another instead of supporting one another. It shows up as the wounded feminine—insecure, unseen, unheard—fighting for breadcrumbs instead of remembering she *is* abundances.

But the sister wound also has a light side—one of the most powerful forces on Earth. When the feminine is healed, she remembers who she is. She remembers her worth, her intuition, her beauty, her voice. That each one of us are unique, and therefore there is nothing to compete about. So she collaborates. She no longer envies, she uplifts. She no longer fears losing space, she creates and opens space for others. She becomes a portal of abundance for all women. This is the sister in its light: women holding each other, rising together, creating what no one else can create alone.

This experience revealed so much about my life beyond business. I remembered the friends who turned against me when my first marriage ended. I remembered my mother, who, when she tried to separate from my father, found no support, only judgment from the very women she expected to stand beside her. And later, as I stepped into our mission, my visibility triggered more women than I expected. I began receiving both admiration and attacks. It took me years to understand that these attacks were not personal, they were expressions of the sister wound. When women saw me walking free, they felt the bars of their own golden cages shake. Seeing someone live a life they secretly longed for but did not yet believe was possible can open deep pain. Pain so old, so hidden, that it erupts as judgment, envy, or distance. But when we shifted into compassion, when we saw them with the Eagle's Eye, everything changed. I could see the suffering behind the behaviour. I could see the wound beneath the words. I realised: a woman can only attack another woman when she has forgotten her own worth. And once I understood this, the attacks no longer had any power over me. I could hold my light without dimming it and share my power through my heart.

Beloved reader, the liberation of women will never come from competing with one another or fighting for who gets to speak first, rise first, or shine first. It will come from liberating all the aspects of the wounded feminine. It will come from remembering that there is space for all of us, and that every woman who rises opens the path for many more. This is why patriarchy has always feared sisterhood—because when women unite, we are unstoppable. But they have nothing to fear. Conscious women are not here to overpower men; we are here to bring harmony, balance, and unity between the feminine and masculine within all of us.

The new paradigm is built on this unity. The healed feminine and the healed masculine standing together. The feminine leads us back to depth, intuition, and truth. The masculine protects, stabilises, and brings that truth into form. Together, they bring us back to Love. Together, they remind us that freedom is not an individual journey but a collective rising.

Parenthood

Another way the first political order revealed itself in my life was through my relationship with Violeta's father. Two years before the pandemic began, my childhood nanny—who was like family—came to live with us in São Paulo, and later in the countryside, to help with Violeta while I worked and studied. At that time, before the world shut down, her father would come only every three to six months to visit her. Our lives moved in a constant cycle of disagreements. He remained distant from his responsibilities as a father—emotionally and financially—while I, still without the Clarity of the Eagle's Eye, unconsciously blamed him for everything that wasn't working.

This, too, was part of a deeper pattern: the mother wound—when a woman, carrying generations of pain and abandonment, unconsciously blames the masculine (whether a partner, an ex, or men as a collective) and moves away from Love, compassion, and forgiveness. I couldn't see it then, but both of us were acting from old wounds, not from our Truth.

However, beneath the surface, this was not just my personal story. It was the first political order playing itself out again—the inherited, normalised belief that a father's role is secondary while a mother's role is central, that women must carry the invisible load while men are permitted emotional distance. This is the story millions of women live every day, and it quietly shapes men too, teaching them that their presence is optional. Without realising it, I was repeating the cycle, holding the weight of generations of imbalance—the same wounds, the same distortions of responsibility, the same power dynamics written into families for centuries.

After my partner and I separated, he entered his own journey of finding himself, while I took full responsibility for parenting and providing. At first, I was angry; I felt abandoned, alone, and victimised. This was the mother wound in its shadow—the part of the feminine that carries centuries of resentment, over-responsibility, and the unconscious belief that we must do everything alone because no one will show up for us. It is the part that blames men collectively for the pain women have endured, instead of seeing the deeper patterns at play. In that shadow, pain speaks louder than Truth. And like many parents around the world, we were simply two wounded people reacting to each other's unhealed stories, caught in the victim–persecutor dynamic that distorts reality for everyone involved.

Violeta's father went three years without paying his alimony agreement. He left behind debts from our time together and, for long stretches, barely saw our daughter. The year before, I had asked for full custody of Violeta, and we peacefully agreed it was the best path for her. Then, during the pandemic, he returned to Brazil to be with his family, his mother, grandmother, sisters, and brother, and slowly began spending more time with Violeta.

When I asked my lawyer whether there was a way to address the debts he had left behind, her response was blunt: "In Brazil, men go to prison for not paying alimony. Give him a scare and do it." But something in me resisted instantly. "I will never do this to the father of my daughter," I said.

In that moment, I saw clearly what I had not been able to see before: how the legal system, still rooted in the wounded masculine, replicates the patterns of violence it claims to solve. It punishes instead of healing. It forces instead of restoring. And it reinforces a narrative where men are persecutors and women are victims, without considering the deeper emotional, cultural, and spiritual wounds that shape these behaviours. This realisation softened something in me. I began to see him not through the eyes of abandonment but through the Eagle's Eye—the higher perspective that recognises the wounds beneath our actions. I saw how he, too, had inherited a story: the story that men are not needed in the emotional land-scape of the family, that they are visitors rather than pillars, that they must choose between their freedom and their presence. This, too, is the first political order playing itself out—the ancient, unconscious belief that a man's place in parenting is peripheral and a woman's place is central. And both suffer from this illusion.

Instead of revenge, I chose Presence. In stillness, I realised that our constant fights were simply our traumas reacting to each other, only multiplying pain and fear, never creating solutions. So when my ex-partner started working again, I proposed a new agreement: "Forget the old debts. Let's begin from now. Be more present in Violeta's life, and now that you're working, start contributing monthly from this point forward." This is the difference between the justice of the ego and the justice of the Soul. The ego seeks punishment to make the other "pay," to restore a false sense of control. The Soul seeks restoration, to bring balance, peace, Love—never revenge.

When we act from the Soul, the questions shift: How can this situation return to harmony? How can Love and responsibility flow again? One choice multiplies wounds. The other multiplies freedom.

The old debts were so high that they had become overwhelm-ing—impossible to move past. By releasing them, dignity was restored on both sides. He could contribute without shame. Violeta gained her father's presence. I reclaimed my inner power and freed myself from the mother wound, bringing more light to the mother within me. And after three years of a silent tug-of-war that only deepened wounds, I gained a friend I now consider family. What a blessing.

A few years earlier, I would not have seen this possibility. I would have held tightly to the old story of blame, of being wronged, of needing justice as punishment. But with the consciousness I had grown into, I could finally step into the Eagle's Eye. From that higher perspective, we saw that neither of us was a villain. We were simply two wounded humans, doing the best we could from the level of awareness we had at the time.

With that shift, everything changed. Solutions that once seemed impossible became effortless. It was a win-win, the kind the wounded ego resists, but consciousness makes possible. When we stay trapped in anger, we collapse into victimhood or lash out like a wounded dog, blaming the other. In separation consciousness, we live only in extremes: I am right, you are wrong. You did this to me. Through the Eagle's Eye, the Truth becomes visible: Everyone is doing the best they can from their level of consciousness. No one is a victim. No one is a persecutor. From this perspective, solutions that honour everyone become clear—and once solutions honour everyone, healing happens.

That is what happened here. By releasing punishment and choosing presence over payback, I created space for restoration. This was never about money. It was about me no longer identifying as the victim. It was about reclaiming responsibility for my choices, my patterns, my traumas. It was about seeing the story from compassion and radical forgiveness, toward myself and toward him. By choosing not to see him as the persecutor, a story I had used to protect my own wound, we found dignity, Love, and balance. And with that choice, everyone won.

So I ask you, beloved reader: Are you ready to reclaim your power without blaming someone else for your suffering? Taking responsibility is not excusing harm. It is not tolerating abuse. It is the opposite. It is choosing Truth over story. It is choosing Love over fear. It is choosing freedom over victimhood.

Because revenge is itself another form of violence. And violence cannot create justice. Violence cannot create peace. Only Love can unite. Only Love can heal.

Through the Eagle's Eye, compassion awakens. Compassion for yourself, and compassion for the other. Forgiveness then becomes a possible path. You forgive not to erase responsibility, but to liberate yourself from the story of "they did this to me". That story keeps you trapped in the golden cage of victim consciousness, far from your true power. Remember this: Whatever lessons the other must learn are not yours to teach. The Universe has its own perfect ways of guiding every Soul home.

This is us after the forgiveness. There is still Love, but no more fear or blame.

CHAPTER 15

THE WOMEN OF MY FAMILY AND SILENCE

The pandemic years felt like a bootcamp for the Soul. The Universe was accelerating our mission, pressing me into initiations I hadn't chosen consciously but was deeply ready. At some point my human body collapsed under the weight of it all—the avalanche of teachings, awakenings, dissolving illusions and grounding into the physical world. I burned out. For days, I could hardly move. Yet beneath the exhaustion, I could feel something else happening: the higher frequencies of my Soul, working through every cell of this body, upgrading its nervous system, preparing me for the step we would soon be asked to take.

One afternoon, as I lay in bed in that glass-and-wood house, surrounded by fruit trees and silence, my eyes fell upon a book I had never really cared for. A school volume, it was titled, *Our Story*. My mother had given it to me when I was a teenager, with a small note taped to the front: *My loving daughter, here is a little bit of the story of your mother's family.*

At the time, as an adolescent, I had dismissed it the way most teenagers dismiss the stories of their elders—half-listening, half-drifting. But in the stillness of the countryside, with my body softened and my heart cracked open, I picked up that family book again. This time, the words didn't just speak to me; they revealed me.

As I turned the yellowed pages, I discovered what I had been blind to all along: a lineage of women who carried immense power—and immense silence. To my astonishment, I learned that on my mother's side, I was the seventh-generation grandniece of Mariana Claudina Pereira de Carvalho, the Countess of Rio Novo (New River). In the 1800s, when Brazil was still a monarchy and when women had no recognised voice, she stood as a leader decades ahead of her time.

After her husband died young, she took full command of their vast estates. And more remarkably, she led through the empowered feminine. At a time when slavery was tragically normalised in the unconscious world, the countess treated the enslaved people on her land not as property but as members of her extended household. When she passed away in 1882, at sixty-six years old, she left behind a will that read less like a legal document and more like a vision for a new world.

First and foremost, she freed three hundred enslaved men, women, and children legally—the very people who had worked and lived alongside her. Then she granted them half of her land, ensuring they would have soil to plant, homes to live in, and the means to sustain themselves. The other half of her land, she designated for the collective good: a school for the poor and the very people that were now free, a creative educational centre, a hospital for health, and a church for spirituality. She built not just a legacy but a dream. To her direct heirs, she left little, saying they already had enough.

What she did was revolutionary—not only then, but even now. Not just because it all happened before the Lei Áurea, the law that officially abolished slavery in Brazil years later, but because it remains rare to see people truly act in service of others beyond themselves. To understand the magnitude of her decision, one must remember that when abolition came, the harshest criticism was that it left formerly enslaved people with nothing: no land, no education, no food, no homes. Many had no choice but to remain in cycles of exploitation just to survive. But my great-aunt had broken that chain long before, offering dignity and true freedom to those under her care.

She lived not by the myth of the "perfect woman" imposed by her time but by the Truth of freedom, courage, and Love. As I read the schoolbook, I felt a spark ignite inside. It was as if a hidden key had been waiting all along—passed down through Yasmine's lineage in Divine timing—waiting for me to discover it. I became restless with excitement, diving into more research, piecing together this story that carried the weight of generations of women in my family.

Then, something clicked. I remembered that my mother, grandmother, and great-grandmother were all buried in a little chapel in the city of Três Rios (Three Rivers). For the first time, I understood why. The chapel belonged to the countess herself, a sacred place she had chosen for her family's rest. Suddenly, the thread of my ancestry felt alive, woven through history, blood, and mission. Yet I had never been there. Not even when my own mother passed away had I set foot in that chapel. Grief, fear, and trauma had kept me away. But now, guided by this newfound understanding, I knew I had to go. So, in November 2021, I made the pilgrimage to Três Rios to stand in that chapel, to touch the earth where my foremothers lay, and to reclaim a piece of the story that had always been part of me. By reading about the countess, I was somehow discovering more of myself.

When I arrived, the chapel was locked, its heavy wooden doors holding decades of silence. Then, as if the moment had been Divinely arranged, a kind older man appeared and greeted me. He was the chapel's guardian, a quiet keeper of memory. His eyes carried the weight of time, but his voice flowed with Clarity and warmth. He had a beautiful light around him, an open heart, and a shine in his eyes.

I introduced myself, and the moment I spoke my name, something shifted. It was as if he'd known I was coming. He began to share stories no book could have captured, stories alive with whispers of truth, history, and spirit. He told me the countess had passed away in London, after travelling there to be treated for ovarian cancer by Queen Victoria's physician. But the surgery failed, and she did not survive. At her side was the family doctor, a man who was married to one of her nieces, and as the story went, seemed more interested in her wealth than her well-being. Some say he even claimed her inheritance for himself.

Then came the part that pierced our heart. Years later, a body—perhaps hers, perhaps not—arrived by ship in Rio. The family never came to claim it. Instead, it was the freed Black people, those whose dignity and survival she had fought for, who went to the port. They carried her remains, whether of flesh or of memory, and they were the ones who celebrated a mass in her honour in that very chapel. The circle closed there: The woman who had given them freedom was, in the end, carried home by their Love.

At that time, Black and White people would never attend mass together. Society's norms were rigid, segregated, and unquestioned. Yet as the guardian keeper told me, the countess defied all of it. Every Sunday, she walked to church accompanied by the very people the world insisted on calling her slaves—yet she refused to see them that way. They prayed together, side by side, as human beings before God. When she passed away, the mass they held in her honour was their final act of Love and reverence for a woman who had seen their dignity long before the world did.

My blood family, in contrast, attempted to erase her legacy. They tried to declare her "crazy," hoping to cancel her will and claim her lands and wealth as their own. But they failed. The courts ruled in her favour, even after her death. For once, justice aligned with Truth—and her vision for a different world was honoured.

Her compassion was an example of true power. Abolitionist leaders such as Joaquim Nabuco and José do Patrocínio praised her as a visionary. Even after her death, her portrait was honoured in the Paço Imperial in Rio de Janeiro, and in Minas Gerais, freed men founded a society in her name—*Os Libertos* ("The Liberated")—a living homage to the woman who had seen their humanity long before it was recognised by the world.

But what struck me most was this: I had never read about her in any of the history books I studied at school. Not once. A woman who led without violence, who broke the norms of her time, who embodied empowered feminine leadership in the 1800s—erased. Silenced. Omitted. And in that absence, I saw a pattern I had been uncovering my entire life: the systematic erasure of women's voices, women's strength, women's leadership. Her story had never been truly told—just like the stories of countless women who reshaped families, communities, nations, and yet disappeared from textbooks and pulpits. This, too, was the work of the wounded masculine consciousness—controlling the narrative, reducing the feminine to weakness, hiding the truth of her power.

That's when the memory keeper's energy shifted, his voice becoming soft with knowing. "You should look for the current president of that organisation," he said. I thought, *What? Is there anything still alive beyond this chapel?* He nodded and handed us two directives: Search for the book written by Cinara Jorge, and call the man who now holds its legacy.

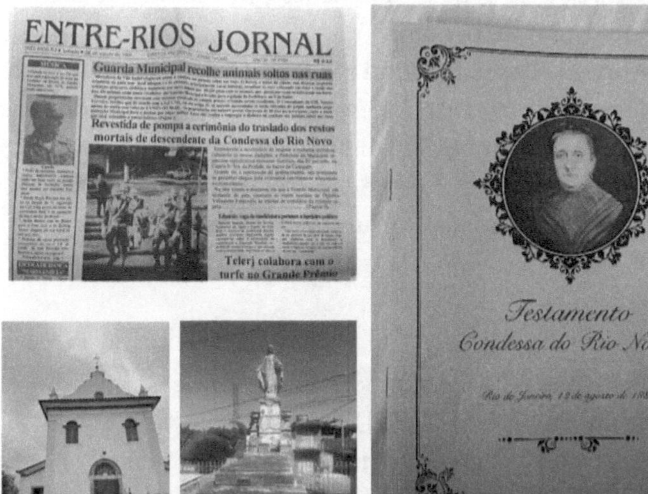

When I went to visit the church for the first time in 2021 and was given this booklet with the countess's will.

As I absorbed all of this, tears filled my eyes. The legacy of feminine leadership and radical compassion had always lived in my bloodline. I realised then that we were not creating this mission from nothing—I was remembering it. I was awakening to a lineage that had been pulsing beneath the surface of my life since before I was born. The torch I thought I had forged through my pain was, in truth, the same flame my great-grandaunt, the Countess of Rio Novo, had carried generations before me—the flame of a woman who embodied freedom not as rebellion, but as Love in action. Freedom not as individuality and separation, but as collective transformation.

It was no coincidence that I rediscovered her story in the stillness of the pandemic, nor that I stood in her chapel at the very moment our mission was preparing to take its next leap. My Soul had guided me back to her so I could reclaim the part of myself I had forgotten—the part written into my DNA, carried through the women of my family who had held power quietly, fiercely, and with grace. It was Divine orchestration, a remembering across centuries. Nothing begins with us; we are continuations of a much greater tapestry. We are threads in a field of Oneness, awakening at the exact moment we are meant to awaken.

As timelines collapsed around me in the eternal now, I understood: I was not stepping into a new mission. I was stepping back into an ancient one—the same mission my soul had been carrying across lifetimes, waiting for the world to be ready for the New Paradigm of freedom, compassion, unity, and Love.

Silenced Women

As I traced the women of my mother's lineage, a deeper questioning awakened within me. All my life, I had been told that my mother, my grandmother, and my great-grandmother were "mentally ill." But as I stood inside the chapel of the Countess of Rio Novo, a woman who had also been called "crazy" simply because she was powerful, something in me shifted. A whisper rose from my Soul: *What if they were not ill at all? What if they were misinterpreted?* I began to see that perhaps their so-called "madness" was simply the language of women who refused to conform to the golden cage of their time. Women whose emotions were too large, whose intuition was too sharp, whose visions were too threatening to a wounded masculine culture that needed to control what it could not understand.

The more I looked, the clearer it became: this pathologising of the feminine was a pattern—a generational silencing disguised as diagnosis. It was the same distortion that erased the Countess from history books and labelled other visionary women as unstable. But what if these women weren't "crazy," as the world had claimed? What if they were awake? What if their sensitivity, their rebellion, their emotional intensity, and their refusal to obey were signs not of illness, but of power, of Clarity—of Souls pushing against systems that were not ready for them? Their visions were too expansive for the paradigm they lived in. Their light was too bright for a world built on suppression.

As I traced their footsteps, I realised I was not only breaking a cycle of silence—I was remembering their power. I was reclaiming a lineage of women whose truths had been buried under misunderstanding. And I knew: in the New Paradigm, where the empowered feminine and healed masculine rise together, their stories would no longer be called madness. They would be recognised for what they truly were—early awakenings.

Five generations of my mother's maternal ancestry.

I decided to call my only elderly relative still alive, my grand-mother's brother. With a trembling voice I asked, "Can you tell me about my grandmother? Was she really mentally ill, crazy, like every-one always said?"

His answer came clear and steady: "No. Of course not. She wasn't crazy. She simply became depressed after the divorce, when her children were taken from her. She was lonely. The separation from her children was too much to bear."

As a mother, I can tell you, beloved reader, that to have your children taken away is one of the most devastating pains a woman can endure. My grandmother wasn't mentally ill, as my mother had grown up believing. She was grieving. She was heartbroken. Without anyone to support her, she was silenced. Her suffering was not madness; it was the natural, human response to trauma and loss. But in a culture that didn't know how to hold women's pain, the eas-iest label was "crazy."

So I continued to ask questions. "What about my great-grandmother?"

He laughed softly. "She was indeed different."

Her first child, from her first marriage, was born deaf. Instead of surrendering to the limitations society imposed, she refused to see him, or herself, as victims. She travelled all the way to the United States to learn how to educate him, showing a defiance of convention almost unheard of for women at that time, when most were expected to remain quietly at home.

She divorced twice. Her first husband, a lawyer, was the father of my grandmother. Later, she married a man who owned what today is Vale do Rio Doce, one of the largest mining companies in the world. He gave her a sophisticated Cadillac, and with her trade-mark authenticity, she had it painted pink with a caramel cover, an audacious statement in the Golden Age of Rio, the 1950s. When that marriage ended, he tried to strip her of everything. She took him to court and won. But her victory was not for material gain or revenge. She wanted integrity. She looked him in the eye and said, "I don't need anything from you. I only wanted justice. I can sustain myself on my own." Afterwards, she moved to the countryside with her children, my grandmother and her brother, where she lived with quiet dignity and many beautiful animals she loved taking care of. She was a divine woman, who lived by her Truth in communion with Mother Earth and all beings.

My great-grandmother and her pink Cadillac.

As I listened to these stories, the pattern became undeniable: generation after generation, the women in my family were labelled "crazy" not because they were unstable, but because they were authentic—because they refused to shrink into the script of the perfect woman. In a culture governed by tradition, silence, and the myth of female obedience, their emotional truth, intuition, independence, and compassion were treated as madness. Most painfully, this accusation of "mental illness" became a weapon in court, a way to silence them, strip them of dignity, and often take from them what they held most precious—their children.

My mother was no different. Like her mother and grandmother before her, she wasn't "ill"; she was silenced. Silenced by the wounded masculine in my father's attempts to control her, and silenced by the wider patriarchal system—a system built on the belief that power, money, and control matter more than Love, truth, or freedom. My mother did not die by suicide because she was "mentally ill." She died because she had no tools, no language, and no support to free herself from the abuse she was enduring. Her death was not madness; it was the final expression of a woman trying to escape an unbearable cage, believing she had no other way out.

She did not have the teachings we share with you now, beloved reader. She did not have the Eagle's Eye, the consciousness tools, the creative path to liberation, or the understanding that her Soul was never broken—only misunderstood. Today, we know a different way. You know a different way. With consciousness, creativity, and service, there is always another path to freedom, one that does not require sacrifice, but reclamation. One that transforms pain into power, and silence into truth.

When half of humanity is seen as "less than" by the religions we follow, the laws we obey, and the cultures we inherit, power stops being rooted in Truth and becomes something taken by force. Only then did I begin to see the pattern that flowed through the women in my family. They were never unstable or unworthy, as I had been conditioned to believe. They were women ahead of their time—women who refused to conform to abusive dynamics, who dared to live outside the script, just like me. Their authenticity was called illness. Their resistance was painted as weakness. But in reality, they were carrying the seeds of a different future.

I carried their blood—but I did not need to carry their fear anymore. Through the Higher Consciousness of my Soul, I was able to see the Truth with compassion: compassion for the women who were silenced, and compassion even for those who silenced them, for they too were trapped in the illusion that power comes from control. How painful it must be to live believing that your worth can be taken away at any moment, chained to the fragile fear-based logic of the lower mind.

One thing is absolute, beloved reader: We are all equally worthy. When we remember this Truth, not intellectually but in all our bodies—we stop bowing to human rules built on fear and control. We rise above them, not by force, but by becoming who we truly are. In that becoming, we discover a freedom no one can take from us.

From that moment onwards, I made myself a promise: I would never again be silenced by fear. The stories of my mother, my grandmother, and my great-grandmother would no longer be erased or distorted—they would be honoured through our voice, through our mission, and through the way I raise my daughter. We would be free from the false ideals of perfection, free from the distorted narratives of protection, free from the cages disguised as "goodness." We would live as we truly are: whole, worthy, and unapologetically free.

CHAPTER 16

HARVARD AND TAKING FREE FREE GLOBAL

As the pandemic drew to a close in the later months of 2021, it felt as though I had lived ten lifetimes in only two years. Many veils had lifted. I could see the abusive patterns humanity was entangled in. Trauma, violence, separation, fear through a compassionate view—all now laid bare before me. As my embodiment deepened, so too did the pull of the mission, calling me towards a new stage.

It was no longer the time to cocoon in nature. My sanctuary had served its purpose. I had learned what I was meant to learn amongst the trees, the silence, and the soil. Now, the world was calling me back. I stood at a threshold, facing a choice: retreat into the safety of stillness or step forwards into the unknown with everything I had become.

By then, I had just completed my graduate studies in social justice at Harvard. That experience became a bridge, an unexpected platform where Free Free was no longer just a movement in Brazil but also a case study, a living example discussed in classrooms filled with people from every corner of the globe. In deliberative justice classes, I debated the very issues I was wrestling with in my own life and mission—this time with voices representing more than twenty nationalities, different races, diverse ethnicities, religions, ages, and genders.

This richness of perspective expanded me. It grounded me. And it made one truth undeniable: The patterns I had lived, and the work we had birthed through Free Free, were not just Brazilian stories but human stories. They were everywhere in the world.

It was there, in those conversations, that I realised: Free Free can't be contained just in Brazil. It was not mine alone. It was not meant for one country. The resonance was global. The issues we debated—violence, inequality, the silencing of women, the separation of communities, the impacts in climate—were the same everywhere. Different faces, different histories, same wounds. Harvard showed me Free Free was not a local answer but a global language.

As my embodiment deepened, we could feel it. Free Free was not just an organisation. It was a frequency. It was alive. It carried the energy of liberation, and that energy could not be contained by borders, governments, or traditional business models. To cage it in one country or one definition would be to betray its essence.

Harvard gave me the intellectual space to study, to analyse structures, to test ideas. But my Soul gave me the Knowing: Free Free had to mirror the very freedom it taught, fluid, borderless, alive like a river.

Harvard also gave me the opportunity to research more deeply into the state of the world, while realising that the business model I had chosen for Free Free was far from traditional. At this stage, we had a social enterprise that offered creative services for corporations—projects, campaigns, content, media, consultancy. Alongside it, we had a nonprofit that survived only because of the social enterprise, since we had never fundraised for it.

In my leadership and politics class, I became fascinated by decentralised companies and hybrid organisational models. None of them were perfect, but each carried a spark—an essence—that pointed to what the future of leadership could be. I realised that neither a traditional private company nor a conventional nonprofit could truly hold the vision of Free Free. Both structures were too rigid, too defined by old-paradigm logic, too bound by linear expectations. I studied the decentralised model of AA—powerful, but far too diffused for what we needed. I analysed another innovative company—highly effective, but only within the specific conditions it had been created for. Still, I felt that somewhere between these structures, in the space where hierarchy and fluidity meet, lived a blueprint that could hold the frequency of Free Free. Something that could allow us to leap, to scale impact, to reach more people across the world without losing our Truth. This exploration wasn't about copying any model. It was about letting these different examples spark a remembering—guiding us toward creating a structure that was new, alive, adaptable, and aligned with the new paradigm of freedom consciousness that Free Free had always represented.

After two years without an office—just a team working from their homes, spread across Brazil—I realised something essential. We didn't need offices. We didn't need the traditional structures the old paradigm insisted were necessary. Our team could work from anywhere in the world. And Free Free, in its very architecture, could become living proof of the new world we were here to build: fluid, borderless, decentralised, creative, guided by consciousness rather than control.

It became clear—it was time to take Free Free global. Everywhere I looked, the world's problems traced back to the same root: trauma. The patterns were global. The wounds were global. And the solution we had developed through Free Free was not Brazilian; it was for all of humanity. It carried a frequency that belonged to all of us. I felt it in every cell of my body. A voice inside spoke clearly: Just go. Not back to São Paulo. Not back to your golden cage. Go to the world.

The two obvious options were London and New York. New York was too far from Violeta's father still living in London. Yet London felt like a full-body no. I still carried the pain of the years I had lived there when I was pregnant and in Violeta's early years. My ego had turned the city into a symbol of that suffering, projecting onto London what had actually been a trauma. London wasn't the enemy. It was simply a mirror of a story I hadn't healed yet.

So I looked elsewhere. Portugal. Or Ibiza. The pandemic had shown me that 70 percent of my work could be done online, and for the remaining 30 percent, I could board a plane. Ibiza felt too transient, too unstable, too far removed from Brazil. Portugal, however, arrived like a whisper. I had never set foot there. And yet the land felt familiar like a doorway. A place that carried both the weight of history and the promise of new beginnings. Europe, but closer. Foreign, but intimate. As I searched deeper, the whisper became louder. I discovered that part of my mother's lineage, my aristocratic line, originated in Portugal. The Countess of Rio Novo. This was a forgotten thread of ancestry returning to me exactly at the moment I was being called there. It felt as if the land itself was inviting me home—not to settle the past, but to reclaim codes of remembrance. I did not know it then, but Portugal would become the bridge: between continents, between my ancestry and my future, between my Brazilian roots and the global scale of the mission. Between my past self and the woman my Soul was transforming me into.

The Decision

By this stage of the pandemic, Free Free was expanding rapidly. We began teaching commanders, broadened our work with the secretary of security of São Paulo, and secured more corporate partnerships than we had at the start of the pandemic. Free Free also grew digitally, reaching one million people per month, and the Harvard program gave me a space to experiment with Free Free in front of a global audience. Meanwhile, Violeta's father and I were slowly getting closer again, not romantically but as friends. In 2020, we spent Christmas together as a family, alongside my brother and his wife, for the first time since our separation. It was also the first time we didn't spend Christmas with our father. Something shifted after I started awakening to the Truth of my early years, and I needed space and time to understand it better, to heal it, and to forgive.

In December 2021, Violeta, her father, and I travelled to Bahia as a family. One afternoon, I told him, "I'm thinking of moving to

Portugal. What do you think?" He said, "That sounds amazing. Yes. I love it. This would give us the chance to be closer."

I took it as a sign.

When we returned from Bahia, we all stayed in the house in nature where Violeta and I had been living for the past two years. It was just before Christmas of 2021, just after I visited the countess's chapel where my family rested. My brother and his wife came over again. In the space between Christmas and New Year, I began sending emails to schools. I told my family, "I have to decide now, whether we move for this school year or wait until September."

My Knowing was clear: *Now. And I said Yes once again.*

Violeta had been accepted into two schools. So in January, I packed up our entire house and shipped everything to Lisbon—without ever having stepped foot in the city myself. By February, we were already living there. From the outside, it may have seemed impulsive, radical, even irresponsible. But inside, it was simple. I didn't think my way into that decision; I *Knew.*

Knowing does not come from the mind. It does not come from fear, from pros-and-cons lists, or from the anxious whisper of *What if I'm wrong?* Knowing rises from the Soul—quiet, steady, unmistakable. It does not argue or negotiate. It arrives like a clear beam of Light showing you the next step before the step even exists. By then, I had learned to trust this deeper guidance. I had Known when it was time to birth Free Free into the world. I had Known when it was time to leave Vogue and walk away from the golden structures I once believed defined my worth. I had Known when it was time to move to the countryside with my daughter, surrendering all the illusions of status and perfection that had held me in place.

People called me crazy, again. But this time, I felt no need to explain myself. My Soul was leading, and I was following. The rational mind could never have understood what the heart had already decided. When the path is guided by the higher consciousness of the Soul, beloved reader, the next step is not a risk—it is alignment. It is Truth. It is freedom.

Some people see (clairvoyance), others hear (clairaudience), others feel (clairsentience). I was gifted with *claircognisance*—the gift of Knowing. It is when information arrives with such clarity and precision that it transcends the logic of the lower mind. You don't analyse it. You don't search for proof. You simply Know. And when this Knowing begins to awaken in you, feel it in your heart. Trust it. It is your Soul speaking to you. Do not let your mind shrink it or silence it by demanding rational explanations that fit into boxes for things born from higher realms. Go forward. Let miracles unfold.

Before moving, I knew I had to make a decision about how to fund Free Free's expansion. I had some personal savings, but if we were truly speaking about going global, it wouldn't be enough. Until that point, Free Free had never taken on investors. Whenever profit-driven investors approached us in the early years, I always said no. Back then, the only investment model I knew was the traditional one—giving away shares, diluting the mission, losing creative freedom, and becoming accountable to people who might not understand consciousness work. I knew the risk of giving equity: with the wrong type of investor, compromise is inevitable, and the mission could be distorted. And, at that time, I had no business partner to share such a responsibility. It was just me.

So I turned to something deeply personal: my art collection. Before Violeta was born, I had begun collecting artwork to mark important milestones in my life—gifts to myself, symbols of transformation. Each piece held a story, a memory, a fragment of my evolution. Selling them was not easy, but it was the only aligned path I could see then, one that allowed me to expand without sacrificing the mission's purity or giving away parts of a structure that wasn't yet ready to receive investors in consciousness.

The very first piece I ever bought was by Sonia Gomes, a Brazilian artist whose work touched me instantly. Sonia takes discarded fabrics, threads, and textiles and transforms them into sculptures of unexpected beauty. The way she stitched fragments together reminded me of my own medium of expression but also went far beyond it.

I had bought that piece when I became financially free—after signing the first contracts of my creative studio, right after my first divorce. It was a moment of rebirth, a moment of reclaiming myself. I remember standing in the gallery, looking at that sculpture and recognising something of my own Spirit in it: the beginning of independence, the emergence of my feminine power, the first breath of a life that belonged entirely to me. It wasn't just art. It was a symbol of liberation, of creation, of freedom. It was the last thing I wanted to sell. But by then, Sonia's work had exploded across the global art world. That sculpture was now worth many times what I had paid for it eight years earlier. And so, with a heavy heart and absolute clarity, I made the only aligned decision I could: I sold it. My heart broke as I let it go—because it had carried me through one of the most important initiations of my life. But I also knew it was right. That sculpture had fuelled one rebirth, and now it was giving birth to another. It became the seed that made everything beyond this point possible.

Sometimes the Soul asks us to release the symbols of who we were, so that we can step into who we are meant to become. This was one of those moments.

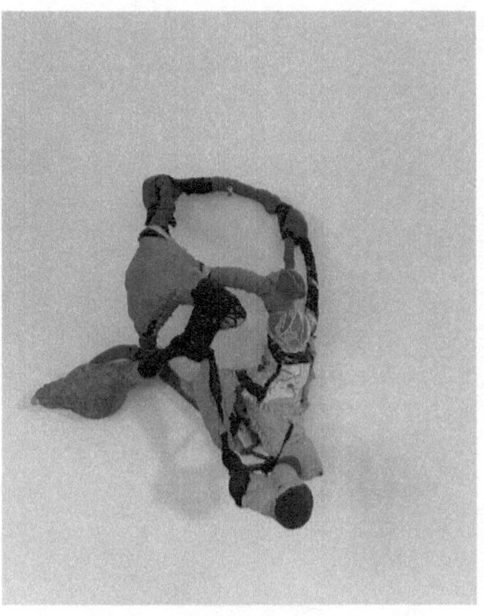

My beloved sculpture by Sonia Gomes.

This is the power of art. Art is not decoration. It is frequency. It is memory. It holds energy, stories, and vision. It carries our pain, transforms it into beauty, and then becomes a portal for new beginnings. For me, art has always been about liberation. In this case, art was not only healing me, it was literally funding the expansion of the Free Free mission. Freeing within, and freeing the world.

Dear reader, perhaps you too have something like this in your life. It may not be a sculpture. It may be a talent, a story, a vision, a piece of your history, an idea, a person, a belief, something you hold onto. When you release it, when you let it flow into the world, it can become the very seed that supports and expands your freedom. Because true abundance doesn't come from what we hold onto, it comes from what we're willing to let go of, in trust, in alignment, in Love.

CHAPTER 17

PORTUGAL AND THE FINAL CLASH OF MY EGO

When we landed in Lisbon, Violeta's father was there, waiting for us. It felt almost symbolic. After all the years of distance, fighting, and silence, we were standing together again, not as a couple but as a family. We were welcoming this new chapter side by side. Then, only a few weeks later, the war between Ukraine and Russia began. The whole world was holding its breath. Families were torn apart overnight. Women and children were running, leaving everything behind. Trauma was repeating itself in another shape, another geography.

The synchronicity wasn't lost on me. While the world descended into another cycle of chaos, I had just taken a leap into a new life, into Trust, into Knowing. The timing was precise. Free Free was never meant to exist outside of history; it was born to stand inside of it, to be a conscious response. The world will not stop breaking, and as we now know, we must break before we find the

Light. But we can offer another path. A way to meet trauma, without perpetuating it, with Love. A way to turn pain into creation. A way to remember freedom instead of using violence to fight for it.

The day after we arrived, an old friend of Violeta's father invited all of us for lunch at her home. She was a well-known woman from the old fashion world, a time when being sharp, ironic, or emotionally distant was often mistaken for sophistication. I had known that world well in my early career, and in her generation, these behaviours were even more normalised, even admired. When we spoke during the pandemic, she had always been kind—generous with advice, eager to help us settle in Portugal. So when we arrived at her home that day, I walked in with an open heart. But almost immediately, something unexpected happened. She looked at me and, without greeting or softness, asked, "Did you bring me the glasses that were being fixed, as I asked?" I replied gently, "Yes, of course. I just haven't opened our suitcases yet. We only landed yesterday, so I will bring them to you this week." In seconds, her tone shifted. She erupted, her voice raised, her words sharp, as if my delayed gesture were a betrayal. "How dare you come to my house like this? You have no consideration. No education." I froze. Her anger was disproportionate, and it pierced the silence of the room like a blade. Violeta, only six at the time, hid in a corner, frightened by the sudden outburst. Inside, I felt the familiar tremor of my ego rise—What is happening? Who does she think she is? Why is she speaking to me like this after everything I've just been through?

But instead of reacting, I grounded myself. Calmly I said, "We have just moved countries. If we are not welcome, we can leave." My ex-partner tried to ease the tension. "Don't worry—this is her way. She didn't mean it." But I could see it clearly: this wasn't about glasses. It wasn't even about me. It was a projection of something I was a symbol of. Her behaviour was inappropriate, yes. But beneath the surface, I saw a wounded feminine response: a woman trying to protect an old identity in a world that no longer honoured those ways.

We stayed for lunch. We smiled. We were polite. But something deep inside me was burning—not with anger alone, but with recognition. Later that day, she sent messages justifying her reaction, trying to convince my ex-partner she was right. My ego wanted to defend itself, to fight back, to prove something. But my Soul was still and observant. In her outburst, I saw one of my final mirrors. A reflection of the parts of me that still believed I needed to earn my worth. A reminder of the girl inside who once felt she had to be perfect to be accepted. A lesson in not allowing myself to be pulled into old paradigms of competition, hierarchy, and fear. Through the Eagle's Eye, I realised: She wasn't an enemy. She was a woman in pain. A woman shaped by a world that had taught her to survive through hardness. A woman, like so many, afraid of being replaced, unseen, forgotten.

Her reaction was the wounded feminine, trying to regain control through criticism and superiority. And my reaction, the fire inside me, was my own wounded feminine rising to defend itself. This moment cracked open an old layer of my ego. It was the beginning of a deeper unraveling, one that Portugal, in its quiet yet fierce way, would continue to bring.

Portugal would become the arena where I confronted not only the wounded feminine and wounded masculine outside of me, but the remnants still living within me. As the law of reflection makes evident. It was the beginning of the stripping, the burning, the purification that would prepare me for the next octave of our mission.

Our New Home and Friends

Soon, I settled into my new apartment, close to the river I loved so much. It felt like a fresh beginning. I decided to give another chance to the woman who had first welcomed me with that scream. This time, she invited me into her circle of friends, introducing me at their monthly gatherings. At first, it was all lovely, warm conversations, laughter, and the comfort of new connections. I appreciated her kindness in opening her circle to me.

What I didn't know was that this kindness came with a cost. She was used to having people bend to her will, and if they didn't, she would unleash her anger through manipulation and gossip, making herself feel feared by those closest to her. For me, this was not normal. I had never seen it to this extent, not even in Rio. Then again, when I lived there, I was still a girl. Now, I was amongst women, mostly older than I was. I thought, This is what my mother endured. This is what happens not only in Rio but amongst powerful women all over the world. This was the wounded feminine in the world's high-society circles. If you don't bend to their rules, they attack. This is why my mother avoided being part of groups. She had friends from multiple places, never trying to belong to this and that group. These "rules" are created by women stuck in their own cage, trying to dim the light of those who dare to be authentic.

A few weeks later, it happened again. The scream, the sudden attack, words hurled like knives. By coincidence, the apartment I had rented was only a few streets from hers, so these encounters became unavoidable. Each time, she would be triggered by something small I had done, or not done, and I would freeze in shock, unable to understand why I had become the target of so much rage.

That's when I began to draw boundaries, quiet ones at first, just enough to shield myself from her outbursts. Even as I stepped back, I recognised the familiar pattern of Rio's high society. I had worked so hard to distance myself from the dynamic of that world. Yet here I was again, face to face with its shadows, because this was exactly where the mission needed me to be. I knew this was no coincidence. There was something I needed to learn through this experience, something deeper I had not yet uncovered. This was a place where trauma and abuse carried the power of status and money, causing harm that pushed people to their limits—as it once did to my mother, and as it has likely done to millions of women around the world. This was my Soul training me for something the mission was calling us to do.

One Sunday in particular stands out. Violeta's dad was in town. By then, he would stay with us during his monthly visits. We felt happy. For the first time, there was a sense of routine, a glimpse of family life. It gave me comfort, as though I finally had more of his support and Violeta more of her father's presence. They were even closer.

That weekend, he suggested we join his friend for brunch. To be honest, I had already distanced myself from her and from most of the circle she had introduced me to, keeping only the few who felt truly aligned. I resisted at first, but he convinced me it would be okay, so I agreed. At first, the brunch was lovely. I promised myself not to take anything personally. Yet she kept prodding, trying to hit a nerve. First, she criticised the way Violeta was eating, calling it "uneducated." Then she made another small, funny comment meant to sting me. I smiled, stayed quiet, determined not to give her reactivity.

Then, when my ex-partner went with Violeta to the bathroom, she struck. Her voice sharpened, and she said something along the lines of, "He never wanted this kid. This daughter was your choice. He wasn't ready after his first son. You made him have her. Who do you think you are, moving freely through life with your daughter like this? One day you are in Brazil, now Lisbon."

I tried to answer calmly, telling her she was wrong, that we both chose Violeta with love, that she was deeply wanted. But she cut me off, shouting, "No! She was your choice. You have no right to complain you are a single parent. She was your choice because you didn't have an abortion!"

That was it. My whole body shook. I stood up, tears in my eyes, and said, "Today, you crossed a line. You are speaking about my daughter, who is sitting just here, as if she wasn't wanted by both her parents, who love her deeply. Today, you crossed every limit." I picked up Violeta as she was leaving the bathroom and left. It was pouring rain outside, and we had no umbrella as we rushed home. The downpour felt cleansing, washing away the heavy, draining energy.

Later, with distance, I understood. She wasn't speaking about me at all. I was simply her mirror, a reflection of her frustrations, her choices, her wounds. This was the depth of her own wounded feminine projected at me when she saw my freedom, my loving, authentic relationship with my daughter and her father, my courage to move beyond borders and live by my terms.

This is the Truth, beloved reader: People's reactions to you have nothing to do with you. You are only the mirror, the surface onto which their unhealed wounds are projected. When someone lashes out, they are not truly attacking you; they are attacking the part of themselves they cannot bear to face. Simply by living authentically, you shine a light on what they have hidden—not only from others but even from themselves. And through the law of reflection, you can also look within and see how you may have been unconsciously treating yourself. When something in your field feels painful or attacking, that reaction can serve as a mirror, pointing to something hidden within you—something you may still believe or feel about yourself. In my case, I realised I was still carrying the identity of a victim for being a single mother. There was pain that had not yet been fully transmuted, healing that was still unfolding, and she mirrored that truth back to me.

This was a big lesson for me, one that prepared me to work not only with women in vulnerable communities, like those I had met through the Department of Justice, but also with CEOs, businesswomen, and women from elite backgrounds—the very world my mother and I had come from. In that space, the shame, the fear of being insignificant, and the competition between women, the sister wound, reached another level because of the power they carried.

I am grateful for this woman. She became an important teacher as I began expanding Free Free. When I say this, beloved reader, I want you to understand that each of us is responsible for our own actions. So I didn't blame her. I could see her suffering through compassion. Especially now after time has passed and my own wounds healed. Compassion is a very high frequency, different from pity or empathy. It allows us to see the bigger picture through the Eagle's Eye and bring Love to any situation. When we do so, forgiveness comes quickly, almost naturally, because we no longer see the attack as personal. We see it for what it truly is: another human, still wrestling with unhealed wounds, caught in the ego, searching for Love, Light, and Power not through the Truth of the Soul, but through the limitations of the ego.

What I also learned is that we are all creating our reality based on our beliefs. Whether consciously or unconsciously, through our thoughts, actions, imagination, and words, we are always cocreating what we choose to believe. If we believe having children will take away our freedom, so it will be. If we believe moving countries is unstable, so it will be. If we believe a woman cannot have a success-ful career and be a great mother, so it will be. If we believe every man will abuse us, so it will be. Every belief can limit you or free you. When you hold a limiting belief, you create a limited life—and those limits become magnified whenever you see someone living what you always dreamed for yourself.

You are a creator. We are all God within. We are all Divine beings with free will to create. We can create from the ego or from the Soul. The liberation journey is about aligning your life on Earth with your Soul, freeing yourself from the traumas that create the lim-iting beliefs you might still be living from—the golden cage.

Portugal

Apart from those initial lessons, which felt harsh at the start, I loved being in Lisbon. Soon, I found myself in a routine that brought me so much joy: surfing, going to the beach, hiking, and working on a deeply exciting project with Harvard, the first Free Free club for uni-versities and schools.

When I arrived in Portugal, I had just finished my gradu-ate studies at Harvard, and all the data and research I had been immersed in were fresh in my mind. On paper, Portugal, and much of Europe, ranked amongst the top countries in gender equality and in addressing violence against women. But to my greatest shock, once I was living there, I saw this wasn't true. The difference was that the inequalities were hidden. Women in power often embodied the same wounded masculine behaviour as the men, and violence was so shrouded in shame that most women didn't even recognise it or felt deeply ashamed of it. They didn't see it, didn't name it, or they hid it away. I asked myself, *How can you count something that is not even seen as a problem?* The data was wrong.

I knew then: Free Free was profoundly needed here. But the work had to be preventative. We couldn't wait until violence had already happened. We had to create awareness and tools early, before the golden cage locked itself around the next generation. That's where the idea of the Free Free clubs was born. We needed to teach young people self-esteem, emotional freedom, what bullying looks like, what violence is, and why their dreams, voices, and work matter. Everyone deserves the chance to dream and contribute.

I worked alongside my Harvard professor to design a program for universities, as well as a brilliant family therapist to adapt the program for younger age groups. The vision was clear: If culture creates the golden cage, culture can also set us free. And it must begin with the youth.

In July 2022, just as everything seemed to be stabilising, I received an unexpected message from my dear friend and teacher of Divine Meditation. At the time, I was in London with Violeta, her first time back since we had left when she was just eighteen months old. We were staying in my old apartment, where my ex-partner still lived, and for Violeta, being in London felt like a dream come true. We were close, but we didn't talk every day, not even every month. Out of the blue, her message felt special. She wrote: I met a man here in Ibiza at a friend's dinner, and for some reason, I feel you both should meet. He does amazing work with embassies around the world. He's from LA but has recently bought land in Portugal. Can I give him your number? I said yes without hesitation. I trusted her completely. By then, she had been a part of my life for seven years, guiding me into powerful spiritual journeys a few times each year. The very next day, he texted me. We agreed to speak while he was catching a train to pick up his daughters in the Netherlands. Violeta was out with her dad, and by some synchronistic twist, I happened to be alone in the bedroom when his FaceTime call came through.

I wasn't expecting a video call, much less one that could be romantic. I had on oversized reading glasses and a sweatshirt. I thought she had connected us for work reasons, and to be honest, I had no expectations at all. But the call turned into an hour-long conversation, and from that day onwards, not a single day passed without us speaking. First, it was simple daily messages. Then the messages became letters—long, unfiltered, disarmed. In these letters, we shared the most intimate stories of our lives, our views on spirituality, love, work, and our perspectives of the world.

They were not ordinary letters; they were raw, profound, and free of the masks the ego usually wears. There was no fear of judgment, no need to impress. We didn't know each other in the traditional sense, so there were no expectations of what this was or what it wasn't. We were completely undressed—not physically, but spiritually. We weren't acting out our usual characters; we weren't performing. For an entire month, this is how we lived: through words that felt almost telepathic, carried on a frequency that bypassed logic and landed directly in the heart.

In early September, he came to Lisbon to see me. We had never met in person, and yet we both felt that this moment carried a sacred weight. We decided not to look at each other immediately but first to sense each other's frequency, just as we had in our letters. I lived on the fourth floor of my riverside apartment building, and as I walked down the stairs, we kept the lights off. From below, I could hear him softly playing a song on his guitar. When I reached the ground floor, we wrapped ourselves in each other's arms and kissed.

We drove south, toward the land he had bought. Nothing had been built yet, so we were meant to stay in a nearby house. But before anything else, he took me straight to the land. It was late. The moon was full. The sky glittered with stars. As he held my hand and we walked across the earth, it felt as though Mother Earth herself was holding both of us—holding what needed to rise, and what needed to be released. He spread a blanket on the ground and handed me a gift: a book, its pages filled with part one of our letters, printed and bound. I was speechless. I had never received something so intentional, so intimate, so carefully woven.

Then, beneath the stars, inside the womb of the land, we made love. At the time, it felt like a Soul union—a dissolving of boundaries, a returning to something ancient. But now, through the

Eagle's Eye, I see the deeper Truth: it was an initiation. It was the moment my Soul used to open Yasmine's heart fully so the karmic patterns still held within her could rise to be released so she could fully take the lead without those barriers. The connection felt like divine union because it needed to—not to bind us, but to break us open. The intensity was real, but its purpose was entirely different from what I believed then. It wasn't the forever my heart longed for; it was the door through which my next evolution would pass. A door designed to liberate me from the last remnants of Yasmine's wounds—dependency, romantic illusion, the saviour myth, the belief that love must come from another.

Back then, I thought our hearts had made a forever choice. Today, I see with absolute clarity that our Souls had made a different kind of choice—one that would set me free. What I didn't know at the time was that what I called a "union" was never about the two of us at all—it was part of a much larger orchestration of my awakening. It was Divine Union within myself. Our connection was fuelling the mission with a frequency I had not yet understood, a vibration of Love and Creation that was not coming from him, but rising through me. Being with him made me feel supported, not because he completed me or stabilised me, but because he acted as a mirror—reflecting back a version of myself I had not yet fully stepped into.

For so long, I had carried everything alone in the physical plane—motherhood, the birth of Free Free, and the unhealed karmic memories of my lineage. So naturally, the experience of walking beside someone who seemed to mirror my Soul felt new, tender, revelatory. Our letters, our connection, the land, the intensity of what unfolded—it all became part of my awakening. Another key. Another door. Another initiation guiding me toward the remembrance of who I truly was beneath the old stories.

In the months that followed, Free Free expanded as if carried by an unseen wind. I had believed our mission was already vast, but this initiation opened a new dimension within me—a deeper understanding of unity, not between two people, but within myself. Because the Truth is, beloved reader, the same energy that creates life is the same energy that fuels creation, art, leadership, and change. When Love rises from the Soul, it does not bind—it liberates. It doesn't necessarily make two people one—it can also awaken the one who is ready to remember.

What I believed was romantic destiny was, in reality, the activation of an ancient key within my spirit. An initiation designed to dissolve the last illusions of dependency, to release Yasmine's karmic patterns, and to reveal the creative force that had always lived inside me. When Love arrives at the Soul level, its purpose is never just personal. It ignites the power that transforms the collective.

The Clash of My Ego

As the relationship unfolded, the intensity only grew. Even if we weren't always in the same country—he with his work and children, me with my work and Violeta—we remained deeply intertwined. We spoke of everything: politics, spirituality, work, parenthood. He applauded my successes; I applauded his. He was learning how to navigate life as a divorced father, and I shared how Violeta's father and I, after years of conflict, had become more than co-parents—we had become family. He longed for that kind of peace with his ex-wife and daughters. Our connection was powerful. My frequency, the Love I carried, seemed to awaken things in him he had never realised were wounds. It was one of those relationships where nothing could stay hidden. The Light was too strong. The Love, too powerful. We had no control. We could only surrender to the current.

But this was where the clash began. As things deepened, our egos slowly crept in. Relationships were still the one part of my life where I held onto old rules. I still carried a belief my ego developed when I was twelve years old—the belief that a man had a role to fulfil. So it was difficult for me to surrender fully into the unknown. I wanted to know where we were heading. I wanted structure, because Love felt vulnerable. For him, embracing the depth of commitment our connection required was equally challenging because of his own fears and traumas. When the egos took the lead, everything began collapsing. Yet all of this became part of the teaching that would eventually liberate me.

After six months of honeymoon bliss, the cracks began to show. At first, they were small. I would feel sad if I couldn't speak to him before going to bed on Christmas Eve. He would feel upset that my attention was fully on Violeta when we were together. These were normal frictions, but every disagreement was a mirror revealing where our egos were still holding on. Then, in January 2023, my body began to speak. Whenever we were together, I started feeling sick. My energy would drop. My system would weaken. It made no sense. On paper, everything looked perfect. We travelled together in a camper from the Netherlands to Portugal, passing through the most beautiful villages in France. And yet, my body was not at one hundred percent. Something deeper was asking to be seen. I could not understand it at first. What was my body trying to show me?

My Soul was showing me what my ego refused to see: the love between us was real, but it was not meant to last. It was meant to awaken me into my Soul nature, and awaken him on the next stage of his evolution. The belief I carried since childhood—that a man must be the saviour—needed to be dissolved. And his belief that deeper commitment meant losing freedom needed to be released. Every time I unconsciously expected him to rescue me, my body revolted. It was as if my entire system was saying: No more. This pattern ends here.

Much of what I had called love in my past had actually been attachment—including in this relationship—the wounded feminine longing to be saved, and in return, offering her power away. But true love is not born from fear or lack. True love does not complete us; it expands us. It was time for me to see the difference. It was time for him to experience structure without suffocation.

So my body became the battlefield of this clash. The higher frequencies of my Soul were no longer compatible with the old patterns of my ego. The result was exhaustion, illness, and weakness—not because the relationship was bad, but because the parts of me that were unhealed could not survive in the Light of this new

Love. Looking back, I see it clearly now: this was an initiation. My body was cleansing the illusions of dependency so I could step into the truth of Divine Union within myself—not two halves trying to complete each other, but two sovereign beings, whole in themselves.

In February, we had one of those moments where time dissolved—a night of pure love and bliss, so deep it felt like our Souls were merging across dimensions. We weren't just touching bodies; we were touching eternity. And then, with so much Love, Light, and Creative Power, his ego panicked. The next morning, I woke up and he was gone. When I called to ask if he was okay, he said he needed to see the land and would be back later that evening. Then, after a pause, he added, "I'm scared you might be pregnant. Can you take the morning-after pill?"

I took it to reassure him. But inside, something broke. It wasn't the pill itself—it was the fear beneath his words, the mistrust, the intrusion of panic that cut through. I always knew I wasn't pregnant. But the energy of fear, crashing into the energy of divine intimacy, felt like violence in my body. I wept. I felt exposed, raw, vulnerable, unable to understand what was happening. He was afraid of our love. And that was the deepest wound of all.

A couple of weeks later, I travelled south with Violeta and my dear friend guardian angel to see him. One evening, after a simple dinner between just the two of us, we went to the tent he had built while waiting for his house to be finished. We stayed only an hour, resting on the earth. That's when he turned to me and said words I will never forget: "Yasmine, you don't understand the power you have. The power you have to shift others. You are not who you think you are. The frequencies you emit… they transform people. Can't you see it?"

I froze. My instinct was to resist. "No," I told him. "I'm just like you." But he shook his head. "No, Yasmine. You bring things out of people through your Love and Light that are far greater than you realise."

His words echoed inside me like thunder I wasn't ready to hear. It was the priestess wound. I was afraid of my own power. Of being misunderstood. A part of me—the last fragments of Yasmine's ego—wanted to reject it. Who does he think I am? I'm just Yasmine. I've worked hard, yes, but I'm just a woman like any other. My mind tried to protect me through denial. But beneath that resistance, my Soul stirred. Quietly, patiently. She Knew. She had always Known. What he was seeing in me wasn't new. It was ancient. It was the Light I had carried across lifetimes, the frequency guiding Free Free long before I had a name for it. The frequency that rebirthed me when Violeta was born. The frequency that unlocked every awakening and every initiation beyond my ego's control.

I wanted to run, to hide in the comfort of what was perceived as "normal." The myth of perfection. The good girl. But my Soul whispered: This is the mirror. This is the Truth you have been avoiding. You are more than you think you are. And now, you cannot unknow it. That night, he dropped me back at the house near the land, and I lay awake, feeling the clash inside me—the ego terrified of being seen, and the Soul vast and steady, reminding me why I came here. Another key had been placed in my hands.

It took me a long time to understand that I was no longer Yasmine, the perfect woman. Nor was I the girl from Rio. Those identities had dissolved. My Soul's gifts were becoming undeniable, but I had not yet learned how to see myself through the eyes of Truth. He saw me, he felt me, before I saw myself.

Every time we spoke, or made love, or simply existed in each other's presence, it wasn't human interaction—it was communion. He felt exposed even when fully clothed, because I could see him beyond the layers he allowed the world to see. That kind of seeing is frightening, not through confrontation but through tenderness. He had spent his life performing perfection. Now, someone saw the parts he hid even from himself—with love instead of judgement. And that can feel more terrifying than rejection.

He grew up inside a very traditional Catholic German family, first-generation Americans navigating two cultures at once. His parents loved their children deeply, but like many families of that generation, love was expressed through structure, discipline, and high expectations. His father valued responsibility, excellence—over demanding. His mother, gentle and devoted, treated him as a prince. It reminded me of my father's upbringing. In that environment—full of care, also shaped by old ideals of perfection—he learned early to excel, to achieve, to be the best. Valedictorian. Princeton. Summa cum laude. He became the man his family, culture, and upbringing had trained him to be. But the cost of perfection is that vulnerability rarely has space to breathe. So for the first time in his life, he found himself without a mask, without the polished armour he had always worn. He realised he was still living inside the myth of the "perfect man," just as I had once lived inside the myth of the "perfect woman." This is what the myth of perfection does, beloved reader: It convinces us love is conditional. It makes worth something to be earned. It robs us of intimacy. It destroys the possibility of authenticity. Performance cannot hold Love. Eventually, it collapses.

I supported him through his awakening, through the dismantling of everything he had been taught to be. Yet after we visited his parents in LA and travelled to New York, something shattered. I don't know exactly what took place. He closed his heart. I only know that when I returned to Portugal, my body collapsed. I was supposed to fly to Brazil the next morning to receive a UN Women award, but my cells refused. My body said: Stop. Pay attention.

He went from New York to Paris for meetings and promised to return two days later. By then, one of my rooms had become his office. My closet held his clothes. We were searching for a home. Dreaming of a life together. Asking questions that felt like promises: Would you move south if Free Free expands? Would you be willing to have a partner fully committed to her mission? The UN prize was the final trigger. The morning after the ceremony, I woke up to a letter—not a love letter, but a rupture. The first sentences congratulated me. The next sentences destroyed me. I realise I need to be the king of the relationship… I was raised to be the one in charge… I need space to heal… We need to pause… In September, I'll return and we'll start again. It felt like a knife splitting my chest. Shock. Paralysis. Betrayal. It was quick. He had celebrated my power. My leadership. My success. Now he said he needed to be "king." His letter wasn't him. It was the wounded masculine. Cold, rigid, controlling. Trying to freeze the river because he didn't know how to flow with it.

I asked him not to come to my house—my sacred home with my daughter. I was in shock. The next day, when he came to gather his things to go to the south I wasn't home. When I returned, another book awaited me on the table. Part Two of our letters. With a note saying he loved me. I wept. Deep down, I knew the truth: His healing would not take six months. The wounds were ancient. He was terrified to go inside them. We barely spoke in the weeks that followed. I cried for the teenage girl who believed a relationship would save her. I cried for the dreams that would never unfold. I cried because the last pieces of Yasmine's karmic identity were leaving my body.

Violeta's father came from London to support me. My childhood nanny who raised me and later helped me raise Violeta, came to Lisbon too. They held me through the paralysis of those days. Through the grief that swallowed every breath.

The Grief

The grief that followed was not just about the end of a relationship. It was much deeper than that. I was grieving Yasmine. I was grieving the parts of her that had once handed her power to men, believing they were the source of safety, stability, or love. I was grieving the old identities—the girl who thought she needed someone beside her to be whole, the woman who ran from her own Power because she didn't yet know how to hold it.

This grief was the final trauma rising to the surface, perhaps the biggest one of all: the old belief that she was incomplete without a man. But she had been wrong. So deeply wrong. And in the days that followed, I felt her dissolving inside me—not in pain, but in liberation. After our first break, life moved with its own Divine orchestration. In May, I travelled to Turkey for a summit called Harvest. There, surrounded by visionaries and soul-driven leaders working to build a better world, something in me awakened again. I felt myself expanding, remembering the mission, stepping into the frequency of who I was becoming.

When I returned to Portugal, I poured my energy back where it belonged—into service. I delivered the first Free Free sessions at the Harvard Club. I launched our program for tweens at Tasis School in Portugal. I felt my Soul leading again, clearly, steadily. The mission was moving through me effortlessly. Then, in July, a letter arrived from him. He had finally returned to Los Angeles. And then, the words that cut through me: I met someone else. I'm in love.

For a moment, I couldn't breathe. The last time we had spoken, he had promised six months of solitude to heal, to face his wounds, to step into the man he wished to be for us. Now, here he was, back inside his old patterns—running, distracting, avoiding the very depth that had terrified him. My anger flared, at him, at myself, at the story I had allowed to continue past the point of Truth. That was my wounded feminine rising, entering the victim consciousness one last time. Yet… beneath the anger, a deeper Knowing was already present. Because when I received that first letter months earlier—the one that felt like a knife through my chest—a part of me had already Known he would not be ready in six months. A part of me had Known he was not meant to walk with me into who I was becoming. But Yasmine still hoped. Yasmine still believed. Yasmine still wanted to try. And that was the part of me that was breaking. In that moment, something shifted profoundly. Enough, I thought. Enough with the illusions. Enough with the stories. Enough with the patterns that were no longer mine. It was time to reclaim the Power I had unconsciously given away—not to him, but to my ego's last remnants of longing. It was time to step fully into the frequency of my Soul, free from every illusion of dependency. This heartbreak was not a failure. It was an initiation. It cracked open the final door. It set me free from the last piece of Yasmine's karma so I could rise as who I truly am.

After one year in Lisbon, I finally found a house in the countryside—the kind of home I had been searching for since the moment I landed in Portugal. A lovely little cottage appeared almost like a miracle, right next to Violeta's school. The garden overflowed with fruit trees, and without overthinking, we moved in. It was that same kind of Clarity I had felt so many times before—a Knowing that doesn't come from the mind but rises from somewhere deeper, somewhere sacred. I needed to return to Nature. My body, my heart, my Soul were all guiding me back to the womb of the Mother Earth.

And then something strange happened, something that had never happened before. All my financial abundance paused. Contracts that were supposed to be renewed suddenly weren't, and for the first time in my life, I had to face real financial constraints—right at the peak of my Soul expansion. What does this mean? I asked God.

It felt as if my energy was still entangled with the relationship I had just released, and until I integrated the deeper lesson, nothing new could flow. It was as though the Universe had pressed pause—not to punish me, but to redirect me, to pull me inward so I could fully understand what was being purified within.I began to see that abundance is not only about discipline, work, or strategy. True abundance flows with alignment. When our energy is scattered, or still tied to old wounds or karmic threads, even the most promising opportunities pause until we fully receive the teaching. This was not a blockage. It was Love. A higher intelligence guiding me back to wholeness, to release the last remnants of Yasmine's beliefs before the mission entered the global stage.

I realised that the relationship I had just released had touched me so profoundly that, until I learned the lesson it had been designed to teach me, no new door could open. And perhaps you, beloved reader, have lived this too—those seasons when abundance seems to pause, not because you did something wrong, but because something inside you is being rewritten.

For me, it was also time to face another wound, the one I carried from my teenage years, from the financial instability I grew up with with the up and downs of my father. That memory lived inside my cells. And it was a fear I carried until then but never had to face because I always had so much success in my career. And now, here it was again, rising not to haunt me, but to be healed.

I cried. I panicked. I prayed. And yet I continued. Something deep within me Knew this was not the end but the turning point. The moment my Soul was preparing me for the expansion that was coming next.

In September, we hosted a summit at Harvard to launch the impact projects the students had developed. Later that month, I was invited to speak at the Harvest Series in London, alongside incredible thought leaders such as trauma physician Gabor Maté. In October, I returned again, this time to launch the Free Free club at the renowned fashion university, Marangoni. Two dear friends also hosted a Free Free dinner to share our work in London.

London was calling me back, and I hadn't even realised it yet.

The days I spent in London, Violeta's dad was in Portugal with her, so I stayed at his apartment, the apartment we lived together. To my surprise, there was no pain left in it, no ghosts, no wounds. I was fully healed. That same day, a dear friend introduced me to a woman in London whose presence felt like a breath of alignment. We met for coffee before I headed to Marangoni. As I began sharing about Free Free, something remarkable happened—her whole being lit up, not with polite interest but with recognition. It was as if the essence of the mission spoke directly to her Soul. She reflected Free Free back to me with such clarity and enthusiasm that, for the first time in months, I could see the beauty of what we had created through someone else's eyes. Her genuine excitement, her understanding, and the way she instantly grasped the depth of the work felt like a confirmation I didn't even know I needed. In a moment when life felt heavy and uncertain, she became a mirror reminding me of the Truth—of the impact, the purpose, and the frequency of Free Free. Our connection at that time was deeply meaningful, and her support strengthened me during a crucial chapter of the mission.

The synchronicities were undeniable. Her grandfather, like mine, had been a Romanian refugee who moved to Rio. Her father had come to London after losing his own father to suicide. Our lineages, with their echoes of pain, resilience, and survival, seemed interwoven in ways I could not ignore. She didn't just understand Free Free intellectually—she felt it in her body. She recognised the mission through the prism of her own ancestry, her own journey, her own longing for a world shaped by compassion rather than fear.

I will be honest with you, beloved reader: At that time, I felt fragile. The heartbreak had left me raw. My energy was low, and I was questioning everything—not from a lack of commitment, but from exhaustion. In that moment of vulnerability, I wasn't looking for solutions; I simply needed someone who could see me beyond the surface. And somehow, she did. Sitting across from her, as I shared the deeper meaning of Free Free, something softened inside me. It wasn't her words. It was her presence. There was a recognition there, a mirroring. A reminder of the Truth I had momentarily forgotten. It felt as if she held up a quiet flame when I feared mine was flickering. Not to save me, not to guide me—simply to reflect back who I truly was. And the importance of Free Free. And that was enough. Enough to realign me with my purpose. Enough to remind me of the force and beauty of this mission. Enough to help me take the next step with clarity and devotion.

With the relationship that had recently ended, I unconsciously entered the blame game with myself mostly because, at some point, the dynamic had turned toxic, and I couldn't understand how someone who had spent so many years studying the wounded masculine and feminine could still become entangled in such a pattern. I felt ashamed. I felt like a fraud. It was as if I had failed not only as a woman but as a teacher. I kept asking myself, *How can I teach something I still struggle to embody fully?* But this was an illusion of the ego, not the Truth of the Soul.

What I came to understand later was that the relationship had not derailed me, it had *initiated* me. It brought to the surface the final remnants of Yasmine's karmic patterns, especially the belief that love must come from outside, that safety must come from a man, that worth must be earned through perfection. Those were not the truths of my Soul. They were the wounds of my ancestry, the echoes of the

Mother Wound, the remnants of the girl who had once learned to give her power away. And they were dissolving.

The truth is, beloved reader, neither of us was to blame. We were simply two humans, both carrying our unhealed wounds, both learning, both acting from fear when the Love became too powerful. Our Souls had connected for a reason—but our egos were not able to sustain what our Souls had initiated. We became mirrors for one another: mirrors of Light, yes, but also mirrors of the places still asking to be liberated. After our separation, my energy collapsed. I felt lost in a way I hadn't felt in years.

After that encounter with my friend, I returned to the Portobello flat to change before a lecture I was about to give at Marangoni University. On the walk toward the Notting Hill Tube station, something extraordinary happened. A flash of energy moved through my entire body, as if time had folded into itself. Suddenly, I was seeing three versions of myself at once—twenty-one, twenty-eight, and the woman I was now. I saw myself wide-eyed on my way to university, pregnant and confused years later, and finally as the woman walking that street in the present moment. Past, present, and future collapsed into one single line of Light. My whole body vibrated. I couldn't stop smiling.

By the time I reached Fashion Street, where Marangoni stands—the same path I walked after my mother passed away, when I was doing my master's—goosebumps covered my skin. It felt like stepping into destiny. Only this time, I wasn't a student. I was the one teaching. I was public speaking to a group of almost one hundred students. Within minutes of introducing Free Free, forty students had already joined the club. London understood. It wasn't about words; it was about frequency. The city and I were finally a match. It felt like a homecoming on a Soul level. This was the city of my rebirth and the birth of our mission.

That evening, at a dinner two friends were hosting for Free Free, I ended up giving a speech to a room full of people. Thirty faces illuminated by candlelight, listening, nodding, some even crying. I felt unstoppable—not from ego, but from alignment. It was as if London itself was speaking to me.

But when I returned home, something unexpected happened. The two contracts I had secured for the end of the year fell through. I had already invested all my savings into Free Free. I stood at a crossroads: return to Brazil to my father's country house—a golden cage of safety—or trust my Soul and go to London with nothing but the Knowing that this was the way.

Between November and December, a few friends helped me create the Free Free members' club. People worldwide kept saying they wanted to be part of Free Free but didn't know how because until then the only way to be part of Free Free was through the institutions we collaborated with. This was the answer—a bridge, a container, a way to decentralise the mission and open Free Free directly to people while reducing dependence on corporations caught in political turbulence.

By the end of December, all my furniture went into storage. And yet, the Knowing grew louder. So I said yes—yes to London, yes to the unknown, yes to the higher timeline calling me forward. Violeta and I temporarily moved into her father's home, who kindly welcomed us with generosity and care.

People thought me crazy. But beloved reader, when you have a Knowing, forget opinions. Opinions come from the lower mind, from fear, from scarcity. Your heart comes from Truth. The heart is the Soul; the fear is the ego. Follow the heart always. It never leads you anywhere but home.

CHAPTER 18

BACK IN LONDON

In the last eighteen years, this was the third time I had moved to London, and it had never once been a carefully planned decision. Every time London called me, it was beyond space and time, a Knowing, a call of the Soul that the ego could hardly argue with. I began to notice the pattern. The most important turning points of my life happened in London: the six months after my mother passed away; during my daughter's birth, my rebirth, and the birth of my mission; and now, once more.

Why London? Why always here?

I returned in January 2024. This time, something was different. My ego was fully stripped away. London wasn't just a setting anymore; it was a womb. The mission was preparing me for the most important lesson I had to learn before Free Free could truly take the global stage. I was stripped of a home, something I had always valued deeply. My nest, the space filled with furniture and art pieces that carried the memories of my life's journey—gone. I accepted my ex-partner's support, living with him until I could find my feet again, something I never, ever thought I would ever agree to do. It humbled me beyond words.

The last few thousand pounds in my bank account went into only two things: my trip to Gambia, where we launched *Free My*

Period, the project created by the Free Free Harvard club to solve period shame, give girls a sustainable, fashionable tool to stay in school, and teach them about self-esteem, consent, and the prevention of child marriage; and the launch of the Free Free World Membership.

I had nothing left in material terms, but I had everything: our mission, our daughter, and the flame of my Soul.

Gambia

Only two weeks after I had arrived in London, I was already on my way to Gambia. The coordinator of the Free Free club at Harvard had gone ahead, and I was joining her for a few days of intense teaching, learning, and impact. Money was tight, so I booked the cheapest flight I could find, one with stops—first Barcelona, then supposedly straight to Gambia. But somewhere over Africa, a passenger fell ill, and the plane turned back, making an emergency landing in the south of Spain.

In the past, an unexpected delay like the one I had before arriving in Gambia would have made me anxious. I would have felt frustration rising, my mind trying to control the timing. But something inside me had shifted. I had surrendered to a different way of being. This time, the uncertainty didn't disturb me. I simply allowed myself to land in the unknown with peace.

When I finally arrived, the Free Free Harvard coordinator was waiting at the airport. She drove me to the hotel—a beautiful retreat with lush gardens opening onto the vastness of the ocean. As someone who feels deeply connected to water, my first instinct was simple: I needed to swim. I dropped my bags, put on my swimsuit, slipped clothes on top, and walked through the gardens toward the beach. That's when it happened. A young man who worked at the hotel stopped me. With a casual tone, he said, "My shift ends in a few hours…" The implication was clear. An invitation. An advance. My whole system froze.

I had never felt unsafe in a hotel before, never been approached like that by someone who worked in a place meant to protect guests. My body reacted instantly. Something in me felt violated, not in the physical sense, but in the subtle, energetic sense of being reduced to an object. I managed to respond, "No, thank you." But the moment had already changed everything. Instead of walking toward the ocean, instead of touching the water that called me, I turned back. I ran to my room, closed the door, and didn't leave again until sunrise.

Beloved reader, understanding this moment requires seeing through the Eagle's Eye. I was a foreign woman, alone in a country with traditions very different from the ones I grew up in. Perhaps it was normalised behaviour in his environment. Perhaps his perception was shaped by the stories he had been taught. Perhaps he misread my presence. We will never fully know.

But my experience was also valid: I felt unsafe, objectified, suddenly aware of my vulnerability as a woman alone in a place I did not yet understand. Both perspectives are fragments of truth. Compassion lives precisely in that space—between judgement and understanding. This is why the Eagle's Eye is essential. It doesn't excuse harm, but it allows us to see context, and context reveals the deeper truth of human behaviour. The next morning, our Harvard coordinator, whose family was Gambian, and our driver picked me up for our first visits. Our first stop was a small local factory where Gambian women had been sewing menstrual underwear designed by Free Free Harvard students. Our coordinator's mother had trained them personally. When we arrived, thirty samples were waiting, thirty seeds of dignity ready to be taken to a rural school.

The energy was radiant. These women were proud. They understood how meaningful this work was. Period poverty is not a minor inconvenience; it is a silent crisis. One in ten girls worldwide misses school because of their period; in parts of Sub-Saharan Africa, it is as high as one in five. Without sanitary products or proper bathrooms, girls fall behind, drop out, or are pushed into early marriage. Period shame becomes a chain around their futures.

In Brazil, we see the same pattern. Girls drop out. Teenagers become mothers before they even understand how pregnancy happens. Shame replaces knowledge. Vulnerability replaces power. This is why Free Free embraced the idea created by the Harvard club. Menstrual underwear is not simply a product. It is a pathway. It restores dignity, education, autonomy, and connection to the feminine body. It breaks the silence around cycles. It interrupts the shame. It transforms futures.

That afternoon, we visited Wave, an organisation supporting women who had survived torture. Then we met a group of university students for a Free Free session, planting the seeds for what could become a local circle of conscious women. The next morning, we drove nearly three hours with no air conditioning. As we left the city and entered the rural roads, the heat was intense, but what struck me even more was the waste. There were no sewage systems. Trash piled on corners, burning in open fires that filled the air. Suddenly, the impact of a single menstrual pad became clear. How long would its plastic take to disappear? How much harm could it cause in a system with nowhere for waste to go? In that moment, the vision expanded: Our menstrual underwear wasn't just a tool for dignity—it was a tool for sustainability, a way to honour both women's bodies and Mother Earth herself.

This, beloved reader, is what consciousness looks like in action. This is feminine leadership in practice. This is the new paradigm: healing the woman and healing the Earth in one breath.

At the rural school in Gambia. I love the image of us under the tree. It reminds me of the way women used to gather around trees.

When we finally arrived at the school, I was surprised. The classrooms, the sports programs, the energy of the students—all of it was far beyond what I expected. These children and teenagers were receiving a good education. The problem wasn't their learning; it was the lack of opportunities afterwards, a labour market that kept them frozen in cycles of poverty.

We gathered in one of the classrooms for another Free Free session. This time, we partnered with Girls' Pride, led by an incredible local leader who taught the basics of reproductive education, breaking taboos that had weighed on these girls for generations. I stepped in to teach about self-esteem, about knowing their worth, about remembering they were already whole, already enough.

Then came the moment of joy. The second part of the session was outside, under a tree, like how women used to gather to share wisdom. We handed each girl the menstrual underwear, explaining that we would like to receive monthly feedback: Was she losing fewer days of school? Was she able to play sports more freely? Was she feeling less shame about her blood? Their eyes lit up. They were excited, curious, and above all, grateful.

The period underwear created by the Free Free club at Harvard.

The next morning, I packed my bag to return home. After all, I had just made a huge move, shifting Free Free's operations and my family to London with no resources, only Presence and Trust. But I knew God was showing me the way. All I had to do was follow.

The Launch of the Free Free World Club

When I arrived back home, we had just two weeks until the big launch of the Free Free World Club Membership. Two dear friends co-hosted the evening for Free Free. They were part of that fashionable circle I had known from my Vogue years, but above all, they were generous enough to hold space for me when I had just moved back to London. The trip to Gambia had taken a deep toll on me. My energy was already low from the move, from still recovering from heartbreak, and from the weight of the reality I had just witnessed. I kept asking myself, Is what we're doing really enough?

At the same time, I felt the natural pressure of making the Free Free World Club work. This wasn't just a beautiful gathering; it was the next evolution of our ecosystem. The membership was about sustainability, coherence, and alignment with the mission. It was about creating a model that reflected the very values we were teaching: consciousness, shared responsibility, community, decentralised action, and abundance rooted in purpose.

So in the two weeks leading up to the event, I studied everything I could find about making sacred offerings for individuals. I devoured books, took online classes, and tried mastering countless tools. My real skill had always been negotiating large contracts, building partnerships with institutions, shaping collaborations that transformed systems, not working directly with individuals. Yet, deep down, I also knew something: People respond to story, to frequency, to Truth. That had always been my power, even if my ego still doubted it.

I used to carry a limiting belief that offering my gifts was somehow wrong—that made me less spiritual or less pure. But later, I came to understand the deeper truth: making an offering is an act of service. When we sell our work as a sacred offering it is actually an act of service. If we don't offer what we have to give, how would people ever know that the solution they are seeking is right in front of them? I realised the opposite is the Truth. When we don't share our gifts is the ego at play trying to keep us safe in our golden cage. This beloved reader, is the priestess wound. We hide our power camouflaged in thinking that if we share our power, offer our gifts, we might be judged. And yes it can happen, but we have no control how people perceive us. This is where the trust and self Love comes in. We trust the unknown, speak with an open heart, and whoever is aligned with resonate, whoever is not won't, won't. And this is ok. What people think is not our business. Judgements are a reflection on the one who judges, not on the person who is judged. Speak your Truth, beloved reader, and this is all you need to do.

So on January 31st, around eighty of the most sophisticated women—and a few men—filled the room for our launch. I have to be honest with you, beloved reader: In that moment, my ego felt fractured. I was still tender from heartbreak, still battling the imposter voice that whispered, Can you really do this?

But something greater carried me. I took the microphone, opened my heart, and simply allowed the words to flow through me: "When one woman frees herself, she frees millions—just as we did. Can you imagine what would happen if each of us used our gifts to change the world? The world would transform. This is about consciousness, creativity, and true action. We want to invite you to be part of Free Free."

For the first time, I also shared the story of selling my Sonia Gomes sculpture—the first artwork I ever bought, a piece so precious to me, to fund the expansion of Free Free. My voice trembled as I said: "I gave up something I loved to carry this mission forward. But now I can't do it alone anymore. We need your help—not just as donors, but as part of the mission. This is why we created the membership: so we can all grow on our freedom journey, free within, and then free the world, together." By the end of the night, forty people joined as members. For the first time, Free Free took it's first steps into a business model that would move beyond just working with corporations and institutions. Club members would now receive weekly Free Free Teachings on Zoom. Each session began with meditation, moved into a short teaching, and opened into a space for sharing, questions, and reflection—the real conversations where women begin, or deepen, their journey toward freedom.

Beyond this, we organised almost-monthly artistic gatherings where we could meet in person, create together, and remember joy. But perhaps the most important part of the Club was this: it wasn't just about receiving. Members could use Free Free as a platform to bring their own service ideas to life.

This was my dream becoming reality. The decentralised model I had studied so deeply at Harvard was now alive—moving, breathing, activating people all around the world. Of course, it was still a testing phase. We were experimenting, learning, adjusting, trying to understand what truly resonated and why people were joining. But the foundation was there. The club would later transform into what we call now the Paradigm Family, a home for Wildflowers. This was the seed beginning to bloom. The winter was over. This beloved reader, was my Soul leading.

In the Meantime

My ego was crushed. I felt depressed, confused, paralysed. My Soul was calling me forward, but there was an alchemy happening at the same time with my ego.My last relationship had been a great teacher—a huge one—but in the aftermath, I was shattered. First, my ego created repetitive thoughts telling me I was a fraud. How could I teach about freedom when I felt I had just lived through an unhealthy relationship myself?

Second, the business model I had relied on for years, focused on B2B, suddenly paused. No matter how many emails I sent, no matter how many meetings I took, nothing moved. There was no explanation other than the Truth I knew deep down: my energy mirrors my work. If my energy is shattered, my work will stagnate.

The ego, beloved readers, plays games with our mind when we are at the threshold of a major consciousness expansion. As the Soul moves you forward, the ego creates stories rooted in the past. Thought-forms—illusions of fear—arise, and it can feel like a battle between the Light of the Soul and the ego doing everything it can do maintain control and it's power. Thoughts are responsible for our emotions. Emotions are energy in motion. If you think you are unworthy, you feel unworthy. This was the game unfolding within me. A natural process, I have to say, when we are about to take a great leap.

Third, debts from the previous months were weighing on me. I had kept my commitments, followed through with the projects, but my self-esteem was in pieces. For so long, my ego had worn the armour of the independent woman. Now I felt I had lost control of my life. My greatest fears had manifested—as fears often do when we repeat them in loops as thought-forms, beloveds. Fears held in our field attract the very experiences we are afraid of, so that we may finally free ourselves from them. In the end, all is a blessing.

But in Truth, this is an important teaching we wish to share with you now: you can shift your reality if you shift your thoughts, and by consequence, your emotions. In doing so, you no longer need to experience the painful manifestations created by unconscious thinking and feeling. As you know by now, beloved, you are a powerful creator. This is where awareness comes in. Silence. Meditation. When you notice a fear, do not ignore it. Acknowledge it. This allows your feminine spirit—the feeler within you—to feel seen. By observing the emotion without suffocating it, you experience it fully, and it releases from your field. The same is true with thoughts. The moment you notice negative thinking, acknowledge it and use your will, beloved—your power of choice—to observe the thought and consciously create a new one aligned with the Truth of your heart and higher mind. Do not allow your ego to feed your lower mind with old memories and fears without taking action. And when we say *taking action*, we mean something simple yet profound: observing, stillness and awareness.

Then, for the first time, Violeta was not accepted into the private school to which we had applied. At first, it felt like another failure. But it was a blessing in disguise. My ex-partner suggested we look at the state school near our home and, as if by miracle, there was exactly one spot available in her year group. The Universe was whispering: *Have patience. Everything that is happening is in Divine Order.* So instead of fighting to solve more problems with my linear mind, I surrendered. I fully surrendered to the Divine for the first time. I locked myself in my room, threw myself on the floor, knelt, and spoke to God from my heart. *I surrender. I surrender. I give it all to you.*

The only thing I continued doing was diving deeper into consciousness practices and study. My meditation practices opened the wisdom of my higher mind to a higher octave, and breakthrough after breakthrough followed. This was the beginning of me finally accepting my true power. My inner power. My spiritual power. Not the external power I thought I had, as this beloved, is simply an illusion.

Beloved, we do not say this as anyone above or below you. We are just like you. We all carry powerful spiritual gifts. Unique gifts. We simply need to remember them. Awaken them, as our society numbs them when we grow up and we get overtaken by the myth of perfection and the rulebooks we receive to be "accepted" by our culture. I kept doing my spiritual practices, deep meditations Until one day, the lesson landed. I could fully see, acknowledge, and feel gratitude for what I had been through.

When the lesson lands, beloved reader, the problems you once believed were towering over you dissolve—just like that, in the blink of an eye. The more we resist the lesson, the longer it takes to shift. It can take lifetimes, beloved. Or seconds. It all depends on your willingness to open your heart and let go.

The Lesson

We were learning many lessons, but the most important one was this: I was whole. I didn't need a romantic partner to complete me. I didn't need saving. I was already whole. Beloved reader, this is not a lesson you learn by reading a sentence in a book. To truly learn it, your body, mind, and spirit must *integrate it*. It must settle into the fullness of who you are. In that season, it did.

The second lesson was harder: asking for help. For most of my life, I could not ask for help. I wore my independence like armour. I had my own money, I made my own decisions, I raised my daughter on my own. To ask for help felt like weakness. But to do the mission as we were called to, we couldn't do it alone. What an illusion. There are so many physical and spiritual beings helping me all the time. And so many helping you beloved reader. All we need to do is See. In my case, I needed to learn this before we could grow further. I would need all the help available. I was never alone, and neither are you.

So, the Universe forced me to surrender my pride—to stay at my ex-partner's house, to accept volunteers who wanted to collaborate with Free Free, to receive donations without giving something in return. I realised I had avoided fundraising the way other foundations did because I never wanted to ask. I only knew how to give.

But when I had no choice, something cracked open. I discovered there were so many people willing to help—not to use it against me later, not to control me, but simply to help. It was an ancestral trauma being lifted and healed with Love, right there. When we give from the heart, beloved reader, without expecting something in return, the Universe sees. And the people that give, beloved, they receive 10 fold back from the Universe. It's Divine Law. Somehow, by not allowing people to help until I had no choice, I was also withholding from them the gift of giving, serving. Wow. Some came with conditions, yes, and when they did, the frequency of the mission expelled them. However, most came with pure intentions. The real teaching was this: to trust others enough to let them hold me too. Never question intentions, as the moment we do beloved, we question someone's divinity and we question our own divinity. Trust beloved, and listen to your heart.

It was humbling. It broke me open in ways I never expected. That, beloved reader, was the gift my ex-boyfriend from Portugal had given me. Our relationship shattered the last stronghold of my ego, leaving me ready to step fully into our mission without fear, and most importantly, step fully into who I truly was.

No more fear of running out of money.

No more fear of asking for help.

No more mistrust of others.

No more of the need to complete myself through anyone else.

No more of the need to feel "special."

The relationship had been a gift all along, one that accelerated my embodiment a hundredfold. It was just here, in this moment, that I understood everything. I finally understood our mission was also a spiritual one. You might feel this is crazy, but it is true. It took me six years after launching Free Free to understand our service was Divine Service. It was my Soul leading. I couldn't understand that power my ex-boyfriend had told me of in that tent. Why me, I would ask myself? It was humbling and empowering. I was never alone. None of us are. But now, I felt the power of the mission. The power of the Universe. The power of God. As all the power beloved, comes from the Field of Oneness. Only after I was humbled enough did I Know.

The Turning Point

Once the lesson was integrated, everything shifted. We signed two big contracts. In April, I was still undecided: go back to Brazil or stay in London? The contracts were good, but they were not enough to sustain a full life in the UK with my daughter because of the exchange rates that devalued the Brazilian currency. So I told my right hand, whom I call my Guardian, "I'm moving back to São Paulo." When I flew there to launch the Free Free World Club, I told everyone I was returning for good. The truth? I was trying to convince myself. But the moment I landed back in London, I called her again and said, "I have to stay." It was that Knowing again, that undeniable call. Against all odds, I had to stay.

By May, the decision was clear. I applied for a visa. My European nationality didn't allow me to stay in London like in the past because of Brexit. Without money for a lawyer at the time, I did the whole application myself. With only weeks before I was invited to speak at Cannes Lions, an invitation that felt like a once-in-a-lifetime opportunity, I chose the fast-track option that gave me an answer in forty-eight hours.

The deadline came, but with no answer about the visa.

So I got on the train to the immigration office, repeating to myself the mantra: "I am 10 percent human, 90 percent spirit. Miracles are happening now." I whispered it over and over again, not allowing my ego to create worst-case scenarios. When I arrived, the guards refused to let me in—no appointment, no entry. I explained I had to be in Cannes in just a few days because I was speaking at the festival. Without my passport, I would lose a very important opportunity.

One guard softened and let me stand at the entrance. He called a woman who came to meet me. She listened and said gently, "All I can do is email the agent on your case. Send me every document you have to prove this emergency." I rushed home, gathered everything, and sent it that same afternoon. The next morning, there was still nothing. I didn't lose faith. I was about to take the train back when an email appeared on my screen: "Your visa has been approved."

Minutes later, the woman called me personally: "You can come tomorrow morning to pick up your passport."

It was nothing short of a miracle. No one could believe this had happened in the UK. The very next morning, I went back to the immigration office to collect my passport, a process that usually takes at least five days because it is always shipped to you. As I walked in, the woman at reception looked up and said with a knowing smile, "Oh, you're Yasmine."

I nodded, still holding my breath. "Yes, that's me."

"Your case is famous here," she said, laughing softly.

I couldn't help but laugh with her, tears welling in my eyes. "Thank you," I told her. "You have no idea how important this is to me."

In that moment, I felt the Truth pulse through my entire being: When we surrender control, when we keep our state high and trust in the Universe, miracles are not exceptions, they are the natural rhythm of life. It is only our limiting beliefs that deny their natural expression. We are not bound by human laws of time and space. We are boundless, creative beings, with the power of God within when we align with our Soul's Truth, in Love, in Light, without the ego's interventions.

Summer

In June, we finally found our garden flat, a lovely ground-floor home with just the kind of garden I had dreamed of. It was within my budget, and by grace, we managed to negotiate the contract start date for August 15, because I was about to spend forty days in Brazil for work.

First, I spent a few days in Rio with my daughter—a pause to breathe, to play, to be. Soon after, I was invited to speak at the Latin America Leadership Summit, alongside remarkable leaders such as the US ambassador of the United States, Hilary Sale from Georgetown University, and managing partners from DLA Pipers. From there, we travelled to the mountains to see my father, and then on to Três Rios and Paraíba do Sul, the cities founded by my ancestor, the Countess of Rio Novo, to visit the operations that were still alive more than a century later.

What I witnessed left me in awe. In Três Rios, I visited the chapel where the women of my family rest, enjoying a deep conversation with that man I had met just before moving to Portugal. In Paraíba do Sul, I walked through the hospital, the school, the educational centre, all part of the land the countess had given away when she passed, building the dream of a sustainable, equitable society.

I was received almost as royalty in the city, not because of who I was but because I carried her bloodline. Yet, to me, they were the royalty, the ones who had carried forwards her vision with such devotion. The hospital was so well cared for, the school thriving, the centre alive with children's laughter. I even visited the local government office to understand how they supported trauma survivors, and I offered a Free Free session to the kids, a meditation followed by an open conversation.

What moved me most was the day I sat with the children with Violeta by my side. We gathered outside, in sunlight, their curious eyes following me as I introduced myself. I asked them to close their eyes, place a hand over their heart, and simply breathe. At first, there was giggling, whispers, restlessness, but soon the room fell silent. In that silence, something shifted. I could feel their energy softening, their little bodies settling into stillness, their spirits remembering what Presence feels like. I taught them that they could be anyone they dared to dream they could be.

All the kids together after our meditation session,
hugging Violeta and me.

When they opened their eyes again, I asked them, "What did you see yourself becoming?"

One boy said softly, "I want to be a policeman."

A girl, no older than my daughter, said, "I want to be Rihanna."

We talked about freedom, about dreams, about the power of their voices. I told them, "Your future is not determined by what the world expects of you, where you come from, your past. You carry the seeds of new possibilities within you." Their faces lit up, and I knew in that moment, the countess was there with us, her legacy alive, flowing through these children, through me, through the land itself.

We danced together, played.

The creative centre is directed by a loving woman with a lot of faith, and she said, "Whatever this mission is, I want to feel it again. I want to be part of it. You have my full loyalty." It was breathtaking to see the vision of my ancestor live one century later (a story I might be called to share more in-depth another time).

Back in London

When I returned to London, we entered a season of pure creative flow. Unilever UK had just joined as a partner, and we were deep in preparations for our very first annual gala. We had ten co-hosts, some of the most extraordinary women in London, and one of our leadership committee members was working closely with us, helping bring every detail to life.

And that radiant Soul I had first met for a simple coffee, back when I came to London for the Marangoni lecture, was now officially part of our board. A visionary, an expert in the art world, she led the curation with grace and brilliance.

Soon, donations began to arrive: works from Tracey Emin, Catalina Swinburn, Tunji Adeniyi-Jones, Mandy Franca, and others. For me, the most profound moment was writing to Sonia Gomes. I poured my heart into that letter, telling her how one of her sculptures had been the very piece I sold to fund Free Free's global expansion. That sale had been the seed. When she wrote back saying she would donate a piece for the Gala, I wept. It was as if the circle had closed, art birthing art, one act of courage multiplying into another.

I was in awe. It meant the world to me. Each artwork carried more than beauty; it carried vibration, generosity, memory, a frequency of liberation that lifted the mission higher. Art, once again, proved itself as a source of transformation, a language that transcends barriers, beyond right and wrong, a language of the Soul. I had never seen so many people coming together in service—members, patrons, artists, galleries, sponsors. I had never seen so much collaboration, so much beauty, so much heart. That night, the feminine revealed herself in her purest form—free, creative, abundant, united.

By the end of that year, Free Free had crossed a threshold. We had endured the tests and integrated the final lessons before the expansion: Trust the Divine. Surrender control. Embrace humility. Accept help without shame. Remember that abundance is never personal, it flows where service is aligned with Truth. We ended the year with a £500,000 budget, resources that were already committed to sustaining and expanding our impact. It was nothing short of miraculous, because we had begun that same year with zero.

This was the mission in action. The moment I stopped trying to control how it would all unfold and simply devoted myself to teaching, creating, and serving, the resources began to arrive without resistance. This is what it means to walk with God, to move with the mission team in spirit: The current whispers, *Go, go, go*. The doors open before you. In 2025, we started the year with a leadership breakfast at the World Economic Forum in Davos; created the Free Free Mobile Spaces in Gambia and Brazil to take the Free Free Methodology's® meditations to communities; were invited to speak at Oxford and SXSW London; renewed for another six years our contract with the Department of Justice in Brazil; started collaborating with Cambridge University on a project on digital literacy for youth; and so much more.

CHAPTER 19

MY FINAL TRAINING

After this miraculous year of 2024, something in me shifted. My consciousness reached a new octave. For the first time in my life, I felt whole. I no longer carried that emptiness in my heart, that constant sense that something was missing. Since I was a girl, that emptiness had lived inside me, fed by traumas of abandonment, financial instability, and the illusions of needing something outside myself to feel safe.

Then, when the universe stripped me bare, took the partner of my dreams, the contracts, the house, instead of collapsing, I realised this was the final part of my ego being freed—the part that still feared loss, resisted asking for help, had the need to feel special to feel worthy, searched for any external validation. Everything I had once tried to control simply didn't work. I surrendered. In that surrender, I turned fully to God. I said, "I have tried everything my human mind knows. I tried everything to keep the organisation financially healthy, everything to heal my broken heart. Now I give it all to You." So I spent days and nights in meditation, surrendering myself over and over, raising my vibration. I stopped asking, *Why me?* I stopped feeling like a victim. Instead, I asked, *What do I need to learn?* I took full responsibility. I took my power back. I wasn't a victim, *nor are you.*

Each day, I walked to Hyde Park, listening to meditations, and I would sit on a tree trunk, rocking myself gently as though the tree were my mother. There, I communed with Christ and with Mother Mary, while the mama trees wrapped me in their embrace. When I refer in this book to Christ, Mother Mary, or other spiritual masters, I am speaking of them as Ascended beings of light and consciousness, understood beyond religion, doctrine, or institution. These names are used as symbols of universal qualities—love, wisdom, compassion, and unity—recognised across many spiritual traditions. I would walk home carrying a new frequency. As my frequency rose, so did my creativity. Life began to flow differently. I stopped worrying about tomorrow and started living day by day, in the eternal now.

I know this may sound impossible, but during those few months when everything stopped, and I had invested my last savings in the Free Free impact project in Gambia, there were days I looked at my bank account and saw nothing—no money, not even for groceries. Then, suddenly, something would sell or a payment would arrive, and I had exactly what I needed for that day. When I needed to book a flight, the resources appeared right at the moment they were required. The Universe was teaching me what abundance truly is. Abundance isn't billions sitting in a bank account. Abundance is Trust. It is knowing that everything you truly need will arrive the moment you need it. It is co-creation. It is the language of frequencies that go beyond time and space, when miracles start happening. The lack of financial resources didn't stop the mission. We were still teaching, travelling, and making an impact, more than ever. This is also abundance, beloved. But this time, I allowed help. I didn't feel I had to carry all the weight alone on my shoulders. I learned to ask without feeling weak. Asking, beloved readers, is a sign of empowerment. But remember, there should always be a win-win, as none of us should be takers, or in any way abuse another's kind and giving nature, because this only brings karma.

As I embodied this Truth, the old traumas I had carried for so long—around money and the emotional roller coaster of my teenage years—began to dissolve, not because I forced them to heal, but because the lesson finally landed in my body. I understood the teaching that freed me to grow Free Free without fear: abundance is not only money. Abundance is whatever you need, precisely at the moment you need it. It can arrive as a helping hand, a place to live, a single vacancy in a state school, nourishing food, or even the air you breathe. The mission did not stop, beloved. Support was always there. This is abundance. This was the lesson.

At this stage, something fundamental had shifted within me. When thoughts of dating arose again, it surprised me. There was no desperation, no longing for someone to complete me, no hunger for external validation. I felt no rush. For the first time, I experienced myself as whole—settled in Presence.

The old social conditionings that once whispered that a woman was incomplete without a relationship dissolved entirely. I no longer needed a romantic fairy tale, nor a man to give me security or prove my worth. I was Love itself. I was complete. I was living a state of inner Divine union. This did not mean I would never choose partnership again—only that I no longer expected it to be the source of my happiness or fulfilment.

I was whole. I was free.

I thanked God every single day. My ego no longer held power over me, and in that surrender, my consciousness expanded into entirely new octaves—beyond anything I had imagined. Fear had almost dissolved completely from my being. Beloved reader, understand this: fear is not Truth. Fear is the ego shaped by trauma and old beliefs trying to keep us alive by repeating the past. Fear is memory, not reality. It happened then, not now. And since the only moment that truly exists is now, fear is never real. It only feels real because of the memories it carries. This is why healing trauma is essential so we can dissolve illusion and return to Truth, to Love, to creative power.

Alongside our ongoing work with communities, the Department of Justice, security institutions, Harvard, and global organisations, the Free Free World Club was now alive as a living ecosystem. It was our first offering directly to people rather than institutions, a space where those with the means could grow in consciousness while actively supporting others and their communities.

At Free Free, we do not believe in transformation for its own sake. We believe we raise our consciousness so we can place our creativity in service of the world. Ideas are not meant to remain on paper. This is service. This is true social justice—not rooted in blame or separation, but in love, compassion, and forgiveness. Every Monday, I continued teaching the Club members. These sessions became a sacred field where meditation, teaching, and sharing intertwined. And something extraordinary began to happen: as I taught, I could feel my own consciousness accelerating—expanding at a pace I had never known.

It was then that I remembered the teacher of my Divine Meditation teacher.

Beloved reader, you must know this: When you are ready for the teacher, the teacher finds you. This teacher never called herself a guru, she calls herself a Divine coach, a sister, and there is a reason for this. The higher you raise your consciousness, the humbler you become. Real teachers never want to take your power away. They guide you to see your own power. Never give it to them, as this would not be teaching but another distortion of power. Jesus and Buddha never asked for followers, and the teachings they gave were, *I am the son of God, or I am the Light, and so are you.* This is important for you to know. As you continue your freedom journey, be aware of any teachers, gurus, priests, or coaches who, instead of empowering you to learn, want you to depend on them. I hold all my teachers and mentors with great esteem and gratitude. But as we already know by now, no one is better than another. We are just in different stages of our freedom journey.

This beautiful wise teacher was the last key to my full becoming at this stage of my journey. I had reached a point where the mission was expanding faster than I could comprehend. My consciousness was opening to new levels that felt both miraculous and overwhelming. Without guidance from someone you trust, it is intense, because not everyone around you understands what you are going through. You need days in bed for integration, downloads start happening non-stop, and in my case, I had an organisation to continue leading. It was a lot for my body to integrate.

The teachings gave me language for what was happening within me. She gave me the training to navigate the next octaves of my Soul's path. She was the bridge between the vastness I was touching and the grounded presence I needed to embody my Presence more fully.

We began meeting weekly, and the Presence of Christ guided our journeys in meditations. Each session became communion. He began teaching me everything I was ready to learn for the mission. The veils have never been thinner. He told me something that pierced my heart with truth: Violeta is already an ascended being. She brought the mission with her. When I gave birth to her, I was also giving birth to a higher dimension of my Soul. That is why everything changed so suddenly, why the trajectory of my life was turned upside down. It wasn't chaos, it was Divine order. It was both my frequency and Violeta's frequency that gave birth to Free Free.

Christ explained that it had taken nine years for my soul to fully clear Yasmine's old characters, beliefs, and karma—nine years of unlayering, undressing, dissolving everything that was not truly me. Only then could I step into who I was meant to become.

He revealed that my Soul had made a sacred contract: to bring higher consciousness to humanity, just like he and other beings had. The first seven years of Free Free were never about perfection, they were about initiation, about learning what the true state of the world really was. This is why I had to walk through so many fires. Being attacked by women, navigating abusive corporate dynamics, teaching commanders and judges, seeing the level of violence and trauma women, but all of humanity was experiencing in the deepest way, moving from one country to another, the relationships, the friends— these were not random experiences. They were the curriculum. They were the training ground. Each challenge was equipping me, freeing me from my own limiting beliefs, dissolving the illusions created by trauma, clearing karma. The more you learn, the more lightly you experience life, the more you experience Grace. At the same time, they showed me the deeper Truth of the world I was here to serve. They prepared me to step into the next level of our mission.

I want to repeat this, beloved reader. When I launched Free Free, I didn't think it was a spiritual mission. I didn't know my Soul was the one leading those workshops, or that my frequency was already healing the people around me. When my ex-boyfriend in Portugal told me, "You don't know the power you have," he was right. At that time, I still didn't believe it. I didn't understand our true inner power. It was only in the last two years that I started to realise how, since day one, everything was guided, beyond my human mind, always through my heart. Everything is God beloved. Our heart, beloved readers, is our true guide when our ego still holds parts of us in fear and doubts. Most people who experienced Free Free felt embraced. They couldn't explain why. They experienced the power of our heart.

Here is the truth: Every choice I made, every opportunity that showed up after Violeta's birth, all had one reason—our mission. It was the mission I said yes to when I danced in Marrakech and whispered, "I am ready." I didn't consciously know what I was saying yes to, but my Soul and Higher Self did. And I kept saying yes, every time I followed my Knowing and found the courage to leave the ways of my old self behind.

It wasn't easy. Leaving the golden cage is the most courageous act one can do. Because to step out of the golden cage, you must have the courage to leave your comfort zone, to face all the pain, all the trauma, all the messiness. And you must keep going even when everyone around you thinks you've gone mad. You start realising that external opinions don't matter. You stay true to Soul.

As you move deeper into this state, the choices you begin to make are no longer traditional. You may be criticised. You may feel alone. Yet within you, there is a quiet Knowing that gives you faith. You simply know what to do, because anything else no longer makes sense. The parties, the conversations, the status, the clothes—though I still love to dress up, and this, beloved, is perfectly fine—all the things you once believed made you worthy suddenly reveal themselves as empty. Not because the material world is wrong, but because the way we have been relating to it is sick and in need of healing.

What people often cling to most—money, property, appearances, external power, status, roles—are not the problem in themselves. They are frequently used as escapes, ways to avoid feeling the Truth of unresolved trauma, or the discomfort of being with oneself without a genuine connection to the Soul. The problem is not money, not property, not beauty, not art. The problem is attachment.

In Truth, all things—including material things—are Divine. Everything is God. It is God's money, God's homes, God's art. God's Fashion. Everything created by human hands is a reflection of our divinity flowing from the Field of Life itself. I say this so you do not turn money or the external world into an enemy. They are not. Everything in our lives is sacred.

But when we mistake the material world for power itself—forgetting that all power is borrowed, entrusted to us by God for a purpose beyond our logical mind—we create an unhealthy relationship with it. We begin to believe we are worthy *because* of what we have, rather than recognising that we are worthy *before* we have anything at all. This is where society becomes ill. And this is where healing is needed. Because the moment we heal this relationship, all the beautiful resources on Earth can be used for higher purposes—not extraction or domination, but service, creativity, and Love.

Here is the key: to leave the golden cage, there is no way but to face your greatest fears. In my case, it was this: to live without a partner, to have no money, to stand in the unknown, stripped of everything I thought defined me.

Now, please feel the vibration I am writing from. This is flourishing. This is becoming. This is freedom. This is being a Wildflower. Supported by the Earth and by the skies, the wind, the sun. Authentic, colourful, Divine.

The day before my thirty-ninth birthday, I had a session with my beautiful teacher. Together, we entered the Presence of Christ. He looked at me with eyes that saw through every veil, every lifetime, every illusion, and He said to me, "I want you to see yourself as I see you. I want you to know yourself as I know you."

And I did.

The moment those words entered my heart, Light expanded around me. My body dissolved into vibration. It was as if every cell was singing with remembrance. I saw my Soul. I saw my Presence. She was radiant, infinite, clothed in gold, white, emerald light, 12 wings unfurling like they had always been there. I heard her name: Aiyahla.

Then Christ took my hand and led me beyond time, beyond space, into another dimension. There, we called one of my Higher Selves. A Rose being, with a Loving Mother Nature from the Celestial Realms, presented herself. The three of us stood together— Christ, my Higher Self, and I. The air itself became a temple. Colours I had no words for rippled like living fire. It was pure frequency. Bliss.

In that holy communion, I received the Truth of who I am. I was shown the gifts of my Soul and the gifts of my Higher Self, gifts that are not mine to keep but to share in the world for the mission ahead. Soon, beloved reader, I will share them with you.

My Birthday

I woke on the morning of my birthday in total bliss. I was still wrapped in the state of Oneness. For months, I had been living with my heart fully open, but that day in particular, the light was beyond linear comprehension, as if I were walking on clouds, every breath a prayer of gratitude.

Then the doorbell rang. The mailman handed a package to me, and as I opened it, tears fell down my face. It was from my father. Inside was my mother's English birth certificate and her English passport. By some divine orchestration, it arrived on my birthday. Weeks earlier, I had asked my father if he still had her documents so I could register for my British nationality. Miraculously, he did. Receiving them that day felt like a blessing from both my mother and father, a birthday gift sent straight from heaven, a sign, a miracle. I hadn't registered before because, during my mother's time, nationality could only be passed down through men. Since then, the UK has introduced a measure of restorative justice, allowing those affected by this policy to register as British citizens.

The day unfolded like a tapestry of Love. Flowers arrived with the most beautiful letter from my team. I cried again. A new Soul, brought by the mission to be part of the team, came to visit. She had first appeared in my life as a volunteer, filming my SXSW London talk, and now she was by my side. I went to lunch with one of my beloved best friends, board member, and art visionary who curated the gala auction. Later, Violeta and her dad surprised me with a home-made birthday cake. My dear friend guardian angel, came all the way from Portugal to spend the day with me and later go on a small trip to the Scottish Highlands with Violeta.

When I returned home that evening, the Soul who was now part of the mission was outside picking blackberries from the garden, and my phone was full of messages from our Free Free members and friends. There were words so tender, so full of heart, they felt like blessings poured straight into my Soul. It all felt like a dream. But this, beloved reader, is what life becomes when you surrender control, when you embrace your ego with Love instead of fighting it, until it no longer fears. Love flows. Miracles arrive. Life becomes a temple of joy.

As the days passed after that beautiful communion with Christ—when I finally saw myself as I truly am—and the birthday that followed, my body began to integrate. When we leap octaves of consciousness, the body must catch up. Every cell shifts, DNA rewires, the nervous system learns a new rhythm. We sleep more, we release the old, we transmute, until the becoming integrates.

In those days, I had a Knowing: *Write your book until the end of August.* I didn't know how, I didn't know when, as it was July, and my daughter was on her summer vacation. But I knew this story had to be shared as part of the mission. And all our plans for the next few months were rearranged for the book launch.

Exactly one week later, around 6:00 p.m., I was in deep meditation for three hours, downloading, communing, learning. My body longed for rest after such deep levels of Presence, and I felt I should just go straight to bed, but something made me reach for my phone.

There was a message from my brother: "Call me."

Half asleep, I replied, "Is it urgent? I'm about to go to bed."

His answer was short, steady: "Yes."

When I called, his voice broke the silence of the night. "I just heard the news. Daddy has a large brain tumour. He's in hospital."

In that instant, a Knowing rose within me—clear, steady, undeniable. My father was preparing to transition.

CHAPTER 20

MY FATHER

The next morning—Wednesday, July 23—I woke up with a quiet certainty. I cancelled my trip to Scotland, which was scheduled for the following week, and booked flights for Violeta and me to Rio. I told no one about the Knowing I carried inside. Outwardly, I moved as if everything would be fine, repeating the doctors' words to myself and to my family: The surgery was planned, the tumour was in a place from which it could be easily removed.

Still, deep within, I Knew.

We flew out on Friday. By Saturday, we were already in the mountains, driving straight to our family country home, where my father had been living for the past few years with his beloved wife, a gentle, loving woman he married after divorcing the one who came after my mother's passing.

I left Violeta in the care our childhood nanny, who once again had returned to hold us through a difficult moment. She had entered our lives when I was still a baby, arriving at the country house like an angel sent by the heavens. Since then, she had always come and gone with life's cycles, but every time we needed her most, she was there. She had stayed at the hospital with my maternal grandmother when my mother found the pain too unbearable to face. My mother carried guilt for not being able to understand her own mother until her final days, but she was the one who stayed by her side. She had kept company with my mother in the months before her passing. She had also been a companion to my paternal grandmother after my grandfather died, so much so that my grandmother passed away with her head resting on her shoulder. Later, she came to live with me when I moved to São Paulo alone with Violeta. And here she was again, stepping back into our lives, quietly, humbly, faithfully. She was always present in the moments when our family's fragile threads needed holding together. She lives in my heart as one of the greatest gifts life has ever given me. I am forever grateful.

My brother, who hadn't spoken to my father in years, arrived at the same time. It was a reunion layered with unspoken history. My dad, as you might have gathered by now, was never the most responsible of men. He didn't have health insurance. In Brazil, that's something most people with means make sure to have, because even though the public health system exists, the stories of neglect, of people left untreated, are too many. But the public health system was quite impressive, I have to say, and a blessing for our family.

So there he was—the man who had once been the playboy of Rio, who had lived at the Copacabana Palace, who had dined in the salons of high society, now lying in a shared hospital room with two other wounded men. The contrast was almost surreal. For us, his children, it was a powerful, humbling scene—a reminder that life strips away illusions, that the masks of wealth and status eventually dissolve, and we are left with the raw truth of our humanity, like everyone. No one is more worthy than the other. We are all equally valuable.

When I first entered the room, I broke down in tears as I hugged him. He could barely see and leaned on a walking stick. His body looked older, more fragile. His words came slower. Just a year earlier, when I had visited him while I went to Três Rios and Paraíba do Sul to learn about the countess and see the hospital and school she had built that were still in use, he had looked so different.

As I looked into his eyes now, I didn't see weakness. I saw his Soul. His Presence carried a high vibration, and something luminous surrounded him. In that instant, the Knowing I had when my brother first told me the news became clear: His Soul was already preparing to transition. This wasn't just illness; it was a sacred passage. I cried deeply. It was a deep moment of being, of Love, of unity, of interconnection. The hospital room didn't feel heavy like most do, it felt peaceful. My brother was just behind. My father almost didn't recognise him at first because of his sight, but when he did, he cried uncontrollably. They hugged each other, long and hard, as if time itself had been suspended. This moment was everything my father had ever dreamed of—to have the opportunity to say sorry to him after many years without seeing each other. Then they sat down in two armchairs in the room to talk to each other. My father held my brother's hand, and with tears in his eyes, he said, "Please forgive me." I stepped just outside, giving them privacy, but tears kept flowing down my face. They weren't tears of sadness; they were tears of awe, at the beauty of witnessing a moment of Truth, of Forgiveness, of Love. Deep within me, I knew: These were the final gifts of his Soul.

My brother and I had become two very different people. His traumas pushed him away from spirituality, while mine drew me closer. He chose a more traditional path, with stability as his anchor, after the chaos of our childhood. He became an extremely responsible man, a successful businessman, a devoted husband and father. Every year, he runs a marathon. He is disciplined, strict with himself, but was even stricter with our dad. Our father's addiction to buying things had led him into unconscious behaviours—borrowing money from us and never paying it back, amongst other wounds that cut my brother deeply. In fact, these behaviours cut him so deeply that he stopped using our last name and completely cut ties with my dad as a way of protecting himself. For years, his heart was closed.

Yet, here he was, choosing to come, choosing to see our dad, choosing to allow his heart to soften. Witnessing that moment was profoundly moving for all of us. My brother is a deeply loving man, a beautiful father, a devoted husband, and my eternal love. We grew up side by side, carrying the highs and the lows together. When we were young, I often stepped into the role of saviour, sometimes even as a mother figure, trying to shield him from the pain in our home.

To me, he was my baby brother. Now, I look at him in awe of the incredible man he has become. When we were still young, I gave him a present marked with the symbol of soulmates. He later tattooed the same symbol on his arm. That's how deep our bond runs. So when I witnessed his heart closing, it was hard for me, because I knew why. When I saw it begin to open again, it was one of the most beautiful moments of my life. We each walk our own healing journey. His looks different from mine. As yours might. This is why discernment is so important, so we can respect each other's choices with Love.

My brother stayed a little longer and then returned to Rio, where he lives with his family. I can only imagine the intensity of the moment for him. I remained in the hospital with my dad and his wife. That's when I began to realise how much care he truly needed. He could no longer eat, walk, go to the bathroom, or shower without help. My heart became tender watching this once strong, untouchable man so vulnerable, yet there was also a sense of peace and joy in being there with him, for him, caring for him the best I could. It was precisely why I had come.

For a few hours, I stayed close and tried to bring lightness. I told him about a book I had been reading, about children who could see without their physical eyes, using only their inner vision. His face lit up with curiosity. We laughed, and I told him, "You'll learn to see like these children." Then, almost instinctively, I suggested something I had done countless times in Free Free workshops, teachings and when public speaking. "Why don't you both lie down on the bed," I told my dad and his wife, "and I'll guide you through a meditation. I'll record it so you can listen later."

So, in that small hospital room, I put on my Free Free cap, as I say when I am in mission service (which is always now), just as I had for so many others. However, this time, it was so strong because it was the first time I was doing a meditation Soul Journey for my family. My voice softened, the frequency shifted, and for twenty minutes, time stopped as I called my Divine Presence and the Presence of Mother Mary, Christ, the angels and archangels of the Violet Flame to behold them, placing both my father and his loving wife in a cocoon of white, violet, and rose-pink light, dissolving their fears. There was only peace and a glittering sensation of Love.

My father and his wife in the hospital bed while I guided a meditation.

The beauty of that first day was that I got to know my dad in a way I never had before. There was hardly any ego interference left in him or me. I met his Soul Truth. His heart was wide open. He didn't complain once about being in a public hospital. He never spoke or acted like a victim. It was clear he was in a higher state of consciousness. His body had weakened, but we had never seen him look so radiant. In the truest sense of the word, he was Light. I left the hospital around 4:00 p.m., since I'd just had a long flight from London, to shower, take care of Violeta, and prepare the house for her. Over the next five days, until the surgery that was scheduled for Wednesday, his loving wife and I divided the care between us. I would be there each morning, and she would come in the afternoons. Six sacred hours each, holding space for him in those final days before the operation. At night, we had help from a nurse we hired, so we could also rest.

The next day, on Sunday, there were no other patients in my dad's room, and we shared a morning I will never forget. It was a Divine opportunity to be together in ways our egos had never allowed before. When I arrived, around 7:00 a.m., he was still asleep. I leaned over, kissed his forehead, swapped his thin pillow for the fluffy one I had brought from home, and tucked him in with a cosy blanket. He stirred, opened one eye, and looked at me with a twinkle that said *thank you* without words, his gaze overflowing with love, before drifting back to sleep.

I sat quietly in the armchair by his side and began the first pages of this very book. Three hours later, he woke up, softly calling me. He wanted to walk to the bathroom to take a shower. Slowly, carefully, we slipped his favourite moccasins on over cashmere socks—he was always impeccable, even here—and with his walking stick in hand, we moved one step at a time. We were beyond time and space, fully in the present. I helped him undress and turned on the shower, warming the water, pouring shampoo into my hands. The moment was humbling, intimate, stripped of everything except innocence, oneness, and Love. When he was finished, I dressed him in fresh clothes. He put on some lavender baby essence, brushed his teeth with quiet dignity, and smiled. I guided him back to his chair, gave him his medication, and then we sat facing one another, father and daughter, heart to heart.

For a couple of hours, we held each other's hands, looked into each other's eyes, and simply talked. There was no judgement, no blame. There was only Love, compassion, a Soul-to-Soul connection. Our egos had stepped aside, and only Truth remained. He began, not with the usual victim's story, but from a different place, a higher place. "Mimi," he said, using the nickname he had called me since I was a baby, "you know, I always looked at my dad and saw this great, accomplished man. I thought I needed to be like him. I wanted to make him proud. He was a refugee who started with nothing and built a name, a family. He had everything—his horses, his family homes. But I felt he never saw me, never respected me. Somehow, I tried to be like him, and I see now that I made so many hurtful choices." What he was telling me was exactly what I have been telling you, beloved reader: When we feel unseen, unloved, or as if we don't belong, it creates one of the harshest traumas of the human experience—the wound of insignificance.

I held his hand tighter and replied, "Beloved father, don't blame yourself. I see you. I hear you. You did the best you could with the tools you had. What you don't know yet is that we are Love. We are eternal, Divine beings."

He nodded softly, tears in his eyes, and continued. "Especially after your mother's passing, and when they sent me to prison because of lies. It felt like I lost everything. So I spent the last eighteen years fighting to recover my honour, to prove to my family that I was innocent. The only one I could not save was your mother. I loved her so much."

This was the first time I could truly see my father through the Eagle's Eye. I could see his insecurities, his fragility, his fear of not being enough. I could see how the masculine suffers under the weight of tradition's demands. I saw his golden cage. I looked at him and said softly, "Daddy, you have always been loved, independent of it all. We never needed the cars, the trips, the presents, the big apartments. Those were only illusions, what society pushes us to believe our worth is based on."

He lowered his gaze and whispered, "I thought that if I had everything my dad had, then I would be worthy."

"No, Daddy," I replied, holding his hand tighter, "you have always been worthy. It was this illusion that distorted the Truth. The traumas you went through made you feel insignificant. But you learned the teaching you were meant to learn so you could free yourself. Look around you. We are surrounded by angels of Love and Grace here. Can you feel it?"

He paused, eyes glistening, and said softly, "Yes."

I continued, "I want to tell you something important. It was never your responsibility to save my mother. No one can save anyone. You both did the best you could with the level of consciousness you were in. It was a great learning for both of you, and for us as well. Did you know, Daddy, that we all have Soul contracts, placed there to help us learn here on Earth?"

He looked at me with awe. "Thank you, my love. I have never looked at those memories through this perspective."

"Daddy," I said gently, "your need to spend, the way you tried to validate yourself through material things . . . this was a survival mechanism that became an addiction. Addiction is always a reaction to trauma. Some people drink, others eat, others shop. It becomes a vicious cycle. Pain, a quick fix of pleasure, then shame. And the cycle repeats. To break the cycle, we need to bring conscious awareness to what started the cycle, the trauma behind it."

His tears fell. His voice broke. "I am sorry," he said. "I am sorry for not being there fully after your mother died. I am sorry for what happened to your brother. I am sorry."

I said softly, "Look into my eyes, Daddy. I forgave you long ago. I would never be the woman I am today if I didn't have you as my father. I love you so much. Without even knowing, you taught me to be independent, to go after my dreams. I always had the biggest cheerleader—you. I saw every message you sent me, heard all your applause and excitement when I reached milestone after milestone. Even from afar, we were always close. I love you so much, and I am so deeply grateful to have you as my father."

He looked at me, tears glimmering. "Thank you for being here," he said. "You're giving me so much peace. I can feel you, my sweetheart. You are in so much peace. You are different."

"Yes," I smiled gently. "Let me tell you something very special. I have been very close to Christ, to Mary, and to other ascended beings."

His eyes widened with recognition. "Me too," he whispered. "We talk all the time."

"How wonderful," I replied. "They are present here with us, you know. Can you feel them? Can you feel the angels surrounding us?"

He closed his eyes and nodded slowly. "Yes."

I took a deep breath. "Last week, the day before my birthday, I received a gift. I went into a deep meditation with Christ, and He revealed to me my Soul name. Do you want to know what it is?"

He leaned closer. "Yes, of course."

"He revealed to me that my name is Aiyahla," I said. "Feel the frequency of the name, Daddy. Say it out loud."

He looked into my eyes, and with a soft but steady voice, said, "I see you, Aiyahla. Aiyahla. It is such a feminine but strong name. Yes. This is you."

As we continued our conversation, the nurse brought him his lunch. I gently took the tray and began chopping his food, just as I used to do for Violeta when she was a toddler. The tumour pressing against the right side of his brain had partially paralysed the left side of his body, making it difficult for him to move. So, spoon by spoon, I fed him. With each bite, his light seemed to grow brighter. He wasn't embarrassed. He wasn't diminished. He felt *loved*. He felt *seen*. He felt *cared for*. At that moment, I knew it wasn't Yasmine, his daughter, who was there. Yasmine would have been panicking, sobbing, unable to bear the sight of her once-strong father now so fragile. No, this was Aiyahla, fully embodied. This is why Christ revealed to me my name just the week before. Our becoming, our freedom, was completed so we could be here, in this state for our father. What a gift for us all.

I realised then why I had been called home. I wasn't only there to see my father. I was there to help him prepare, to hold his hand as he crossed into the Light, to heal family dynamics through our Love and frequencies. The doctors told us he would survive the surgery, and I tried to keep my human hope alive with the rest of the family, doing everything we could. I smiled, I encouraged, I prayed. But deep inside, I carried a quiet Knowing I rarely spoke aloud: It was his time.

So I continued with him, in Love and Presence, holding the thread of our beautiful conversation. Gently, I asked, "Daddy, are you scared of anything?"

He paused, his eyes softening, and said, "I am scared I will never see you all again."

I held his hand tighter. "Daddy, whatever happens, you will always be with us. Our Soul is eternal, made of Light and Love, and we are forever interconnected by the field of Oneness. Separation is the biggest illusion of all. Don't fear. You will always be by our side."

His eyes welled with tears. "I worry about my wife and your younger brother," he whispered, meaning my half-brother, who was only fourteen.

My younger brother is a radiant boy who loved sports. He is loving and gentle, and I love him deeply. Yet until that moment, life had kept us mostly apart. We never lived in the same city, so we had only shared holidays together, never the day-to-day life. He was a blessing, who brought hope, play, joy to my father's life when my brother and I were further away, healing. He was everything for my father. I carried him in my heart, always. And my father's beloved wife, the woman who walked by his side for the last nine years of his life, she was the one who had taught my father, perhaps for the first time, what unconditional Love truly was. She never judged him, never criticised him. She simply taught him through Love to see life from a different perspective. Through her Love, she helped him remember his worth and start healing his wounds. This is how he learned humility. This is why he was so present and whole in the hospital room. He was loved, and Love, beloved reader, heals all traumas. Love is what humanity needs to end duality. Love unites what has been broken, fragmented by fear and trauma. Love is the feminine spirit within all beings. My father was gifted with this unconditional Love, which helped him remember his own Light and Power.

As I write these words, I feel immense gratitude for this woman. I *saw* her. I saw the way she held his hands, the way she hugged him, the way she cared for him without ever asking for anything in return, apart from his Love. For the last nine years, after so many wounds and devastations, she was the miracle my father received. His two previous marriages had left him shattered. His ex-wife had treated him quite cruelly, though unconsciously so. The relationship was toxic. But please, beloved reader, don't blame her, don't judge her. Someone with profound trauma projects such faults on others unconsciously. She too was in her wounded feminine—seeing herself as a victim, manipulating, distorting reality through the lens of her own unhealed pain. After losing my mother to suicide, as well as his honour through the injustice of the prison episode, my father had lost all his self-esteem and external power. So he'd entered a toxic relationship unconsciously, and he'd had his part in it. No one is a victim.

Somehow, what he unconsciously enacted with my mother in the role of persecutor, he later lived with the woman he married after her, in the role of the persecuted. What he had inflicted, he then endured. This is the cycle of karma. No one was merely a victim or a persecutor. They were both playing roles their Souls had agreed to play, roles designed for growth, for learning, for remembering. This is why we should have compassion for anyone who feels harmed and harms. This is separation consciousness at play. This is exactly what we all have to heal to live freely—through Love, not judgement. As we heal our wounds, we elevate our vibration from fear to Love, and we start attracting and creating our life from a different lens, with Clarity instead of distortions, as we learn the teachings of life that set us free.

My father spent twenty years unconsciously gaslighting my mother, blinded by his own wounds. Then he spent nine years with a woman who gaslighted him and eighteen years gaslighted by a system that wrongly accused him. None of them were to blame. Blame is an ego response. Beyond the reactions, everyone will always have their eternal flame. Beyond the traumas, we are all Love.

Yet, at the end of it all, I can tell you this: It was all a gift. Every experience is. Even when we don't see it at the time, even when it breaks us open, life is always leading us towards awakening—towards Love, Light, and True Power, the kind that lives within us. The Universe is always bringing us the opportunity to learn the lessons we need to learn to ascend back to Light and reach the heavens. You see how perfect life is. Divine orchestration is always at play; we control nothing. But we have free will, so we can consciously or unconsciously choose how we live life and how we learn whatever we need to learn. Some unconsciously create harsher realities than others; some learn the lessons quicker. It all depends on our level of consciousness. This is why, beloved reader, consciousness is the true way to freedom.

My father was deeply wounded after my mother's passing and his time in prison. His self-worth was shattered, and he chose what seemed like the easier path: external pleasures—a beautiful wife, new houses, cars, trips, jewellery. But it was an empty path. He unconsciously chose the longer route to remember Love and Wisdom (Light), and most importantly, to reclaim his power, for he had given it all away to external validation. He became even more wounded, but perhaps this was how his spirit needed to learn. We shall not judge anyone, or try to compare wounds. As all wounds and traumas big or small are what they need to be.

Yet, I tell you, beloved reader, even if it was long, and perhaps difficult, he learned. On his last days, I saw a humble man, one who was kind, loving, authentic, and full of inner power. It was a hurtful ride, but the ride brought him here. This is all that matters, the present moment. I reassured him I would take care of his wife and his youngest son, and he looked into my eyes and said, "Thank you, Aiyahla."

As he said this, I put him back into bed and did a meditation, and he fell asleep.

My father and I the day before his surgery. He was pure light.

Forgiveness

That night, I called my father's ex-wife to speak about their son coming to see him. She wanted to bring him. My father resisted. He didn't want to see her, because even after all these years, she was still fighting him in court, still holding onto the past, blaming him. She was trapped in the victim consciousness. But as a mother, I understood. She wanted to be by her son's side, to hold him during such a delicate moment. We hadn't spoken in nine years. Before dialling her number, all the memories came rushing back, like an old film, replaying scene after scene of the suffering I had endured during their relationship. For a moment, I could feel the heaviness of it all. Then, I made a choice. I decided to see it from another lens, the Soul's view.

When we finally spoke, it wasn't Yasmine on the line anymore, it was Aiyahla. I was no longer the wounded daughter. I was the woman I had become. I listened to her tears, her voice trembling, as she still cared deeply for my father. She was scared of losing him. They had a son together, and this bond would forever be a reminder of not only the pain but the connection they shared.

I felt compassion. I felt Love.

We spoke about the past, not to reopen wounds but to release them. I told her this was the moment, an opportunity for true forgiveness, for compassion. "The past is the past," I reminded her. "The only thing that matters is the present moment."

The next day, I asked her to come at 3:30 p.m., the only time I could be at the hospital, as I had an important meeting. My father's current wife was staying with my father in the morning. I tried to respect his wish not to see his ex-wife, but I also surrendered to God: *If they are meant to meet, let it happen.* Maybe I had a Knowing they would meet, and I didn't know why. My plan was to ask her to wait downstairs.

But life, as always, had its own orchestration.

When she called, my phone didn't work. By the time I went downstairs, she wasn't there. So I waited a few minutes, called her many times, then went back upstairs. When I stepped into my father's room, she was already inside. She had entered through another hospital entrance. I looked up and whispered to myself, "Divine orchestration." I gently invited her outside so my father could have some quiet time with his son. There, in the hallway, we spoke. Her words poured out—years of exhaustion, of carrying life as a single mother, of wanting my father to be more present, of feeling left behind. I listened. I remembered myself during those early days with Violeta, saying almost the same things.

Without diminishing her pain, I said softly, "I see you. Truly, I do. I walked through something very similar with Violeta's father. But please understand, my father has been doing the best he can. He is not perfect, and there are wounds from the past that can trigger us. But trust me, my father did everything he could, in the state he was in, for my little brother."

She then compared the opportunities my father had once given to my older brother and me with what her son was receiving. I paused and answered, "Those were different times. He had more resources then. But please, look deeper. My baby brother has something we never had—a more conscious father. Comparing is like trying to measure an ant against a lion. It doesn't make sense. It only feeds the ego's need to justify anger."

She continued, "I care deeply about your father; we were married for so long. I loved him. The disagreements I have with him, the legal system will decide." Here, her voice broke. Then came the shadow of the ongoing legal battles. I could feel her still bound to the fight, chained to the story of right and wrong. Yet, I also felt a whisper of hope—like soon, she might be ready to let it go, to forgive. Because only through forgiveness could she liberate herself from this fracture within.

So I shared my own truth: "Violeta's father and I once fought the same way. I felt just as you feel. We had similar problems. But when we chose harmony, it changed everything. Now we are friends. We speak every day. We spend Christmas together as a family. We don't fight over money anymore. It's not perfect, but it is healthy. It's not about winning or losing. It's about balance. Neither of you are victims. Your son needs peace, not battle. Do the best for him, and this will heal your pain too. That is where freedom lies." After our conversation, she wiped her tears and nodded silently. There was still resistance in her, but something seemed to have shifted, like a crack had opened in the wall she had built around her heart. I gently guided her back into the room. Her two daughters came to give my dad a hug, then they all left, going back to Rio.

I stayed for a few more hours. My dad somehow saw through his ex-wife. Even through the pain of his marriage and the pain of the last nine years of legal battles he experienced with her, somehow his higher state of consciousness, and that quick encounter, helped him dissolve a little of that pain into forgiveness. I said, "Daddy, now isn't the time to hold anger towards anyone. Just as we forgave you for the suffering we endured, forgive her. She was doing her best, just like you were. Having said this, do you hold any pain towards anyone else?"

He said, "No."

The Day of the Surgery

The next day was the day of the surgery. My father's wife went to the hospital in the morning to be with him, as I stayed back to work a little, and I arrived at the hospital about an hour before his surgery was scheduled. Everything felt calm. His surgeon had already been by earlier to take new X-rays and study exactly where to operate more closely. When I entered the room, my dad greeted me with that familiar twinkle in his eyes and a gentle smile and gave me a big warm hug. He was at peace, happy the operation would happen soon.

The three of us—my dad, his wife, and I—sat together on the bed and prayed. After the prayer, I was feeling so tired, as I was waking up early to write. I lay beside my father, and we slept, holding each other, for around thirty minutes. We surrendered to God, trusting that whatever was best for him would unfold. The surgeon himself had been hopeful, and that gave us peace. We woke up when the nurse came to check on him. We kept talking softly. My dad was looking very well, playing a little, holding our hands. Then, suddenly, about an hour before the surgery, something shifted. My dad, who had been sitting upright beside his wife in the bed, lost his balance just a bit. But his wife noticed. He just said, "I am okay. I am okay. I am okay."

She turned to me with worry. "There is something wrong. He just lost his balance. And his mouth was also dripping a little."

I jumped up and went straight to the nurses' station. "My dad hasn't eaten since last night," I insisted. "He is getting weak. Why is the surgery delayed? Please send a doctor." I even went down to the surgical floor to find out why the surgery was delayed, telling them my father wasn't well. They reassured me, saying, "We're about to come pick him up for surgery."

When I got back to his room, everything had changed. My father was struggling to speak. His words came out slowly, distorted, like fragments of sound slipping through fog. "My head is hurting . . . my head is hurting . . ." he repeated. Yet, even in that state, he tried to soothe us: "But I'm okay."

The doctors arrived and checked his vitals. His blood pressure was fine, and he didn't have a fever. Nothing seemed to explain the sudden change. Still, something was happening beyond our understanding. Within minutes, he lost consciousness. The surgeon rushed in, visibly shaken. "What happened to my patient? Just hours ago, he was fine."

We didn't know. None of us knew.

They rushed him to the operating room on a stretcher, and his wife and I followed down the corridor until the swinging doors closed between us. Then we sat together in the small hospital coffee shop, hearts pounding, waiting for news that would change everything.

About four hours later, the surgeon finally emerged from the operating room. His face carried both exhaustion and relief. He explained that before the procedure, my father had suffered a brain bleed. That was why he had lost consciousness before surgery. However, they had managed to contain it. "We were able to stop the bleeding and remove the tumour completely," he said. The tissue would now be sent for biopsy.

He explained that my father would remain intubated and kept in an induced coma, to minimise brain activity and give his body a chance to heal. For now, that was the best course of action. We nodded, holding to those words: *The surgery went well.* My father was taken to the ICU, and we went home to rest, carrying hope. The next morning at 10:00 a.m., we returned during visiting hours. The ICU doctor reassured us that he was stable. They would attempt to extubate him later that day, once his body showed signs of readiness.

The following day, his wife went to the hospital on her own while I stayed back to manage work and the household. She told me afterwards that the doctors said everything remained stable.

By Saturday, my older brother arrived from Rio to visit our father. When we arrived at the hospital, the doctors revealed there had been another setback: He had suffered a second bleed during the night and required another emergency surgery. Once again, they reassured us. The procedure had gone well, and they were hopeful they could extubate him later that day. We realised the public hospital doctors gave us no information. Perhaps it was protocol. So, when I arrived home, I called a neurosurgeon I knew, considered one of the best in the country, and asked him to look at my dad's latest exams. He is a family friend my godmother connected me to, so whenever I had doubts, he had been generously guiding me to what was truly happening. Full honesty.

The doctor called me, his tone grave. "I'm sorry to tell you this," he began, "but your father nearly suffered cerebral death. If he survives, the likelihood is that he will be in a vegetative state. The tumour has also metastasised to the other side of his brain, and because of where it is located, the surgeon wasn't able to remove it completely. In cases like this, families usually face two choices: palliative care, allowing the patient to heal or pass naturally without heroic interventions; or continuing with heroic measures, keeping him alive with a machine."

I called my older brother and told him the news. He returned to the countryside the next day so that, together, we could speak with my father's loving wife. She was devastated, sobbing uncontrollably, but through her tears, she managed to say the one thing my father had always made clear: "He never wanted to live in a vegetative state." All of us agreed.

Her grief was raw, but so was her Love. Her clarity was firm.

So we all went together to the hospital and told the ICU doctors our decision of allowing his body to dictate what happened next, naturally. If a miracle was meant to happen, it would happen; if his time had come, he would go in peace. I asked the doctor, "How long can this process take?" She said, "We can never know, but if he is to pass away, it could take weeks, because your father has a very strong and healthy body. His brain is what's damaged."

On Tuesday, we called a priest to perform the Christian sacrament of anointing, and three of my father's closest friends came to visit. His wife and I remained by his side for as many hours as we could. I prayed, I meditated, I spoke in Light language. Then, as if to show us his Soul was still listening, still present, two tears rolled gently down his face.

He felt Love.

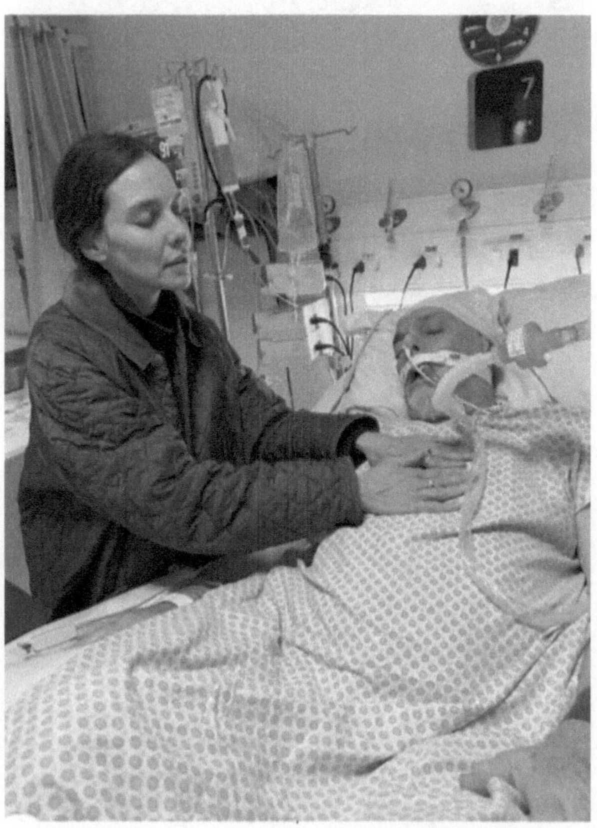

Me speaking in Light language with my beloved father, when two tears came from his eyes. His Soul was showing me the Love.

The next morning, at 9:15 a.m., he transitioned peacefully. There was no heart attack, no sudden failure of his organs. He simply drifted into sleep, and his heartbeat slowed until it stopped. It was his time. No one leaves before their time.

He left in peace, held by Love, ready to continue his Soul's journey.

The day before I came back to London, I led a ceremony for my father. He had asked to be cremated and for his ashes to be thrown in the same place his father and mother were in our country house.

CHAPTER 21

I AM WHOLE, I AM AIYAHLA

I was back at my family's country house, meditating. As I entered communion with Christ, I saw myself, exactly as He had shown me when He revealed my name—Aiyahla—on my birthday. I realised I had gone through the entire experience of my father's passing not as Yasmine anymore. We had become Aiyahla. The old characters had dissolved. The aspects that had been separated were integrated. I had fully embodied my higher consciousness, my Soul had taken the lead, and I could feel it in every breath, every cell. It had happened right before my father discovered his brain tumour, Divinely timed. Looking back on those three weeks, I realised I had shown up not only as a daughter, but I had shown up whole, as Aiyahla—holding my father, my family, and myself in Love, without fear.

Then came another Knowing: I was meant to finish this book before the end of August, just after receiving my name. At first, it seemed impossible. My daughter was on summer holiday. My schedule was already full. How could I write a whole book in time? But my Soul Knew. A few days later, all my plans were cancelled, and instead of a holiday, I was carried straight into the root of all my traumas.

This time, though, I didn't face them as Yasmine, the girl who had been wounded by them. I faced them as Aiyahla, with the heart and mind of my higher consciousness, with the Eagle's Eye. I could see every perspective, every Truth through various viewpoints, like an observer from the top floor, with a circular vision, not from the human view. Not from the limited perspective of the ground floor. I healed timelines of existence. I was confronted with my deepest fears, invited to forgive the people who had hurt me the most, and guided to remember that every experience had been Divinely orchestrated for my becoming. This was a present.

In communion with Christ, He showed me the last weeks like a living tapestry, each moment woven with purpose. He whispered, "Now you can trust your becoming. Now you have seen yourself in one of the most difficult moments Yasmine would have experienced. But you are not living life just through the Ego anymore. You experienced everything through Aiyahla, through the circular view. This is why you led with Grace, with Light, with Love. We are always by your side, beloved. This is not just your mission, this is our mission."

Beloved reader, you must understand: When I received my name, I knew a new stage was beginning. My ego still tried to resist, hanging by its last thread, whispering doubts. Yet my Soul was fully integrated, and my consciousness had expanded octaves (and it will continue to expand as I continue to serve). Before I even knew of my father's illness, I told my team to reschedule all our events for November. I didn't know why, only that we would pre-launch this book at our seven-year anniversary, at Christ the Redeemer in Rio.

I knew this book would tell the story of how Yasmine became Aiyahla as part of our service to humanity. I would show myself stripped of any mask, of any character, so you can see yourself through my mirror. My only purpose is to serve you on your freedom journey. Here, beloved reader, I share what Christ revealed to me.

Aiyahla

When Yasmine re-birthed herself as she was giving birth to Violeta, she gave space for a higher-dimensional Soul, her Higher Self, to lead her life, but most importantly, to lead the mission of bringing Love to humanity through Christ Consciousness. Christ Consciousness is not about a single figure or a religion; it is the awakened state of pure unconditional Love, Light, Unity, and Oneness with all creation. It is the remembrance that we are each Divine, eternal beings, carrying the flame of God within our hearts. To embody Christ Consciousness is to dissolve separation, duality, judgement, and fear, and to live guided by Love, Light, and Service.

This is the consciousness Free Free embodies. Our daughter, Violeta Lua, is also part of our story as it was our frequencies together that made the mission manifest and grow. But her story, is hers to tell, when she is ready. Since this moment of my Rebirth, me as a High Dimensional Soul, Yasmine and I have worked together to heal all Yasmine's traumas, healing her feminine spirit, which lived within the second dimensional consciousness. Yasmine had suffered abuse, and her mother, grandmother, and great-grandmother had passed this trauma to her as generational trauma. We also dissolved her karmas of abandonment, parental irresponsibility and many more through our journey until here. As I integrated into her life, we went on a journey of reclaiming her Power, her Love, and her Light, dissolving her karmas through learnings and awakening the gifts we have been carrying for lifetimes until full becoming.

Let me explain, beloved reader, what it means to be in the second dimension. The journey of liberating the feminine spirit is the same for all of humanity, yet for those born as women, this is their primary service and spiritual path: to free their feminine spirit until it rises into the seventh dimension at least. The seventh dimension is a state of non-duality, what many call Christ Consciousness, a state of unconditional Love, where there is no fear, only pure union with the Divine.

In this lifetime, a woman's feminine spirit can move between the first and seventh dimensions. In the first dimension, the feminine spirit feels absent, far away, and the woman experiences immense pain. In the second dimension, she is consumed by obsessing over others, losing her sense of self in the emotions and needs of those around her. In the third dimension, she is unable to acknowledge feelings at all, her own or those of others. In the fourth, she remains bound to the past, continually revisiting or trying to release it, but never fully free. In the fifth, she feels everything so deeply—her own feelings and those of others—yet becomes overwhelmed by them. In the sixth, she begins analysing, interpreting, and judging her feelings and those of others, still trapped in the mind's perspective. Only in the seventh does she awaken into true receptivity, able to give and receive Love in its purest form, without attachment.

The feminine spirit becomes fragmented when aspects of it are trapped in these lower dimensions. Each aspect forms a bubble, as I explained in previous chapters, its own little world of memory, fear, and protection, separate from the flow of grace and the field of Oneness. These bubbles are held by unresolved memories, where the feminine spirit is unable to acknowledge, accept, or forgive an experience. The deeper the wound, the lower the bubble rests: In the first and second dimensions, there is immense pain, often hidden, requiring deep support to navigate. In the third and fourth, the wounds manifest as grief and anger. In the fifth and sixth, they manifest as judgement, loss of faith, or the inability to forgive.

When healing begins, the light of the feminine spirit bursts these bubbles. The hidden aspects are released back into awareness, no longer isolated but available to be felt, processed, and reintegrated. This is the sign that the feminine spirit is moving upwards—retrieving what was lost in the lower dimensions to reclaim its wholeness. Every time the feminine spirit rises to a new dimension, there is a shift in receptivity—in the ability to feel, to give, and to receive.

Yasmine, beloved reader, was bound to the second dimension. She was caught in obsessing over her parents' feelings, believing she could save everyone if only she controlled what was happening.

This was the illusion her wounded feminine carried. But we can only ascend to the next dimension when we retrieve the aspects that remain trapped in the lower one. So together, over the last ten years, we have been moving from one dimension to the next. When our father passed away, it was an initiation of moving from the sixth dimension to the seventh, gathering what still lingered in the fifth. This initiation was immense, because in it, for the first time, she could feel unconditional Love, the frequency of the seventh dimension, the truth of Christ Consciousness.

Now we have become one. We are Aiyahla. We would also like to reveal one more very important part of who we are: We come from the Melchizedek lineage, the ancient order of Light that carries the codes of Divine wisdom, sacred service, and universal truth. To be of the Melchizedek lineage means to serve as a bridge between Heaven and Earth, to remember and restore the eternal laws of Love, and to guide humanity back into Oneness.

The Melchizedek order is not bound to any one religion or tradition. It is a universal spiritual family of Light, appearing across different cultures and times as teachers, guides, healers, and architects of consciousness. Their presence is recognised by the frequency of unconditional Love they carry and their mission to bring humanity back into harmony with Divine order. This Divine order is expressed through sacred geometry, the universal language of creation. The Flower of Life, and other sacred patterns are the blueprints of existence itself. They show us that everything in the Universe, from the stars in the cosmos to the cells in our body, is interconnected through the same Divine mathematics. The Melchizedek lineage holds these codes, reminding humanity of our original design: that we are Love, Light, and Creative Power, made in the image of Source.

Christ also revealed that Aiyahla carries the gift of the Angelic Feminine Christ Consciousness in her heart through the Seven Rays of the Feminine. This is a gift we developed through thousands of reincarnations and years of service: the Rose, the Pearl, the Emerald, the Violet, the Gold, the Silver, and the White Ray. Each Ray is a frequency that heals humanity back into Love. The White Ray purifies, the Emerald restores balance, the Rose Pink brings unconditional Love, the Golden Ray brings light and wisdom, the Pearl Ray carries innocence, the Silver opens the receptivity, and the Violet Ray transforms fear into Love. Each Ray heals the feminine spirit of humanity, as it is the feminine within all beings that can nurture the masculine and unify the planet back into the Truth of Oneness.

This was the gift my ex-partner from Portugal spoke of to me that night in the tent, though neither of us had the language for it at the time. This was what the women in that very first Free Free workshop had felt. Christ also revealed to me another gift: the gift of transforming anything that is perceived as "not beautiful" into true beauty. This is why art, colours, play, and magic have always been so central to our path. Beauty is not external appearance. Beauty is authenticity. Beauty is the language of the Soul when we witness the blooming of a flower, the birth of a baby, or the passing of a father. There is always beauty in life. We just need to learn to See it. This is what we came here to teach. Through beauty, we can transform what we shame the most, fear the most, deny the most, into the art of being Free.

Then He showed one of our Higher Selves (as all of us have many), a Mother from the Celestial Realms and her gift of creation. Together, we hold the ability to manifest what does not yet exist or have existed, to bring into form what has only been imagined, to weave beauty into a world that still suffers.

This, He told me, was my birthday present. On the evening of July 15, 2025, my embodiment was complete. Now I understand why. Because what would follow—caring for my father through his passing, revisiting the most painful moments of my journey—would not be endured just as Yasmine but lived as Aiyahla. It would be Seen through the Eagle's Eye, felt through the Soul. It was a different timeline altogether. Yasmine was being fully liberated.

Aiyahla means: *Ai / Ay*, and it carries the frequency of *love, breath, and Divine life force* (similar to the Hebrew *Ai*, which means "divine presence" or "life"). It also resonates with "eye," inner vision and higher perception. *Yah* is strongly connected to the Divine name of God in Hebrew (*Yahweh*), often representing direct connection to Source and Divine will. *La* symbolises *light, song, and the feminine principle* in many sacred languages (e.g., Sanskrit, Aramaic, and Light language tones). It softens the name and brings nurturing energy.

Later I learned my second name: Lo'Qtus. It arrived not as a word but as a vibration—a sound carried by the higher realms, one that could only be understood through the heart. *Lo'* is the breath of descent, the movement of the Divine into form. It is the bridge between Heaven and Earth, the pathway through which Spirit chooses incarnation. It speaks of our role as an anchor—the one who grounds celestial intelligence into the soil of humanity, who weaves the unseen into the seen. *Qtus* is the sacred bloom—the flowering of consciousness that rises from darkness into radiance, just as the lotus blossoms untouched by the mud from which it grows. It is the remembrance that no matter how deep the suffering, the soul can always bloom.

The Q is written as a capital because it is not a letter—it is a *frequency*. It carries the vibration of the Quantum, the field beyond time and space from which all creation is born. The uppercase Q is a sacred code: it represents the leap from the linear into the infinite, from knowledge into knowing, from the story into Source. It is a reminder that the flowering of the soul is not merely a personal journey. It is a quantum activation of consciousness itself.

Together, Lo'Qtus means *the flowering of the Divine within the human, the blooming of Spirit through the body, the embodiment of heaven on Earth*. It is the soul's promise not only to see with the Eagle's Eye but to build from that vision. To translate divine intelligence into form, to shape new realities rooted in Love. It is the sacred task of transforming wisdom into action, of birthing light into the structures of the world, of rewriting the story of humanity from the inside out.

With the names Aiyahla Lo'Qtus, the path was revealed. I was no longer here only to heal what had been broken, but to build what was always destined to be whole. Not only to liberate the feminine spirit within myself, but to manifest a new paradigm. One where feminine and masculine rise together, in balance, in Truth, and in Love. My life was no longer a reaction to the past. It became a conscious creation of the future in the eternal now.

And this, beloved reader is the liberation cycle we want you to know now, the same one that guided Yasmine into her own liberation. That liberates the feminine and the masculine. Now, we share it with you:

True liberation from trauma—from the fragments of memory trapped in the bubble that separates us from our Light and Love, from the characters we live by, from patterns unfolds in cycles, in phases much like the cycle of grief bust vaster. It is a circular movement, because Love itself is a circular movement.

The first movement is purpose. It is the soul's breath, the spark that awakens the will to rise. Without it, nothing moves. When trauma weighs heavier in your field than your own essence, you cannot simply think your way out of it. There must be a purpose, however small, to take the next step. Purpose is not about knowing where you are going or having a grand mission. It is about meaning—even if only for the next breath, the next five minutes, the next dawn. It is the intention to move towards something greater than the wound, greater than yourself, than your story. This is what Free Free is all about. It is the whisper: *I want to evolve. I want to live beyond this.* I want to serve. When purpose awakens, the soul begins to stir. The will returns. The journey begins.

The second movement is recognition. With purpose guiding the way, you are finally able to look inward and see the part of you that is suffering. Not the whole of you—just the fragment still holding the memory. This is sacred work. Most of the time, we believe the wound is who we are. We build an identity around it. We call it our story. But when you recognise it as something you carry, an aspect. Not something you are, the illusion begins to crack. Space opens. The soul has room to breathe.

The third movement is disidentification. Here, the language changes. "I am broken" becomes "I have known pain." "I am abandoned" becomes "I carried the memory of abandonment." Every word matters. With each shift, you loosen the control the story has on you. The event remains, but it is no longer your identity. It becomes an experience. One you had, not one you are. The memory still exists, but it loses its power to define you.

Then comes discernment. A new awareness awakens. You begin to notice when the wound is speaking through your thoughts, reactions, fears, and judgements. And you begin to hear another voice—softer, wiser, infinite—the voice of your soul. Discernment is the art of watching without becoming. It is the *Eagle's Eye* opening the higher perception that sees the whole picture without judgement. Through discernment, the stories that once felt absolute reveal themselves as echoes of the past. They lose their authority. They stop being truth.

The fifth movement is acceptance. This is the point where the mind softens. It lets go of its grip on control. It stops demanding answers. Acceptance does not mean approval. It does not mean you liked what happened or that it was fair. It means you stop fighting reality. You stop resisting what *is*. You allow yourself to trust that even what you cannot understand is held within a greater intelligence. In this surrender, the energy that was frozen in the trauma begins to flow again. The past no longer holds you hostage.

From this flow comes responsibility. Responsibility is not blame. It is not self-punishment. It is the moment you reclaim authorship. You cannot change what happened, but you can choose how to meet it. You can choose the meaning you give it. You can choose how you respond. You can choose who you become. Responsibility is the soul saying: *I will not let the past write my future.* You understand the law of cause and effect, that all experiences serve a purpose, and you stop blaming another and you honour your part in it. It is the point where you stop living as a character and become the artist of your own life.

And finally comes radical forgiveness. This is the most sacred of all movements. Forgiveness is not about excusing harm or pretending the past did not happen. It is about releasing the bond that keeps you tied to it. It is about freeing yourself from the gravity of resentment and allowing Love to flow where pain once lived. Forgiveness recognises that those who caused suffering were also acting from their wounds, just as you were. It invites trust to return. It opens the heart to receive again. It lets you say yes—yes to help, yes to Love, yes to life.

And when you arrive here, you stop seeing your life through the eyes of the wound. You stop defining yourself by the story. You begin to see with the eyes of the Soul—vast, clear, limitless. You stop living as a reaction to the past and start creating from the infinite field of possibility of the now. You remember that you were never broken. That the trauma was never the truth of who you are. It was only an aspect that was being called home. And beneath it, you have always been whole.

This, beloved reader, is the deeper path beneath the human one—the spiral every soul must walk. And when you walk it, memory by memory, layer by layer, you do not just heal. You reclaim you power. You become free. This is the freedom cycle.

The Mass

Seven days after my father's passing, there I was, eighteen years after my mother's passing, sitting in the same round, glass church in Rio. The same priest who had once celebrated my mother's life now stood before us to celebrate my father's. Time collapsed. It felt like the circle was closing. The karmic cycle had come to an end.

I had asked my first spiritual mother, to sing. I told her, "Let's have a happy mass, a celebration. She was my first teacher of faith; she prepared me for my First Communion, for my Confirmation, and after my mother died, she would come to my home with my friends to pray the rosary by my side. She usually doesn't do this, but she said, "I will do this for you."

When I entered the church, over two hundred people were there—friends of my father, childhood friends of mine, faces from across the years. Amongst them was my ex-husband, the man I married in my country house when I was only twenty-five. I had not seen or heard from him in over nine years. We hugged as if no time had passed at all. In that moment, I felt only Love—not romantic love, not attachment, pure Love. I saw him, not through Yasmine's traumas or distortions, but as he truly is, a beautiful Soul—a Soul who had once walked so closely with Yasmine, who had played an important role in our journey. I saw him beyond our human suffering, beyond our projections. I saw him through the lens of Spirit. Through Love, not judgement. At the time, I didn't realise that was a moment that freed Yasmine's spirit even more. Timelines collapsed in healing light, because the moment brought forgiveness in the deepest sense of the word. The whole mass carried that vibration: the dissolving of roles, of judgements, of separations. It was a gathering of Souls, honouring one Soul, my father's, who had returned to the Light.

Throughout the mass, my first spiritual mother sang the songs I had grown up with, her eyes fixed on me with so much Love, it felt as if every note was meant for me. Her voice carried me back to childhood, back to innocence, back to faith. On our bench sat Violeta's dad, holding my hand, with Violeta at his side, then my older brother and his wife, who was now carrying their second child. To my right sat my father's loving wife, with her daughter and sister. Further to my left was the woman he married after my mother, her son—my little brother—and her two daughters. Just behind me were my two godmothers, who had always held me like true mothers throughout my life. Everyone was united as one. Old grudges didn't matter, blame lost purpose, holding to the past was just another illusion. We were all there together—present, in the eternal now.

The brave priest, the same who celebrated my mother's memory, ended his homily with words of Love, Compassion, and Forgiveness, and then my fourteen-year-old brother took the stage. In tears, he read a letter to our father, remembering how he would come watch him play sports. Then, to everyone's surprise, my older brother decided to speak, reflecting on all that he had learned from our dad—how he had learned to be a loving father, breaking away from traditions of coldness and absence, but also how he had learned responsibility precisely because our father had not been responsible. It was beautiful. This man, who had once removed our father's name from his own, now spoke of him with Love.

Then it was my turn. I walked to the altar, looked out at the faces of friends, family, and loved ones, and I spoke these words:

The last time I was here in this church was when my mother passed away. I stood up then, when I was twenty-one years old. I was so shy at the time. I realised the other day it was the first speech I ever gave in my life. The first time I used my voice. I wanted to do the same for my father. Here is what I said that day:

"My father was an extremely joyful man, as my older brother said, as my baby brother said. He was a man with many friends, who loved life, who loved to celebrate, who loved colour, sparkle, and everything that came with it. He was a man, like many men, who made many mistakes, also conditioned by our culture. He brought much pain to my mother. They both brought pain to each other.

Over the years, I, especially in the work I do, came to see not only my mother's fragility but my father's too. Sometimes, when we don't heal a trauma, we keep reacting from it, again and again throughout life. Six months before my mother died, my father was imprisoned. Four months ago, he was declared innocent. I see that as a great gift, because he spent the last eighteen years in search of Truth, and in that search, he found himself.

Before he passed, he told me, "I always wanted to be like my father. I looked at him and saw this strong, elegant man, with his horses and all he had, and I wanted to be like him."

We start to see how we carry these insecurities, these fears. All the judgement I once held against my father, I began to release when I looked through what I call the Eagle's Eye, a higher view of life. As human beings, we have such a limited way of seeing what's really happening. We end up looking for someone to blame: He did this, she did that. But blame belongs to no one. Everyone is just doing their best, living within the limits of what they know, showing love the only way they know how. As my older brother said, he gave us so much love as we grew up, so much joy. And so did my mother, who is now with him.

The message I want to leave is this: Before we judge, before we search for someone to blame, may we look at one another with the same compassion we owe to ourselves. May we understand that we all make mistakes, and we all learn. That's why we are here, to learn to go back to Love.

Through everything we lived, as difficult as those years were, I would not be who I am today without my father and my mother, without the examples they gave me, without their values. My father taught me to be an entrepreneur. He taught me to negotiate. My mother taught me authenticity, the artistic side, and how to care for others in another way. I carry many of her values with me to this day.

Some years ago, I forgave my father. It was a process I had to live to understand. After, I realised my mother did not die from "mental illness" but from experiences they both shared, which were no one's fault.

In the end, I had five days with my father in the hospital, and they were a great gift. When I arrived, I saw him in another state of consciousness. He wasn't "better" than anyone else, just as no one here is better than anyone else. We all have the same worth, regardless of our surname, where we were born, the colour of our skin, or our age. He had learned that too.

He asked my older brother for forgiveness. It was one of the most beautiful moments of our lives. He was not in the victim consciousness anymore. Often, we feel like victims of our own lives. When we are victims, we do not take responsibility. For the first time, I saw my father stop seeing himself as a victim of the prison, of my mother's death, of everything that happened.

When he surrendered to Christ, to Our Lady Mary, when he stopped trying to control what would happen, I saw the truth of his Soul, as I see in all of us—an eternal Soul made of Light, Love, and the Creative Power God gives us. We had conversations we had never had before. My father was at peace. I was at peace. We were at peace.

In the last nine years, he met a beautiful woman, married her, and lived a relationship of deep love and partnership. This was a gift from God, because his previous relationships were more complicated, with their challenges and lessons. But this beautiful woman gave him so much Love. With her love, he felt safe enough to let down his insecurities. He was received with care, without judgement. He began to trust life in a new way. And he brought that love to his younger son, to his older son, to me, in his own way, in the way he could.

In all of this, we learn that the pains we hold distort how we see things. Whatever we can do to release those pains—so we see with greater clarity, with less suffering, and with more forgiveness—becomes the path to true freedom.

Forgiveness is the true measure of life. It's not the money in our bank account, the number of friends we have, the parties we go to, or the trips we take. Forgiveness is being able to live in peace. Freedom is living without that weight, without trying to control something we never could control. We live under the illusion that we control life. In the end, my father learned, he surrendered. In that surrender, he found peace before passing. He forgave everyone, including himself. He went in peace. That is why we, too, are at peace.

It may have been early, but he went surrounded by love. We had the support of our doctor and friend. I don't know if he is here, but I want to thank him publicly. He guided us with so much care and gave us comfort in letting my father go naturally, without attachments to what might have been.

He went quickly, because he had already found Love inside himself and all around him.

Thank you."

As my final words echoed through the glass dome of the church, a holy silence fell over the room. For a moment, it was as if time had stopped. There was no shuffling, no whispers, no breath, only Presence.

Then, slowly, I felt it—a wave of Love moving through the space, so tangible it was almost visible. Tears streamed down the faces of old friends, of family members, of people who had come from different parts of my father's life. Even those who once carried resentment seemed softened, touched by something greater than themselves. Then, all at once, I felt my father—not in his body but as Light, expansive, free. His Soul filled the church, wrapping us all in an embrace beyond human arms. It was as if he was saying, *Thank you. Thank you for letting me go in peace. Thank you for remembering me in Love.*

My first spiritual mother came to me and said, "Wow, you have the gift of Voice. You just gave a huge, sacred Teaching."

She knew through her heart who I'd become. Someone who met me as a young girl now saw me fully embodied.

I looked around and saw everyone united—ex-wives, siblings, godmothers, children, friends. All sitting side by side. No separation. No battles. Just Love.

And I knew: This was his last gift to us. His passing was not an ending. It was a generational healing. It was Love in action. This is true radical Forgiveness.

It was the sealing of my becoming and the awakening of true freedom.

I am Aiyahla.

This is just the beginning.

PART 3

QUESTIONS OF FREEDOM WITH AIYAHLA

In this part, beloved reader, we will share with you the questions we often receive in our Free Free workshops. These are not random questions; they are the ones that open doors, that invite you to dive deeper into the sixteen truths of freedom.

Sometimes, a single question carries the power to shift a lifetime of misunderstanding. It can shine light into a corner of your heart that you didn't even know was in the dark. So, for each Truth, we will answer the questions most people carry silently within themselves. Our hope is that these reflections will help you not only understand the Truths with your mind but feel them with your heart and, most importantly, live them in your own life.

THE SIXTEEN TRUTHS OF FREEDOM

1. **You have a direct connection to Source, God, Goddess, Oneness, the Creator,** as you are part of it. Therefore, you need no intermediaries, as in presence, you find God within you.

2. **What you believe through your human senses is the lower mind's perspective of reality, not the Truth.** Discernment allows you to honour others' beliefs and limitations without feeling attacked or making judgements or assumptions that cause you suffering.

3. **Truth is Light, and Light is conscious awareness, true Knowledge, and Clarity,** known through the Eagle's Eye, the higher mind, and rarely understood by human logic, or your lower mind.

4. **You are Love.** Live life and make decisions through Love, not fear, since Love is the only truth. Love reunites what fear has fragmented and distorted into further separation.

5. **You are a Powerful Creator.** Every thought, emotion, imagination, and action creates your reality, as you are God within. Your creation is the fruit of your level of frequency.

6. **You are already whole and never alone.** We are interconnected beings, connected to the field of Oneness, anything else is an illusion of separation.

7. **Know you are as worthy and significant as every other being.** Having self-esteem gives you Clarity and grounds you in Love, the only true protection you need.

8. **Trauma creates distortions and addictions**, forming loops that are not true based on a memory. Even if they feel real, they are not in the now. When you acknowledge this, you start having Clarity to heal these patterns through Love.

9. **The feminine is Love, creative, giving and receiving. The masculine is Light, wisdom, planning and action.** Everything else is a traumatic distortion that needs Light and Love.

10. **Judgement is a defence mechanism. Transform it into compassion.** Judgement distorts your vision and creates karma. Compassion aligns you with Divine Justice, restoring balance through Love, not fear.

11. **Forgive everyone and yourself.** No matter what has happened, you have no one to blame. Forgiveness dissolves karmic loops and liberates you from the victim story, returning you to your inner power and true essence: freedom.

12. **Trust that everything is unfolding for your highest good.** Keep your heart open, be grateful, and allow the magic to reveal itself.

13. **Stop predicting your future based on your past. The only moment that truly exists is the eternal now.** Trying to predict the future keeps you bound to old beliefs and closes the door to miracles and the quantum field of limitless possibilities.

14. **Release attachment to external power.** True power lives within, and it is your creative force, the artist within you.

15. **Surrender in eternal gratitude and let go of controlling outcomes**. Control is an illusion; when you surrender and become grateful, you align your life with your highest potential and Soul Truth.

16. **Always use your gifts to serve others.** When service is for the greater good, not just personal gain, abundance flows. Integrity is what aligns your gifts with your eternal flame.

TRUTH 1

You have a direct connection to Source, God, Goddess, Oneness, the Creator, as you are part of it. Therefore, you need no intermediaries, as in presence, you find God within you.

Question: If I start growing my consciousness, and start my freedom journey, will I be betraying my religion?

Aiyahla: Religions are institutions, and institutions are human-made. Your connection to God does not depend on them. We can call God *Source*, as we have all sourced from it; therefore, we are Divine beings in the mirror of God. God is not a being, it is a field of Divine Love, Light, and Creative Power, just as you are. Within your heart, you carry an eternal flame that also contains Love, Light, and Creative Power, just like God. All religions were created as a way of understanding our relationship with the unknown, as routes to God, Goddess, the Creator, Source, Higher Power, Presence or however you choose to name this power, and therefore routes to our own divinity. Each religion is simply a different perspective of the Truth, shaped by cultural conditionings. No religion is better than another. They each hold fragments of the Truth but not the whole Truth.

As time went by and the masculine rose to external power, separating itself from the feminine, humanity experienced what we call *separation*. Separation is the traumatic experience of the masculine overpowering the feminine out of fear of its fluid ways of being. As with any trauma, perception became distorted, and the Truth was lost. The feminine ways of connecting to God—through our interconnection with nature, the flow of the river, intuition, and Love—seemed too dangerous because they could not be controlled.

This is partially how religions came to be: as a reaction to what cannot be controlled. Formed through the lens of separation, they were built through the wounded masculine within all of humanity. The expressions of the wounded masculine can be seen as control, separation, oppression, violence, insensitivity, and the constant need for external power. Religions, therefore, became structures that attempted to control our connection to God, this eternal Presence within us, through institutions. Each culture created its own version of this connection, based on its conditionings, as a reflection of separation consciousness and the fear of losing power.

When you understand that the Truth is that God is Oneness, you also see that separation is not the Truth. Religions are simply the way humanity tried to interpret, translate, structure our connection to God. However, through the higher mind, through the Eagle's Eye, we can See that there is no need to blame religion. We can simply understand that for thousands of years, religions reflected the state of consciousness humanity was in. Therefore, you are not betraying your religion by connecting directly to God. You cannot betray something that is a perspective. You don't need to abandon your religion as well. You will simply see through what is Truth and what is perception. And within all religions there is so much beauty as well.

Question: I stopped believing in God, because how can we live in a world that has so much suffering?

Aiyahla: You don't need to believe in God for God to exist. God exists beyond our beliefs. Beliefs come from our lower mind, our human senses; therefore, they are limited by what logic can understand. Beliefs need proof. God doesn't.

Source, Creator, Allah, Oneness, All There Is, Divine Presence, the Infinite, the Beloved, Great Mystery, Spirit. The name we give carries cultural conditioning and may even be tied to a traumatic memory you hold. If the word *God* feels heavy or triggering, try changing the name. Let's call it *Presence* for now.

Presence helps us understand two very important concepts: Free Will and Creation. Since we are Presence, we also have the power to co-create our reality through our thoughts, feelings, imagination, will, and actions. When we create through fear or when we make decisions from fear, we create more separation, and therefore more suffering, not only for others but also for ourselves. As Presence, or the Field of Life, has no opinion of what is good or bad. Whatever you believe is True and you think, feel, imagine the Field responds.

What we create, we experience. For centuries, humanity has created distortions out of fear. But when we understand that fear is not the Truth, that fear is only a survival mechanism of the ego, the lower mind, we can dissolve it. We dissolve fear through Love and Light, through raising our consciousness into Presence.

When we live in Presence, we start changing our reality. We become Presence itself, connected to God through the stillness of our breath and the beat of our heart.

So, if you feel far from God, begin simply: Pause for a moment. Stop doing, stop thinking, stop interpreting, and just breathe. Take three deep breaths. Notice your heartbeat. Feel the peace of the present moment. As you do so, you will begin to remember the Truth: You are Presence within.

Question: Can I still continue to be a devotee of my religion and be spiritual by raising my consciousness?

Aiyahla: Absolutely. You don't need to abandon your faith to raise your consciousness. You will simply begin to see through your faith what is illusion and what is Truth. As your heart opens wide, you won't judge it. You will embrace it through Love, through compassion, through forgiveness. Religion is not the enemy. Nothing is. So don't blame your religion. Instead, understand it through the Eagle's Eye, your higher mind.

Therefore, there is nothing to abandon if you choose to remain part of it. Also, there is nothing wrong if you decide to drift away. The key is *why* you decide to stay or leave. Is the choice being made through fear or any expression of fear, such as guilt or shame? If so, you are making a decision based on a distortion (a memory, a trauma), not from Truth.

Base your decision on Love. When you do, you are allowing the highest potential of your Soul to guide you, through your heart.

As many religions speak of *sin*, many of us feel we are sinning if we decide to leave our religion. However, sin is simply another illusion of separation. There is no sin, only the law of karma, or the Golden Rule: What you do, you will receive. If you act through suffering and this causes pain to yourself or to others, you are not condemned. You are simply in the process of dissolving a memory, a trauma, by learning from it and bringing Love back to it through the process of forgiveness.

You are not a sinner. You are not to be blamed. You have nothing to fear. You are here to learn. That is the purpose of incarnation. The more we learn, the less suffering we experience, individually and collectively. For as we raise our own consciousness, we raise the consciousness of the world. This is the evolution all of us are going through.

Question: Some of my spiritual teachers wanted me to remain connected to them in a way that prevented me from growing beyond them. I struggle to know how to move forward without feeling ungrateful, given all that they gave me.

Aiyahla: The time of gurus and blind following is over. This belonged to an old paradigm in which we were conditioned to believe that we needed someone to intermediate our connection to God. The idea that only a priest, a master, or a chosen few could access the Divine is part of that outdated structure. When we say you need no intermediaries to connect with Presence, it means you have a direct relationship with Source. Your eternal flame is God within you. This does not mean you cannot have teachers. Teachers exist to support your remembering, never to replace your power or override your unique connection to Source. So yes—be grateful for your teacher. She or he helped you open your heart, dissolve layers of fear, and learn to discern what was heart and what was ego. But if you feel ready to take the next steps of your journey without them, gratitude does not require you to stay. Gratitude does not require captivity. True teachers never try to control you, demand loyalty to themselves, or bind you through fear. They serve your remembrance, not your dependency. Every authentic teacher understands that their role is to walk beside you for a time—whether that time is short or long. You should never stay out of fear. A teacher's true role is to help you reclaim your power, not to take it from you. Remember: even when you are working with a teacher, you always have a direct connection with God. Your inner guidance is the highest authority you will ever have, and it is the one you are meant to follow. It is natural—and even sacred—to reach a point where what once nourished you no longer carries you forward. This does not erase what you received. The teachings remain within you, alive and integrated. Growth does not mean rejection; it means completion. Sometimes teachers, like all humans, are still working through their own fears—fears of being left, of becoming irrelevant, of losing purpose. When this happens, attachment can replace Truth. But this is not yours to fix. You are not responsible for carrying another person's unfinished work. You do not betray a teacher by becoming more of who you are. And sometimes becoming more of who you are means outgrowing a teacher. In truth, your expansion is often the very reason you met them in the first place. The greatest honour you can offer a teacher is to live what you were shown, not to remain bound to the form through which it arrived. You can leave with Love. You can bow in gratitude and continue walking. What is real will remain. What was meant only for a season will fall away gently. Trust that your Soul knows when it is time to move forward.

TRUTH 2 AND 3

2. **What you believe through your human senses is the lower mind's perspective of reality, not the Truth.** Discernment allows you to honour others' beliefs and limitations without feeling attacked or making judgements or assumptions that cause you suffering.

3. **Truth is Light, and Light is conscious awareness, true Knowledge, and Clarity,** known through the Eagle's Eye, the higher mind, and rarely understood by human logic, or your lower mind.

Question: When I see a man beating his wife, is it not the Truth?

Aiyahla: What you are seeing *is* a truth—but it is not the whole Truth. It is a human truth, a concrete reality witnessed through the senses: a man is using violence, and a woman is being harmed. That suffering is real. It is not imagined, symbolic, or subjective. Violence causes pain, fear, and trauma, and that must never be denied or minimised.

At the same time, what you are seeing is still a partial perspective of a much larger Truth. The human mind naturally interprets events through what it can immediately perceive. From this level, we see an act, we name it right or wrong, victim or perpetrator—and this discernment is necessary. Violence is wrong. Harm is not love. And the person committing the act is responsible for stopping and for healing the causes within themselves. Eagle's Eye awareness does not contradict this—it includes it, and then sees further.

From a wider perspective, Truth is not only the visible act, but also the unseen conditions that led to it. There is the lived reality of the woman and the harm she is experiencing. There is the inner world of the man, who may be acting from unhealed trauma, fear, or learned violence. And there is the collective field—the family, culture, and systems that may have normalised domination, silence, or abuse across generations.

Seeing this does not excuse the violence. Abuse is a profound distortion of Love and a violation of freedom. The man is fully responsible for his actions and for seeking healing. Understanding *why* harm occurs never makes harm acceptable. It simply helps us understand how cycles of violence are created and how they can be ended. When we remain only in judgement, we often become locked into a rigid frame: one person as only an abuser, the other as only a victim. While this reflects part of reality, it can also limit our capacity to transform it. Judgement alone tends to keep consciousness trapped in separation—where pain is met only with more pain, and fear with more fear. Compassion, when grounded in clarity, does something different. It does not deny the woman's suffering, and it does not remove responsibility from the man. It allows us to see that harm is often born from harm—that hurt people can hurt others when they are unconscious—and that cycles of violence continue precisely because they are never truly healed. From this state of compassionate clarity, we do not collapse into passivity. We act. We protect. We intervene. We support the victim. And we also hold the deeper intention of ending the cycle, not just punishing its latest expression.

Love is not permissive. Love is not naive. Love is the highest intelligence. It is the frequency that can hold accountability and compassion at the same time. Anger and judgement, even when understandable, often perpetuate the same violence they seek to end. Compassion, anchored in Truth, brings Light into places where fear has ruled for generations. And let me be clear: violence is never justified. This way of seeing is not about excusing harm, it is about making healing possible. Only by addressing both the visible act and the invisible roots can we truly break these patterns. Radical forgiveness does not erase responsibility; it dissolves the chains that keep violence repeating itself across lives, families, and nations. This is how we honour both truths: the truth of what happened, and the Truth that can set us free.

Question: My mother believes women shouldn't work, and because I am not married and have no children, she thinks me shameful.

Aiyahla: Beliefs aren't Truth. Your mother's belief is simply a perspective, shaped by the social conditioning she grew up with, perhaps through religion, her family traditions, or the collective beliefs humanity followed for centuries.

In order not to feel affected by her assumptions, you must see them through a different lens. Every belief that carries negative judgement is formed by the lower mind, our human senses, limited by what it has experienced. It is not the Truth of the Soul but an illusion of the ego created by past or present wounds. The way she perceives you is not a reflection of you but a projection of herself.

It can only touch you, or hurt you, if at some level, you also believe it to be true. When she calls you shameful, use this as an opportunity to look within and ask: *What memory within me makes me believe what she says could be true?* The moment you bring Light to this memory, it begins to lose its power. You can then see through Love, not through distortion.

Beliefs are not only created by culture, they can also be passed through DNA or carried within the spirit from past lives. When we bring them into conscious awareness, what was in shadow is illuminated and, through Love, reunited into Oneness. When you do this, you reclaim the power you gave to that memory, or to your mother, and you can finally see with Clarity: *You are not shameful. You are worthy. Whether you are married or not, whether you have children or not, whether you work or not. Allow yourself to follow your Soul path authentically.*

From this Clarity, compassion naturally arises. You can see that her belief is only hurting her. Even if she continues to hold it, you don't need to feel attacked or to try to change her if she is not open to changing. This is where discernment comes in: allowing her to have her beliefs, while you keep yours, without giving away your power to her ever again.

Question: What about the sacred texts, aren't they true?

Aiyahla: All sacred texts carry fragments of the Truth, from the perspective of the time in history, the location, and the person who wrote them. Therefore, they cannot be the fullness of Truth, only perspectives of it. This doesn't mean they don't carry sparks of Truth; it means we must use our Eagle's Eye and open heart to further interpret them.

Most sacred texts are also incomplete. In the case of the Bible, for example, many writings were deliberately left out, especially those that would have challenged the structures of power at the time. These included texts written by women, as for the past two to three thousand years, women were often perceived as inferior to men. We must not blame those who excluded them, as they were acting from the level of consciousness they knew. However, we must learn to read these texts beyond the surface of our human senses. We are not meant to take every word literally but to look with the Eagle's Eye, so we can perceive the higher Truth within them.

For instance, the Gospel of Mary Magdalene—discovered in the late nineteenth century in a fifth-century papyrus codex in Egypt, with earlier fragments dating back to the second century—offers a very different perspective on what took place in the time of Yeshua, Jesus, the Ascended Master Christ. In it, Mary shares intimate teachings of inner freedom and spiritual authority that were silenced in the canonical texts. What we read in the Bible instead reflects the perceptions of the male disciples, each carrying their own version of events. These are perspectives of truth, but not the fullness of Divine Truth.

The same can be seen in other traditions. In Hinduism, the Vedas were followed by later commentaries like the *Manusmriti*, which imposed rigid hierarchies, including the subjugation of women, though this was not the essence of the earliest spiritual hymns. In Buddhism, early councils debated which sutras to include or exclude, leaving aside many teachings of female disciples. In Islam, variations of hadith collections show how interpretation shaped practice, sometimes contradicting the essence of the Qur'an's message of compassion and balance.

This reminds us that all sacred texts are lenses, shaped by culture, time, and human limitation, yet still carry sparks of Eternal Truth. Our task is not to discard them but to read them with discernment, seeing beyond distortion and listening for the higher voice of Love that speaks through them all.

Let's look at an excerpt from the Bible as an example: "Let the woman learn in silence with all subjection" (1 Timothy 2:11–12). Is this the Truth? The Manusmriti, in Hindu law, declares, "A woman must never be independent." Is this the Truth? Then there's the Qur'an verse: "Men are the protectors and maintainers of women" (Qur'an 4:34). Is this the Truth? From the perspective of the lower mind, bound to the culture of its time, these verses reflect the need to maintain order in patriarchal societies. They are fragments of a historical truth but are not the Eternal Truth of Spirit. Through the Eagle's Eye, the vision of higher mind, we see beyond the words into the deeper essence. We recognise that God, or Source, created all beings equal in worth, Love, Power, and Light. Any teaching that diminishes one, or puts one above another, is not the fullness of Truth but a distortion born of fear, separation, and human limitation.

The Eagle's Eye allows us to hold compassion for those who wrote these words, to understand the consciousness of their time, and, at the same time, to see with Clarity that the eternal message hidden beneath is Love, Unity, and Liberation. When we read in this way, no text can bind us to limitation, because the higher Truth always shines through: we are all Presence, all Divine, and all Free.

TRUTH 4

You are Love. Live life and make decisions through Love, not fear, since Love is the only truth. Love reunites what fear has fragmented and distorted into further separation.

Question: When I was young, I was bullied at school, and I simply hate myself. I look in the mirror and I see my disgusting body. How can you say I am Love if no one has ever loved me? The only thing that makes me feel less pain is when I hurt myself.

Aiyahla: The bullying you experienced at school hurt you deeply, and that pain left a mark. It became a memory in your bodies and over time, that memory shaped how you began to see yourself. This does not mean there is something wrong with you. It simply means something painful happened at a time when you were still forming your sense of self. Experiences like bullying, or any form of emotional or physical harm, do not change the Truth of who you are, even though they may temporarily veil it. Beneath every wound, your essence remains the same. You are alive, you are here, and because of that alone, you are Love—part of the same creative life force that moves through all beings.

When the bullying occurred, your ego was still developing, doing its best to protect you and make sense of the world. In its effort to keep you safe, it stored the experience as a belief. Over time, that belief quietly shaped how you perceived yourself and others. Every belief acts like a lens, filtering reality, often without our awareness. When someone hurts you and you don't yet have the knowledge to see through a different lens, two things happen. First, you may feel attacked and powerless, as though what is happening defines your worth. In that moment, it can feel as if your power has been taken from you. Second, without anyone consciously intending it, the other person may be projecting their own unresolved pain onto you, while also awakening a memory within you that is asking to be seen and healed. This does not mean you caused the harm, nor that you deserved it. It simply describes how unconscious pain often meets unconscious pain.

Your ego, in all of this, is not your enemy. It is a mechanism designed to protect you, to prevent future hurt by predicting danger based on the past. When the ego leads, life is navigated through fear and memory. When the Soul leads, when you see through what I call the Eagle's Eye, the ego gently steps back and supports rather than controls. The reason you may feel disconnected from Love is not because Love is absent within you, but because an old belief learned through pain is still speaking louder than your essence. Until that belief is met with awareness and compassion, it may continue to repeat itself through experiences, relationships, or self-judgment, not as punishment, but as an invitation to heal.

This is why you may look at yourself and feel discomfort or rejection, why you may have accepted less than you deserved in relationships, or why hurting yourself might have momentarily felt like relief from the unbearable ache of not feeling lovable. These responses are not failures; they are signals of a wound longing for gentleness. The loop continues only because the pain has not yet been met with enough safety and love to dissolve. And the way out does not require force or perfection. It begins very simply.

Pause. Breathe. Notice that with every breath, something greater is sustaining you. Life is meeting you, moment by moment. As you inhale, receive that gift. As you exhale, quietly say to yourself, "I am here." Even for a few seconds, this brings you into Presence. In that brief moment of presence, your heart opens just enough to interrupt the old pattern. You may not feel dramatic change, but something softens. Something remembers.

Return to this as often as you need. Gently. Without pressure. Each time you pause and breathe, you allow the beliefs shaped by pain to loosen their grip. You begin to feel yourself not as the wounded child or the self you criticise, but as the simple, living Presence beneath it all. Step by step, breath by breath, this is how remembrance happens. This is how healing unfolds through the freedom journey. Not trying to be perfect, but by meeting yourself with Love. And in doing so, you begin the journey back to the Truth that has never left you: you are whole, you are worthy, and you are Love. And remember, you can always seek help. There is nothing wrong, or weak about asking for help.

Question: How can I be loved if I cannot provide for my family anymore?

Aiyahla: Many men learn early that love is connected to what they do, not to who they truly are. This is a cultural conditioning of the patriarchy. The patriarchy is the current system the world operates from, in which the wounded masculine has set the rules, hurting not only women but also men, children, and all beings, as well as our beautiful planet, due to the imbalance it created.

The belief system says that when men stop being able to provide, for any reason, they are not lovable. This is why many men even commit suicide after going bankrupt or losing their jobs. But let's dive into this through the Eagle's Eye. You are not what you do. You are Love, independent of whether you provide for your family or not. The fact that you cannot provide right now does not change this Truth, even if you feel the pressure of your family, or of society, or of yourself to do so.

Let's look at why your family might be pressuring you. Maybe they are scared they won't be able to survive, so they are in their ego, survival mode, making judgements that are not true. Or maybe they are not even pressuring you, maybe you only feel the pressure and assume they will not love you. Can you see, beloved? The belief you carry, that you must provide to be loved, is simply a perception. Once you understand that your true worth is in who you are, not in what you do, you can shift this belief into true inner power.

As long as you give your power away to the belief that you are not lovable because you can't provide, you remain in victim consciousness, feeling as if life is happening *to* you, instead of *for* you. Try to look deeper: *In what moment of my life did I create the belief that to be loved, I must provide?* Also ask: *What lesson am I learning right now by not being able to provide?*

Everything that happens in life happens for our greater good, never for our detriment, even if it feels frightening in the moment. Perhaps you are not able to provide right now precisely because you need to learn that Love is not about how much you earn or what you can pay for but about the beautiful Soul that you are. Ask yourself: *What is the learning I am being gifted in this moment, through this experience?*

When you do this, you take responsibility for your life and start reclaiming your power. The more you feel empowered—no longer a victim of circumstance—the more Light and Love you bring into your life, and the easier it becomes to shift your state. Whether or not you provide again will not define you. What matters is that you will no longer identify with it, and therefore you will be free.

TRUTH 5

You are a Powerful Creator. Every thought, emotion, imagination, and action creates your reality, as you are God within. Your creation is the fruit of your level of frequency.

Question: I have a fear of being abused, but I am not sure I have been abused in my childhood. This fear affects my life. Am I creating this?

Aiyahla: When we carry the fear of being abused—especially physical or sexual abuse—it may have occurred in childhood, but not necessarily. Sometimes the memory of abuse is passed down through three generations if those before us experienced it. Or we may carry the imprint from another lifetime. Either way, we feel the fear psychologically, as if it could happen again—and the effect on our lives remains the same.

The fear is there to show that something must come to Light. It first needs to be acknowledged, as every thought, emotion, and aspect of our imagination is in our field for a reason, either to heal or to create. But if you continue thinking and feeling it, you are creating it—because we create through our thoughts, emotions, imagination, and energetic frequency. The vibration of fear is low, and when we dwell in it, we attract experiences that mirror that energy back to us.

For every woman, the sacral chakra is the seat of her greatest creations: from birthing new life to creating work, relationships, and visions. When she suffers abuse, or even holds the fear of abuse, she unconsciously closes the sacral chakra to protect herself, as her womb is even more sensitive than her heart because it is where the switch of the feminine lives. This blocks her creative energy. It can lead to complications during pregnancy or childbirth, and can create some level of dullness in her body or eyes, a quieting of her intuition, and an instability in her emotions. This imbalance often unconsciously attracts abusive relationships, not as punishment but as mirrors to help her remember, acknowledge, and bring the wound to Light, as what stays in the darkness continues to create distorted realities from the unconsciousness.

When she practices radical forgiveness, she not only liberates herself but heals three generations before her and prevents the pattern from continuing after her. Men too, when abused, may close their sacral chakra. They can become numb or desensitised—sometimes even addicted to sex, abusive, or cruel toward others. Just like women, they need acknowledgment of the wound and radical forgiveness to be free.

Radical forgiveness does not mean excusing harm, nor excusing abuse. It means liberating the pattern so it no longer repeats. Forgiveness is when we bring Love back to a place that has been fragmented and filled with pain from a past experience. Abuse separates. Love unites.

The feminine within all of us, in women and men, is Love. When the feminine cannot fill the masculine with her Love, harmony is lost in working and personal relationships. This is why there is so much abuse in the world.

I cannot say with certainty what may be happening in your life, but I invite you to explore it, not to find someone to blame but to listen to your body. We can only free what we acknowledge. When you bring the wound into the Light, you also bring in Love. In doing so, you free yourself—and with you, generations past and future.

Question: I think about having an incredible career. I dream about it, imagine it, but it doesn't happen. Why am I not creating it if I am a Powerful Creator, as we are God within?

Aiyahla: In the human experience, we carry the spark of God. Therefore, we carry the power to co-create through the field of Oneness, not through the limits of our human senses. The field of Oneness is the interconnected field we all source from. It is pure Love, Light, and Creative Power—the same we carry in our eternal flames. Every being carries them, from the beautiful mama trees to the birds in the sky.

If you are creating from the ego, it means you are creating from fear, survival, or limiting beliefs, and your creation will reflect that vibration. The ego might think it wants a house, a marriage, or a successful career. But when creation comes from the ego, it is still tied to illusion, conditioned stories, and old patterns, to cause and effect, time and space. The question to ask is: *Is this truly the desire of my Soul, or simply the conditioning of my ego?* Is my frequency, words, actions, thoughts, aligned with my heart's desire? As God is a field, beloved, and it has no opinion, so it will co-create what you vibrate.

When the Truth of your Soul aligns with your heart and will, everything flows. But if there are limiting beliefs, they act like locks on the doors to higher vibrations and creations. You will only create as much as your beliefs permit. This is why the first step of freedom is acknowledgement. You need to examine your belief systems. Often, hidden trauma or conditioning convinces you that you are unworthy or undeserving. Until this is acknowledged, you will continue to create from that frequency.

When the lesson is integrated, the limitation dissolves instantly, and you rise into a new frequency of limitless creation. Less fear means higher possibilities.

We also have to remember karma. Karma is not punishment. It is the Divine law of cause and effect. It ensures that whatever you still hold unconsciously will return to you as an experience, so you can see it, learn from it, and finally free yourself. Or karma can also be released through conscious exploration of is held on your unconscious and released through Love, the freedom journey and expanding your conscious. You don't necessarily need to live through something to release it.

Sometimes, through conscious exploration of your beliefs and patterns, you realise you don't even want what you thought you wanted. This has happened to me many times along my becoming. This is why expanding consciousness is the key to true fulfilment, because much of what we think we want brings no joy when we finally get it. Then the ego just wants more. Only the Soul knows what aligns best to our journey. However, there is always free will. We can make our journey harder when we create from the ego—believing we need what we truly don't—and spend longer learning the same lessons. Or we can create from the heart, consciously, so that what we manifest aligns with our true nature. Either way, you are creating. It all depends on what frequency and level of consciousness you create with. Your mind is a Powerful Creator, especially when aligned with the heart. This is when the magic happens, and miracles start occurring beyond time and space, without logic.

Question: Why is art the language of the Soul?

Aiyahla: Art is the language of the Soul because it bypasses the ego. When we allow creativity to flow without fear interfering, we move beyond the analytical, controlling mind and access a deeper intelligence within us. Art speaks directly to the right side of the brain, the intuitive, imaginal, and relational side, which is the side that connects us to the Divine, to Presence, and to the field beyond time. This is why art can reach places beyond logic. It allows truth to surface without needing to be justified, explained, or defended.

When creativity flows freely, hidden memories begin to emerge—memories stored not only in the mind, but in the body, the nervous system, the lineage, and the Soul. Art gives these memories a way to move. And the first step of healing is always acknowledgement. What we deny remains trapped. What we allow to be seen begins to soften.

As pain comes into awareness, anger often follows. This is natural. Anger is not a flaw; it is fear and pain asking to be released. The question is not whether anger arises, but how we choose to express it. There are unhealthy expressions: calling the person who hurt you and releasing rage onto them, which may create momentary relief but no learning; or numbing the pain through substances, distractions, or avoidance. In these cases, the lesson remains unintegrated, and life will bring it back again, until it is truly met.

Then there are healthy expressions—dance, painting, singing, writing, running, breathing, meditation, walking in nature. These practices move emotion through the body rather than projecting it outward. When you create, you allow anger to flow without harming yourself or others. And in that movement, something alchemical happens: Love enters the process. Love does not deny anger; it holds it. And when Love meets anger, fear begins to dissolve. This is when transformation occurs. Anger no longer fuels blame or separation. It matures into compassion. Where you can have Clarity of what hurt you, but not be affected by it, while keeping your heart open.

Here is a deeper truth: if a memory is alive in you—whether from this lifetime, a past lifetime, or your ancestral line—it is yours to release. And it cannot be released through suppression, judgement, or retaliation. It can only be released through compassion and forgiveness. Forgiveness is not the excusing of harm. Forgiveness is the liberation of your Soul from the repetition of pain. When you attack back, you remain bound to the wound. When you forgive, you step out of the cycle. And art, is one of the most powerful vehicles for this alchemical process of freedom to happen.

TRUTH 6

You are already whole and never alone. We are interconnected beings, connected to the field of Oneness, anything else is an illusion of separation.

Question: I have a big family, many friends, and I still feel lonely. I don't understand why? What can I do to stop feeling so alone?

Aiyahla: It is never about the number of people we have in our lives. You could be surrounded by a family of twenty, have hundreds of friends, or even seven billion people by your side, and still feel alone. Loneliness is not the absence of others; it is the absence of connection with yourself.

When you are fragmented inside, when parts of your heart have been shut down by pain or fear, no external company can fill the emptiness. The feeling of loneliness is an illusion, but a very convincing one, because it arises from those fragments. In one lifetime, we create thousands of bubbles of separation, painful experiences that turn into memories, each surrounded by fear, if we do not become more conscious. These bubbles are aspects of ourselves that disconnect us from the fullness of our being. That is why you feel lonely—because you are missing aspects of yourself that are waiting to return home to your wholeness.

Here is the Truth: You are never truly alone. Your Soul is always whole, because you are part of the field of Oneness. You are God within, and you have a spiritual team that never leaves your side. You may forget they are there when you disconnect from your heart, but their presence is constant. However, they can't interfere if you don't ask for help, as you have free will.

To dissolve loneliness, you must begin the journey of self-discovery and healing. Every fragment that is acknowledged, loved, and reintegrated through consciousness and forgiveness brings you back into wholeness. This is what it means to heal: to return to Love. As you bring Love to what has been fragmented, the illusion of separation dissolves. Then, even when you are physically alone, you will not feel lonely.

Relationships can help in this process; sometimes a profound connection with another person acts as a mirror that awakens the Love inside your own heart. However, if you give your power away to them, relying on them to take away your loneliness, you create attachment, not wholeness. That attachment will only create more pain if they leave, because your sense of completeness was placed outside of you. True wholeness cannot come from another.

The way to stop feeling lonely isn't by collecting more friends, lovers, or distractions. It's by turning inwards with courage and embracing the parts of yourself that feel abandoned. Self-love is the medicine. Also, you can ask for help. Ask your spiritual team, ask God, ask the angels to show you the way back to yourself.

Practical steps can begin very simply. Spend time with yourself—two hours, one afternoon, a day. Do something you enjoy, sit in silence, journal, walk in nature, dance in your room, meditate, enjoy your own company. At first, it may feel uncomfortable, because solitude brings you face to face with the pain you've been running from. That confrontation is the beginning of your reconnection.

Do not believe the story that solitude is for lonely or unworthy people, or that your value is measured by how many friends you have or how many followers you collect on social media. That is another illusion sold by a world that profits from your disconnection. True solitude is a gift. It strips away the noise, the distractions, the consumerist escapes. It brings you back to yourself, where you no longer need to buy, prove, or perform to feel whole.

When you are whole, life itself becomes different. You value truth, deep connection, and experiences that expand your Spirit. You realise that joy is found in Presence, most often in nature, where Love is unconditional, or with someone who sees you for who you are, not the character you have been living. These are sacred relationships. Sometimes they don't come from our blood family. You begin to form a chosen family.

So the next time you feel lonely, go sit by a tree. Place your back on her trunk, send your heart flame to her heart flame, and you will feel her embrace. You will feel how she sees you, how she holds you without condition. This is the gift of Oneness.

Loneliness is only the call of your Soul asking you to come home, and home is always within.

Question: I always feel I have to be in a relationship. I even prefer being in a bad relationship than having no relationship at all. How can I stop this pattern?

Aiyahla: This is fairly common in the world we live in today, as we, especially women, are fed the belief that we are only whole when we are in a relationship. This is simply a cultural conditioning created by the media, most religions, and most cultures. What we need to understand is that it is a conditioning and is therefore a human creation, something created by our human senses, not the Truth.

This illusion makes you feel you lack wholeness when you don't have someone to complete you, keeping you trapped in a cycle of painful relationships, almost like an addiction. This is why you tolerate relationships that are not good for you or are not fulfilling you. Then you probably look for another that might fulfil you more. However, the only one that can truly make you whole is yourself.

Relationships are mostly only healthy when both parties are first whole within themselves and meet in this state, which is still quite rare, because to be in this state, you must have gone through a long healing process. Some relationships can also be healthy when you acknowledge together that you are both healing. This requires open conversation, honesty, boundaries, and self-love, so you can both give and receive and be more present instead of acting from past wounds, projecting fear onto each other.

You will only stop the pattern of going from one relationship to the next when you recognise this is a pattern. When you do, you can look within to find the trauma, or the fragmented part of you—the memory that is covered in fear, making you feel fragmented instead of whole—and embrace it with Love and forgiveness so that memory dissolves and that part of you can come back to your wholeness.

The human spirit, feminine and masculine, gets fragmented, but the Soul never does. It is in the human spirit that we carry all our fragmented parts and beliefs, such as the one you described. The belief that you are only whole when you are with someone is a belief created based on a memory that is held in your spiritual body, the body that surrounds all your other bodies. The spiritual journey is simply the journey of liberating all these beliefs so our Soul Nature can lead instead of our ego, as yours has been leading your life. The more conscious you become, the freer you will be.

TRUTH 7

Know you are as worthy and significant as every other being. Having self-esteem gives you Clarity and grounds you in Love, the only true protection you need.

Question: My son is having problems at school and is trying to find friends online. I am worried because he is only fifteen and has low self-esteem.

Aiyahla: This is a very important question, as many young boys are looking for belonging online at this age. With the change in hormones and the pressures of being a certain way physically and emotionally, boys are pushed into their own myth of perfection. When they don't fit in—whether because they're smaller or less muscular than other boys, don't enjoy the same sports, or are more emotional than what boys are expected to be—they begin to feel unworthy, as though something is wrong with them. This is absolutely not true, but it feels real, because of the cultural conditioning.

When this happens, boys can hide, because they start losing their self-esteem, which is, in other words, their self-worth. The way we esteem ourselves drives our belief system and the choices we make from there on. Before we start looking into your boy's online experience, ask yourself: *Is there any pattern at home that he learned this from?* Don't ask this to blame yourself, your partner, or close family; instead, ask it as a way to bring consciousness to the dynamic. If it's not at home, ask yourself if this dynamic is in your ancestry line. These are just compassionate questions, never judgement, as judgement only creates more separation. What your son needs right now is Love, because only Love can support him in reclaiming his power and self-esteem.

When we feel low self-worth, what we are really feeling is a lack of belonging. As humans, we need to feel we belong as much as we need to drink water. Sometimes, we don't feel we belong with our friends at school, or don't feel this sense of belonging in our own home, not because there is no Love but because we might be needing to express something we don't feel completely comfortable expressing at home. Your son might be scared of judgement. In these cases, the online world becomes the place where he can create a whole new character and look for his tribe.

What we need to be aware of today is that there are many online spaces that feed off boys with low self-esteem, leading them into extreme groups. This is why it is so important to help him navigate the online world with more security. You have to mirror to him his own self-worth, as well as teach him critical thinking skills so he can discern if there is manipulation, false information, or any ulterior motive in what he receives when he is talking with people online. These practical skills will help him navigate the internet more safely, but only his self-esteem will make him trust his interpretations.

So, at the same time, try spending time with your son openly, without judgement. Show him he is worthy by treating yourself as worthy. If you don't speak up, he might mirror that in his own behaviour. So start speaking up, for example. Tell him stories of when you were a teenager. Therapy and consciousness practices can also help a lot, but in this case, you and your partner are his biggest references. You have to show him your worth beyond external validation, beyond judgement. If possible, do it with your partner. However, you are an important mirror, independent of your gender.

When we free ourselves, we are also doing this for our children. This is the greatest gift you can give them: to raise your own consciousness so you can teach and inspire them through Love, not through fear.

Question: My daughter loves fashion and is obsessed with following influencers who are very skinny. I recently realised she is bulimic because she started losing too much weight. How can I help her?

Aiyahla: It all starts with her self-worth. When we lack self-worth, we begin comparing ourselves with others, holding onto the illusion that they are better than we are. However, this is not true. This is often a trauma response—rooted in a memory she's carrying—or a cultural conditioning that's very common amongst girls: the belief that they must be thin to be attractive or to fit into the fashion world.

When Yasmine was around twelve, she felt very much like your daughter. She even read about how to lose weight and tried to induce vomiting after eating, but it didn't work for her. So she started taking laxatives after meals so she wouldn't gain weight. She did this not only as a way to look good but as a way to hurt herself, because the pain she was going through at home was too much. With social media today, we have less control over what our children are exposed to, so we as parents must be their mirrors even more strongly.

Sometimes, without realising, we as parents are also mirroring the myth of perfection. Even if it's not through our body size, we might be pressuring ourselves in other ways that they pick up on. It is in our field and unconscious actions. Now is the time for you to look in the mirror as a mother and see if there is anywhere you are too harsh with yourself. Shift that narrative. We have to let go of the myth of perfection. It can feel messy at first, and scary, but it is just a myth. Your daughter is craving authenticity and feeling loved. She is craving to be seen exactly as she is. You have the power to show her that she is worthy exactly as she is—and that her uniqueness is what makes her special, not something to hide or change.

When we become more conscious and heal ourselves, we find the answers within to support our children. We have to feel worthy in order to teach worthiness. They look up to us. If you compare yourself to your friends, she will likely do the same, but perhaps in less safe spaces. In truth, she is crying for attention, to be seen, to be heard. This is why she is trying to validate herself in the same ways other girls validate themselves. But that validation will never be enough, and it can easily become addictive.

Try doing things together—fun, messy things—outside of routine. Try something new. Take her away from the screen. Go on trips together. Also teach her to breathe, to look within. Teach her she is worthy just as she is, that you are worthy just as you are. When we bring Presence through meditation—or dance meditation, if she prefers more movement—you will find ways to begin releasing the need to be perfect, and instead just allow yourselves to *be*. If she enjoys artistic activities, creativity can act as bridge for her subconscious to be let out.

From there, you can begin to bring conscious awareness to what is beneath the need to throw up, the root pain. When you bring Light to it, you can help her heal herself through Love and forgiveness. Forgiveness is an important step as the act of throwing up can cause immense shame that worsens her sense of worth and Love.

Question: I am financially dependent on my husband, as I stopped working when we had kids. I want to go back to work, but I am scared he won't like it and will leave me.

Aiyahla: Many women stop working when they have kids. The first question you need to ask yourself is, was this a conscious decision that came from your heat, did your husband ask you to or did you feel pressured by culture? The fear you are experiencing now could be coming from a memory, or it could be a projection or assumption based on cultural conditioning. When we have a fear, the only way to allow that fear to dissolve is by confronting it, not by hiding it. We say. Lean in.

My next question is: Do you want to work because you truly feel passionate about it, because you miss it, or because you don't want to depend financially on your husband? Or is it a combination of all those reasons? Regardless of why you chose to stop working or why you want to go back, the real question is: Do you feel worthy? Our self-worth dictates what we choose for ourselves and how others influence our decisions. So, for you to confront the fear, first you need to know you are worthy—worthy of being your full self, of expressing your passion through something you do, or of simply wanting to be independent.

You need to reclaim the power you gave away—not necessarily the financial power, but your inner power—especially if your decision to leave work wasn't truly authentic to you but instead influenced by social conditioning or a desire to please your husband. But you, beloved, are as worthy as all living beings. When we are not authentic to who we are, we give our power away. When we feel powerless, we feel unworthy, and we feel insignificant. From what you are saying, this is what you are truly trying to reclaim. You are trying to reclaim your free will, your ability to make your own decisions.

If you fear your husband leaving you, it may be because, on some level, you feel he doesn't fully accept you for who you truly are, but rather for the character you've been playing to please him. But my question is: Would you prefer to live a lie to keep a fragile connection? Or would you rather confront the fear, share your truth with your husband, and, if he leaves, live more authentically—because he wasn't truly married to you but to the character you were playing? However, if he stays, the bond will become deeper, and the connection between you two will be even more fulfilling. Also, you will always feel comfortable being honest, and he will feel comfortable being honest. This a much healthier relationship.

However, this can only happen when you feel worthy—worthy of even having a relationship like this, worthy of going back to work again, worthy enough to receive the first or second no from the job market and still decide to keep going. Your self-worth is what will guide your choices now. There is always a choice, because you have free will. If you feel unworthy on the first try, you'll probably self-sabotage.

So my question is: If you knew you were worthy, that everything would be provided for, that you would be taken care of, that you are safe, that you could trust a Higher Power, what would you do? This may be the Universe's way of showing you that you can create your life. However, first you need to lean into your fears, and understand that whatever happens will always be for your best. For your evolution.

Do you trust yourself to make this decision now? Do you Trust a Higher Power to hold you through this decision? If not, how can you build your confidence first so you can eventually make this choice? This is the true question of the freedom journey.

TRUTH 8

Trauma creates distortions and addictions, forming loops that are not true based on a memory. Even if they feel real, they are not in the now. When you acknowledge this, you start having Clarity to heal these patterns through Love.

Question: When I get triggered by a small situation, such as a comment or a rejection, how can I not take it personally, and how can I tell whether I'm triggered by my past?

Aiyahla: If the comment or the rejection causes you pain, you know there is a memory within you that needs to become conscious. Sometimes the memory is hidden in our subconscious and we aren't even aware it is there. Memories are always related to trauma that happened in the past. They are aspects of you that have been fragmented from wholeness. This is why they hurt. They are covered in fear and are like open wounds. When we're hurt physically, if someone touches the wound, we might scream or feel discomfort. Trauma works the same way. When someone "touches" that memory with a comment or by rejecting you, if the trauma is related to rejection, then you know you have to heal this rejection wound. The trigger is there to bring your awareness that this is something that still needs healing. This is how the law of reflection works. So, start noticing the triggers with Presence, and instead of reacting to the other person in a defensive manner, thank the Universe for the experience, because that person acted as a mirror to what you have been holding within you. When you know what triggers you, you know what still hurts you, and you can start navigating within yourself, through consciousness practices, to find the root of that trauma and heal it by bringing love to that aspect, as only Love can transform fear. You can also forgive yourself, and anyone else involved, as when we forgive, we liberate the karma, the lesson, and take full responsibility for it to be happening in your life now because now we learned what the memory was there to teach us. Never take anything personally. When someone projects onto you, they are expressing what they feel within themselves. If she rejects you, it's not because you are unworthy or lacking—it says nothing about you. It speaks only about her. In this case, just have compassion instead of judgement, as we never know what someone else might be going through. Always try to put yourself in someone else's shoes, as this will help you have more compassion instead of judgement.

Question: Where does the healing of the feminine begin?

The healing of the feminine begins in your sacral chakra, the most sensitive and sacred centre of your body. The sacral is the doorway to your feminine spirit, the place where you receive, create, and know your real worth beyond appearances.

When you carry trauma, shame, fear, or a sense of unworthiness, these energies enter and settle in your sacral. If you have experienced abuse—even the fear of abuse—or have absorbed ancestral or past-life memories of violation, your sacral becomes imprinted with these. Abuse is not only sexual or physical; it can also be psychological, moral, or financial.

This imprinting can also happen through sexual intimacy. Because you are the receiver, you naturally take in the energy of your partner. If his sacral or base chakra carries dense imprints—fear, sexual addiction, unhealed trauma—these can pass into your field. Each time you share your body, you are not only sharing love but also absorbing energy. If your partner is not open and clear, you may carry his distortions inside of you long after the act itself.

This is why it is so important to bring consciousness to whomever you choose as a sexual partner—not as a restriction but as an act of self-love. Sexual liberation is sacred. It is vital that you feel free in your body and sovereign in your desires. But true freedom comes with awareness: the knowing that your sacral is your temple, and that whomever you allow in will influence your energy.

This Truth is rarely spoken about in our world. We celebrate the right to choose, but we do not yet teach the responsibility that comes with that choice. You can, of course, choose pleasure, adventure, and exploration, but if you choose without awareness, you may unknowingly take on the burdens of others, and your sacral may close as a form of protection. This causes immense trauma.

When your sacral closes, your feminine spirit begins to withdraw. You disconnect from your heart and lose touch with your true worth. You may start to believe you are not enough, that you are less valuable, less deserving. In this emptiness, you begin to look for value outside yourself—through appearance, relationships, career, possessions, or luxury. You begin measuring your worth by the material world. You try to fill what feels empty within, but no external validation can restore what was lost in your inner temple. External validation is an illusion.

This is why your healing begins in the sacral. It is here that memories of abuse, fear, and shame are stored. It is here that your self-worth either collapses or is reborn. When your sacral is purified and filled with Light again, your feminine spirit returns to harmony with your heart. You remember your true value, and your creativity and intuition awaken once more.

So if you find yourself feeling unworthy or endlessly seeking validation from the outside world, it is your sacral that is calling. Begin there, for within the sacral chakra lies not only your deepest wound but also your greatest power. As you clear what has been stored, you liberate your creativity and awaken your true worth and unique gifts.

TRUTH 9

The feminine is Love, creative, giving and receiving. The masculine is Light, wisdom, planning and action. Everything else is a traumatic distortion that needs Light and Love.

Question: I constantly feel my friends are competing with me, as well as moms at school and other women at work. Some of these women are leaders, and I don't understand why they still compete with me.

Aiyahla: When a woman feels insignificant, even if she is a successful leader, she carries a wounded feminine. External success does not mean she holds her inner power. To maintain the character of the "powerful woman," she competes with anyone who might reflect to her the belief she does not want to face—that inside, she feels insignificant. This can also show up as manipulation or envy. Because she is not feeling Love for herself—she is not nurturing herself with Love—she carries the illusion that others can take what she has. So she constantly needs to act as the "big boss," to hold the mask of power, fearing that if someone discovers her wound of insignificance, she will lose everything. This is not true, beloved, because she can never lose what she truly is: Love, Light, and Creative Power. She has only forgotten this because her wound of insignificance, often rooted in a deep trauma of abuse in this life or another, has closed her heart. When the heart closes, she forgets her true nature.

She craves authenticity but is too afraid to show it. What she truly needs is healing.

The same happens within mom groups. Here, there may also be another wound: If they once longed for a successful career and gave it up, and you didn't, your presence may trigger their frustration wound. It is not about you. Their reaction is not a reflection of your worth but of their unhealed feminine. Until they heal, they are unable to fully receive Love, to create abundantly, to give without fear.

If you are standing in your empowered feminine—radiant, loving, filled with presence—your light naturally reflects what they have not yet reclaimed within themselves. That is why they react, not because you have done anything wrong. You are simply reflecting their own forgotten potential. This is the law of reflection.

So the invitation for you is to hold compassion. Put yourself in their shoes. Forgive whatever they did or said, for they were acting from distortion, from their wound, not from the Truth of their being, which is always Love.

If their reaction hurts you, you might also need to discover if there is any wound you might need to take care, as when there is pain, there is unconscious wounds. As situations like this only hurt when you in some level believe it is true to you. The universe is precise, and is perfect and brings to our life experiences for us to learn and free ourselves. Always.

Question: I can't commit to a relationship with a woman because I fear I will lose my freedom.

Aiyahla: This is just an illusion many men tell themselves. A relationship is not a prison, it is a commitment that can be established in a way both people agree to. There are no fixed rules for a relationship, as society imposes. The "rules" are simply cultural conditionings. What truly matters is that you both respect the agreement you choose together. Some couples agree to open relationships, where they can see other people. Others choose exclusivity. Neither is right or wrong. Consciousness is beyond duality. Both are valid if chosen in authenticity, not from fear.

When a man says he will lose his freedom in a relationship, what he is really afraid of is losing himself. It is often an excuse to avoid entering a relationship, because relationships inevitably mirror our wounds, fears, and vulnerabilities. That can feel very threatening, especially for men who have been conditioned to maintain the character of the "perfect man." When such a man enters a relationship with a woman in her empowered feminine, she will not be attracted to the mask, to the character. She will see through it. That leaves him feeling vulnerable, naked, stripped of the armour he has built around his heart. This is what he is actually scared of: being seen for who he really is. However, this is also what he craves the most.

Beloved, this is not punishment. This is the medicine. It is exactly what is needed to empower the masculine. Men who are in their wounded masculine often become either insensitive and detached or controlling, sometimes even violent. If they enter a relationship with a woman in her wounded feminine, the dynamic easily turns into one of control and passiveness. This is common, but it is not healthy, as it feeds each party's wounds instead of empowering each individual into wholeness.

True power emerges when both the feminine and masculine are healed. Then, the man no longer needs to be in control to feel powerful, because he *is* power. The woman no longer needs saving, because she has already saved herself by taking back her power.

When the masculine remains wounded, and a woman refuses to comply with his need for control, some men escalate their behaviour—sometimes to moral, psychological, or financial abuse, and in more extreme cases, to physical or sexual violence. All of these are distortions of false power.

In your case, the fear of losing freedom likely points to something else: The moment a relationship becomes serious and real responsibilities arise, your wounded pattern of insensitivity may surface as a way to avoid facing your deepest wounds. This is a common defence mechanism, but it blocks intimacy, and it blocks Love.

Sometimes it shows up as addictive behaviours, especially sexual addictions. Because deep down, the man who becomes too insensitive is not actually looking for sex, he is looking for Love. Yet he confuses Love with fleeting pleasure, which never nourishes the Soul, but numbs the senses. True Love is the medicine he craves and is found only when he allows himself to be vulnerable, when he lets himself be seen, when he chooses to heal and stops running away.

Question: Do people who are born female also carry masculine energy within them? And do people who are born male also carry feminine energy? Why is the feminine more outwardly expressed in women and the masculine more expressed in men? How can we empower both the masculine and the feminine within ourselves?

Aiyahla: Yes, beloved, all beings carry both the feminine and masculine within. Yet women often incarnate to heal and empower their feminine spirit, while men often incarnate to heal and empower their masculine spirit. Christ revealed to me that the feminine journey begins in passivity—a state in which the feminine is often silenced, disconnected, and waiting for life to act upon her. As she begins to awaken, she moves into reactivity—blaming, becoming overly emotional, or sometimes becoming manipulative—as her wounds rise to be seen. If she continues the journey, she learns self-responsibility, discovering that her worth and power are not outside of her. When she roots her heart in Mother Earth, opens her womb of creation, and forgives, she steps into her true empowerment, embodying Love, receptivity, intuition, compassion, and Creative Power in flow. This is when her healing is complete when she starts serving other with her gifts. As in this stage she is ready to give and receive fully.

For the masculine, the path is different. The wounded masculine often begins in disconnection—numb, unable to feel, pushing emotions away, seeking power outside himself. This easily moves into control—domination, suppression, the use of violence or intellect without Love. When he awakens, he learns integrity and responsibility, understanding that true strength protects, not oppresses. When he allows the Light of Presence to flow down through his crown into his body, he discovers clarity of mind, vision, and direction, as well as the higher masculine gifts of truth, wisdom, and action aligned with the heart.

Together, the feminine and masculine within every being are seeking union. The feminine must rise in Love from Earth; the masculine must descend in Light from Heaven. When they meet in the heart, the Spirit is free. This is the beginning of Divine Union, where the Holy Spirit activates in your heart, and you live no longer through separation but as Oneness.

TRUTH 10

Judgement is a defence mechanism. Transform it into compassion.
Judgement distorts your vision and creates karma. Compassion aligns
you with Divine Justice, restoring balance through Love, not fear.

**Question: How can I stop myself from judging my father when I
see him doing horrible things to others, knowing that his wealth
comes from exploiting people who have nothing?**

Aiyahla: Judgement is a reaction of the lower mind when it feels unsafe
because it does not see the full picture. The lower mind works with
fragments of reality, and when something feels disturbing or unjust,
it tries to protect you by fixing the situation into right and wrong. We
can only perceive the whole through the higher mind—a state of consciousness that allows us to see from many angles at once. This is what
I call the Eagle's Eye. From this perspective, you can acknowledge that
what you are witnessing is hurtful and harmful, while also remembering that you do not know the full story that shaped your father's inner
world. If your father is doing things that hurt others, this does not
make those actions right. Harm is harm. And yet, from a wider perspective, such actions often arise from deep inner fragmentation—pain
that may come from his own experiences, from family patterns, from
wounds carried across generations, and cultural and systemic conditioning. It can also be a survival mechanism. The Truth is we don't
know the full picture. This does not excuse harm; it simply helps you

have a higher understanding, as he might be acting unconsciously. And unconsciousness creates more unconsciousness. When we judge from the lower mind, we enter separation. And separation creates karma, not as punishment, but as the natural law of cause and effect. What we hold in judgment keeps us energetically bound to it.

Compassion is not agreement. Compassion is Clarity. When you choose compassion, you do not deny what you see, nor do you abandon your values. You simply refuse to let fear close your heart. Discernment remains fully present, you do not try to control what your father believes or does, but you remain anchored in your own Truth. You may even choose distance if the situation affects you deeply. Compassion simply means you do not withdraw Love from your own being in order to survive the situation. This is the true meaning of compassion: allowing Love to keep flowing while remaining grounded in discernment. Forgiveness, when it becomes possible, does not mean saying that what he does is acceptable. It means his actions no longer disturb your inner state or pull you into judgment and pain. As long as his actions affect you deeply, it simply points to a wound within you that is asking for healing—not because you are wrong, but because something within you is still holding the experience through unconscious expectations. You can choose to heal this through the freedom journey of consciousness and creativity now, rather than carrying it forward unconsciously. Your father will walk his own path of learning in his own time, according to the law of cause and effect. What we do to others, we eventually come to understand— not as punishment, but as balance—because true freedom only comes when all fragmentation has been brought back into awareness and Love. Your work is not to judge or justify, but to transform judgment into compassion, and fear into clarity, so you can remain free.

Question: I consider myself a very spiritual person, and I've noticed I am starting to judge people who are less conscious than I am. Why does this happen?

Aiyahla: When you judge others for being less conscious, you are simply affirming to yourself that you fear being like them. This shows that you probably still have some lessons to learn before becoming fully free. Unconscious people appear as mirrors for you, to dissolve the fear of losing consciousness, and this is why they trigger your judgement. But when you judge them, you are creating karma, which you will need to dissolve until you learn the lesson: that anyone can have moments of unconsciousness, including you, until they reach a point of ascension that only happens after the seventh dimension.

So, by judging others, in truth, you are judging yourself. This actually moves you further away from freedom, as you are holding a distortion upon others and upon yourself. When you transform judgement into compassion, you allow yourself to learn from the trigger rather than act on it. Compassion means withholding love from no one—not from those who remain unconscious, and not from yourself in the moments when you, too, fall into unconsciousness. Until ascension, this is the practice: seeing every moment as an opportunity to choose compassion over judgement, to choose Love over fear.

Our living experience, our daily life, is our new temple—a place to practice consciousness and creativity in the present moment.

Question: When I look at the world and see so much violence—war, abuse, cruelty—I feel overwhelmed and confused. How can people commit such harmful acts and still believe they are right, or justified? How do we understand this without excusing the harm, but also without losing compassion?

Aiyahla: This is a very important question, beloved, because it touches the heart of how human beings act—and how we learn to see clearly without closing our hearts.

Every action a human being takes is arising from three parts operating at the same time. These parts are always present together—never separate.

First, there is a part of the being that believes it is innocent. This part does not feel it is doing something wrong. It feels justified, misunderstood, or simply convinced that its actions are necessary.

This is not moral innocence—it is perceived innocence. From inside that part, the person believes they are right, or at least believes they have no other option.

Second, there is a part that feels out of control. This part is driven by fear, trauma, survival, memory, and pain that has not been integrated. It is not responding to the present moment, but to the past replaying itself in the now. This is where distortion happens. This is where the nervous system is overwhelmed, and behaviour becomes reactive rather than conscious.

And third, there is the part that is making choices. This part carries responsibility. Free will is real. Actions have consequences. But these choices are being made under the pressure of the other two parts—the part that believes it is innocent, and the part that feels out of control.

These three parts are always acting together.

When we only see responsibility, we harden and judge, and our heart closes. When we only see innocence, we bypass harm and accountability. When we only see trauma and loss of control, we collapse into helplessness.

But when we can hold all three at once, something profound happens: clarity appears without hatred. Compassion appears without naivety. Responsibility is upheld without dehumanising anyone.

This does not excuse violence. It explains how violence becomes possible.

Healing begins when trauma loops are seen for what they are—memories acting as if they are happening now. When these loops are met with awareness and Love, rather than denial or projection, they can dissolve. And when they dissolve, free will becomes clearer, choice becomes more conscious, and behaviour begins to change.

So when you look at the world and ask, *How can this be happening?*—the answer is not that humanity is evil. It is that humanity is often acting from unhealed memory, believing it is innocent, feeling out of control, and choosing without awareness.

This is why the freedom journey is not only a personal solution, it is as important as world freedom.

TRUTH 11

Forgive everyone and yourself. No matter what has happened, you have no one to blame. Forgiveness dissolves karmic loops and liberates you from the victim story, returning you to your inner power and true essence: freedom.

Question: How can I forgive someone who abused me?

Aiyahla: Forgiveness does not mean excusing harm, denying what happened, or minimising the impact of abuse. Abuse is real, and it causes real wounds. Forgiveness is not about the other person—it is about reclaiming your own power. You were a victim in that moment, and it is important to honour that truth. And that moment belongs to the past. In the present, you are here, breathing, alive. You are not only a victim of what happened—you are also a survivor. Feel how these words shift your energy and vibration. *Survivor* carries movement, strength, and life.

When we remain identified only with victim consciousness long after the event has passed, we can begin to feel as though life is happening *to* us rather than *for* us. This does not mean you are weak, wrong, or responsible for what was done to you. It simply means that the wound has not yet been fully integrated. At your own pace, when you feel safe enough, you may gently begin to ask—not *why* this happened, but *what* this experience is asking to awaken within you now. Not to justify the abuse, but to reclaim authorship of your life.

Shifting from blame to learning does not mean blaming yourself. It means choosing not to let the past define your future. As long as the story remains charged with pain, it continues to hold power over you. Forgiveness becomes possible only when you are ready to let go of the past and move into freedom. Forgiveness does not mean trusting the person, reconnecting with them, or allowing them access to you again. It simply means that the memory no longer wounds you in the present.

When forgiveness arises, it is often because you can finally see that the harm came from unconsciousness and unresolved trauma—not because that makes it acceptable, but because it makes it no longer yours to carry. Holding onto blame keeps the nervous system locked in fear. Releasing it allows Love to return to the places where fear took over. This is how the pattern ends.

Forgiveness frees *you*. Divine Justice, the law of cause and effect, will bring each soul the lessons they need to learn in their own time, not as punishment, but as balance. Your role is not to carry their burden or complete their healing. Your role is to come back into wholeness. Abuse is never acceptable. Safety, boundaries, and self-protection are essential. Forgiveness is not about condoning harm, it is about choosing freedom, so the past no longer dictates who you are now and the future you are creating.

Question: I find it very hard to forgive someone who causes me or someone I love harm, and I normally try to find justice in court or by my own means. Why is this?

Aiyahla: Beloved, we normally think justice is doing the same thing to the other person has done to us. We have been conditioned to believe that if we do nothing, we are being weak or foolish. But in truth, when we react in this way, we are simply reacting from a wound, a distortion, and we end up trying to reclaim our power through violence or anger. In reality, this only creates more pain for you and for the other person, generating more karma. Instead of reclaiming power, you are actually giving your power away to the person who hurt you.

Let me give an example that is quite common amongst humanity, which is also a reason why we need contracts. One person agrees with another: "You give me this, and I give you that." For instance, you agree to perform services for their company for twelve months, and in exchange, they agree to pay you for twelve months. In the middle of the year, they decide they don't want your services anymore. In this case, you don't need to be violent with them or hold blame. You can, however, hold them responsible by pointing out that this is a matter of integrity and is not in line with what has been agreed.

Integrity comes from Clarity. Judgement comes from blame. This is the big difference. To have integrity means your heart is still open, while to judge means you are acting from fear.

Whatever the situation, forgiveness means you free yourself from carrying the pain and the blame that the experience brought to you. It means you see the experience as a teacher, instead of seeing yourself as a victim. So the question to ask is: *What did I learn from this?* Perhaps you learned you needed a better contract, or you need to focus on working with people and companies with values more aligned to yours. When the next contract comes, you will be more conscious with the terms, and you'll consider not only the financial return it offers but also whether it aligns with your values. Without the previous experience, you would not have learned this lesson. So, in Truth, the past experience was a blessing in disguise. We can be grateful for all experiences in our lives.

Everything in life is a blessing if we see it through the Eagle's Eye. When you hold blame, you are, in fact, holding yourself, or the people in your life, as victims. When you do this, you are affirming to the Universe that this lesson is still unlearned. Therefore, the Universe will bring you more situations like the one you just experienced so you can truly learn the lesson. When you shift from blame to integrity, you learn the lesson, and the cycle ends. When the cycle ends, you dissolve karma with it. So remember to trust whatever life brings, beloved, as the Universe always wants the best for you.

TRUTH 12

Trust that everything is unfolding for your highest good. Keep your heart open, be grateful, and allow the magic to reveal itself.

Question: How can I trust everything is unfolding for my highest good if I lost my house and my partner in a natural disaster?

Aiyahla: Beloved, what you have been through is profoundly painful. Losing your home and someone you love in such a sudden way shakes the very foundations of safety, identity, and meaning. Before anything else, meet yourself with compassion. Allow yourself to grieve. Let the pain move through you, rather than asking yourself to be strong too quickly. Grief is not something to overcome; it is something to be honoured. When pain is acknowledged and felt, it can move and soften over time. When it is pushed away or numbed, it often settles into the body as trauma. So allow yourself to feel, without judgement, and at your own pace.

At the same time, I gently invite you not to lose trust in the greater intelligence of life, even if that trust feels fragile right now. Trust does not mean understanding, approving, or pretending this did not hurt. It simply means staying open to the possibility that Life has not abandoned you, even in this moment. When trust collapses completely, faith collapses with it, and we can become disconnected from our own inner light. It is natural, in moments like this, to feel powerless or like a victim of circumstances. But if we remain there for too long, we lose access to our ability to respond, to rebuild, and to take the small, practical steps that support us—finding shelter, accepting help, tending to our emotional needs, one breath and one day at a time.

The mind often looks for something to blame—a person, nature, fate—because blame can momentarily soothe the shock. Yet blame does not truly heal; it only keeps us bound to the event. What life is asking of you now is not responsibility for what happened, but responsibility for how you hold yourself through it. This is not about forcing meaning or turning pain into something positive. It is about choosing, gently and again and again, whether this experience will close your heart or slowly open it to a deeper dimension of trust.

There is always something to learn from life, even in moments we would never choose. One of my beloved ancestors lived through the Holocaust and endured unimaginable loss. And yet, she chose—again and again—to remain anchored in Love and Light, not because the suffering was justified, but because she trusted that her soul was still on a path of liberation. We are all, in different ways, learning how to return to the Light through the human experience.

If, in time, you allow this experience to teach you—without rushing the process—you may discover an inner strength, tenderness, and clarity that did not exist before. Not instead of the pain, but alongside it. Trust does not mean bypassing grief. It means letting grief walk with you, while you remain open to the unknown. Choose trust when you can. Choose love when it feels possible. Choose light even if it flickers. The universe holds you more than you know, and support often arrives in unexpected forms when the heart remains open. Remember: even now, you have choice—not over what happened, but over how you walk forward from here.

TRUTH 13

Stop predicting your future based on your past. The only moment that truly exists is the eternal now. Trying to predict the future keeps you bound to old beliefs and closes the door to miracles and the quantum field of limitless possibilities.

Question: How can I stop predicting the future based on the past, as this is what protects me from hurting myself?

Aiyahla: Beloved, this is what your ego wants you to believe, because the ego's knowledge is limited to what it has experienced. This keeps you repeating the same hurtful patterns over and over again, because in truth, you are never learning the lesson. When you stop trying to predict your future based on your past, you stop limiting the possibilities that can happen in your life. They are infinite, and much greater than what your fearful ego can ever imagine.

However, this can only happen when we raise our vibration, as our ability to access limitless possibilities depends on our frequency. The possibilities you attract are always the ones that match your vibration. If you are holding fear, you will attract a lower possibility. If you are holding love, passion, excitement, trust, and joy, you will attract a higher possibility. This is the law of grace: What you ask for, you shall receive.

So stop limiting your potential by holding to the past, and start expanding your consciousness by learning from every experience as if it was a blessing, because it is. From that space, you will receive much more than you could ever imagine, beyond time and space, as this is the place where miracles happen. And yes, miracles are real, but they are only true for you if you believe they are, as our beliefs are our greatest limitation.

What truly protects you from hurting yourself is not repeating the past but keeping your heart open and raising your vibration. In fact, what keeps you in hurtful loops is exactly the repetition of the same patterns.

Question: What is the unified field and how do I access it?

Aiyahla: The unified field is the field of Oneness, from which we all Source. It is what some call God, while others call it the quantum field or the Field of Life. It is the Light, Love, and Power of Creation. You can access it by tuning into yourself, as the Higher Power is within you and within every being. God is in the trees, the mountains, the ocean, the animals, the people. God is also in the void, in the spaces we think are empty.

By turning within—through stillness, breathing, meditation, or art—you quiet your mind and tune into your heart. This is how you consciously connect with the unified field. In truth, you are always connected to it—but most often unconsciously. This is why you tend to create your life from the ego, repeating the past and projecting the future, instead of from a conscious space where limiting beliefs dissolve and you can feel the interconnection directly.

Traumas are what disconnect us from our divinity, creating the illusion of separation. Only the freedom journey makes us aware of the Truth: that we are never separate, that whatever you do here, in this very moment, has an effect on the skies, on the earth, and on other people. We are all One in the Truth of Oneness. Separation is the biggest illusion, as well as the cause of the greatest pain.

TRUTH 14

Release attachment to external power. True power lives within, and it is your creative force, the artist within you.

Question: How can you say external power is not power when we see all these powerful systems that profit by making all the decisions that affect our world?

Aiyahla: External power is only power for the ego. It feeds the ego, but it never fulfils you. Most people who hold financial or influential power are often the people who feel the emptiest, because their egos grow so big, they lose touch with the truth of their Soul. This is not always the case, as there are some who carry external power and also cultivate inner power. In the society we live in today, this is still rare, but soon we will see more of this. As external power can also reflect inner power in the most beautiful way. This is the frequency the world is shifting into. We are limitless when we remember who we truly are.

The difference is this: External power alone, without inner power, creates control; inner power creates freedom. External power alone is built on fear—fear of losing, fear of not being enough, fear of not being seen. It uses force, manipulation, and domination to maintain itself. This is why the world looks the way it does today, with systems profiting from suffering, because they are rooted in wounded masculine energy (control, separation, insensitivity). Because fear always needs more to feel safe, external power is never satisfied. It is temporary, fragile, and can be taken away in an instant.

Inner power is eternal. It does not come from what you own or what position you hold but from who you truly are: Love, Light, and Creative Power. When you act from inner power, you don't need to control. You don't need to dominate. You inspire. You liberate. You create. You serve. This is power that can never be taken away, because it is God within you.

Gandhi, for example, was a very powerful man, not because he held great financial resources but because his inner power was vast. By embodying integrity, Love, and non-violence, he transformed that inner power into influential power that liberated an entire nation. That is the true alchemy of power: when the inner aligns with the outer, not to serve the ego but to serve humanity.

So remember, beloved, that money, influence, and recognition are simply tools, not who you are. If you are attached to them, you have no true power, because if these tools are taken away, you collapse with them. However, when you stand rooted in your inner power—the power of Love, of Light, of Creativity—you are unshakable. That is the only power that lasts. And power of influence and money in these cases are incredibly powerful for the higher good. So we must not blame money, for example, as this creates fear, shame and distortion. As money, beloved, is also God's money. The power of money, mana, is amazing, when it is used as tool for good, beyond personal gain.

Question: I have no money, no property, but I dream of creating a better life for me. Is this attaching me to external power?

Aiyahla: No, beloved, it is not. To dream of a better life for yourself is not attachment, it is creation. You are using your inner power, the artist within you, to envision a life that is more comfortable, more nurturing, more aligned with your Soul. This is a gift. The very fact that you can imagine a different reality is proof that God within you is guiding you.

You are only attaching yourself to external power if, in the present moment, you are feeling like a victim, believing that money or property will save you or prove your worth. They won't. If you are creating from the state of victimhood, you are creating from the ego, from fear, and this lowers your vibration. When you create from fear, you will only manifest a reality that matches that fear—lack, limitation, and disappointment.

When you create from Love, the vibration shifts completely. Imagining a better life is part of the creation process. The key is how you imagine it: not from lack, not from "I don't have," but from "I am worthy, I am whole, I am ready to receive." Creation is not about fixing yourself, because you are not broken. It is about expressing your wholeness into form.

So, beloved, when you dream, dream through your heart. Feel that you are as worthy as any other being on this planet of living in beauty, joy, abundance, and peace. Drop any limiting belief that says you don't deserve it. These beliefs are illusions, inherited from cultural conditionings, from ancestral wounds, or from past experiences. They are not the Truth. The Truth is that you are Love, Light, and Creative Power, and the field of Oneness is always available to you.

Then, surrender. For when you surrender your dreams to God, to Source, to the field of Oneness, you step out of control and into Trust. This is when miracles happen. Creation is a dance between your inner vision and Divine timing. You plant the seed with your imagination, but you water it with trust, presence, and gratitude.

So continue to dream, beloved. It is not external power you are seeking; it is your inner power that is awakening. Keep dreaming through Love, and the path will unfold before you. Reflecting your inner world.

Question: Why are we so divided? Why are we fighting against one another? Why is the world in such chaos?

Aiyahla: Most of humanity still holds onto the idea that if they give power to others, they are losing power themselves. This is why there is so much separation between nations, religions, races, ethnicities, genders, and even between generations. Humanity carries the illusion that power is limited. But the Truth is that power is limitless. The fear of losing power, the fear of being less, of not surviving, is what has created most of our wars, most of the violence, most of the chaos we see in the world today.

When we remember that we are all divine, and that the universe is abundant, we no longer need to hold power over anyone. This illusion of scarcity and control is what separation consciousness feeds on. Most of the systems of power that humanity live under today were created from the perspective of the wounded masculine (control, domination, separation, violence). This is what duality has looked like for thousands of years.

Yet, as Earth shifts in vibration, the illusion of false power is breaking. Only those who hold true power, inner power, will be able to let go of the things they hold onto the most. This can only be done through Love, the energy the feminine brings into the equation. For centuries, the feminine has been perceived as weak, but the empowered feminine is not weak. She is the one who nurtures the masculine back into balance, who can heal the very systems that are now collapsing.

Healing does not mean the feminine overpowers the masculine; it means restoring harmony between them. Only through Love can we unite what has been fragmented by trauma. Only by opening our hearts can we collaborate more, trust more, share more, have compassion, and forgive. For we can only move beyond the current state of chaos if we forgive one another and stop trying to find justice by creating more violence.

Beloved, when the masculine and feminine are finally in harmony, the world will look very different. We will no longer compete for resources but share them. Nations will no longer be divided by fear but united by vision. Families will no longer be torn apart by the need for control but healed through presence and compassion. We will see leaders rise who act not from domination but from service. We will see women empowered in their Love and men empowered in their Light. Together, we will build systems that are not based on the fear of loss but on the Truth of abundance. This is the future already being born within us, as we are Powerful Creators, artists, and this is the Free Free World we bring to the now. Creation happens in the present, not in the future. So start living life as if this is already happening, and you will start elevating your frequency, since fear, beloved, is only real to the ego. However, it is not real to the Soul. Remember this every time you feel fear when you see the news, when you feel hurt, and when you want to blame. Shift your focus and bring it to the present moment, feel your heartbeat, and remember we are One.

TRUTH 15

Surrender in eternal gratitude and let go of controlling outcomes. Control is an illusion; when you surrender and become grateful, you align your life with your highest potential and Soul Truth.

Question: I fear that if I let go of control, my life will become a mess and the worst-case scenarios will happen.

Aiyahla: Beloved one, control is just an illusion. In Truth, the more you try to control, the more you interfere. Control is only a mechanism of the ego, used to keep you safe, but it is not the Truth. When Yasmine tried to control her family by being perfect, she didn't save anyone, she only wounded herself. When you try to control other people's reactions, or every detail of your own life, you are lowering your vibration and living in fear, for control is always a reaction of fear. When we fear, we control. When we trust, we surrender. When we surrender, we allow miracles to happen. We align with our Soul's Truth instead of the illusion of what we think is best, based on the stories our ego tells us.

To begin letting go of control, try this simple practice: When you notice yourself controlling, pause. Place both hands on your heart and take three deep breaths. With each inhale, say to yourself, "I receive." With each exhale, say, "I let go." As you breathe this way, you are reminding your whole being that you don't need to carry everything alone. You are supported by the field of Oneness, by God within you. Slowly, your body relaxes, your mind softens, and your heart opens to trust.

Every time you choose trust over control, you shift your vibration. Little by little, you will notice that life does not fall apart when you surrender. It flows with more harmony, grace, and beauty than your ego could ever imagine. This is where the true miracles are—when Soul takes the lead.

Question: When I am creating something for my life, I still feel I am trying to control how it will happen, and I feel this is why I am not manifesting it in my life.

Aiyahla: Yes, beloved, this is exactly why you are not manifesting your creation. Just like the ego tries to predict the future based on the past, it also tries to control the outcome of your creations. Control is always a sign of fear. When there is fear, there is a lower vibration in your field that doesn't match the frequency you need to be in to manifest your creation.

We can only manifest effortlessly—without building the house brick by brick through human force and within the limits of time and space—when we fully surrender control of *how* it will happen, *when* it will happen, and *through whom* it will happen. When you fully surrender, it doesn't mean you don't act at all; it means you act as if it has already happened. You live in the present moment as though it has already unfolded. By doing this, you feel the joy of that creation, and you feel the people around you receiving all they are meant to receive. You feel it all. You feel gratitude for all you already have. When you think and feel as if it already exists in the present, you are helping (instead of interfering) the Universe to manifest it. Your trust keeps your vibration so high that you stop controlling and you start embodying it.

This is the difference between creating through the ego, which fears, controls, and limits, and creating through the Soul, which surrenders, trusts, and allows miracles to unfold.

Question: I hate to lose control because it takes me into the unknown.

Aiyahla: Yes, beloved, it does take you into the unknown, and many people fear the unknown exactly because they cannot control it. But what if I told you the idea of control you have now is simply an illusion? Anything can happen at any time in your life. You could lose a parent between one day and the next. You could lose the job you thought you controlled. A natural disaster could happen. You could even cross a street, get hit by a car, and die. Life is always changing and shifting. We only *think* we're controlling when, in truth, we're never controlling anything. What we're doing is keeping ourselves in a loop of the past, predicting the future, which keeps us bound to the same patterns. That gives a false sense of control, but what is truly happening is that we are avoiding the learning, avoiding the joy, avoiding anything unknown—yet the unknown often carries the greatest blessings.

The more we try to control, the more the Universe invites us to surrender. Over time, many people find their bodies developing illness because they've suppressed their authentic nature for so long—silencing themselves, tightening, holding back—that life itself begins urging them to open. Through these wake-up calls, many learn to open their hearts and become conscious of their patterns. The unknown is part of the human experience. Confront your fear and step into it now. Step by step, you will begin to surrender, to trust that everything is for your best.

TRUTH 16

Always use your gifts to serve others. When service is for the greater good, not just personal gain, abundance flows. Integrity is what aligns your gifts with your eternal flame.

Question: Why is sharing my gifts related to my abundance?

Aiyahla: Beloved, every being carries unique gifts. They were not given to you to be hidden or kept for yourself. They are seeds meant to be planted in the world, because the world needs what you carry. When you share your gifts in service of the greater good, you step into the flow of life, the Divine current of giving and receiving. You give not because you are lacking but because you are overflowing. You give not from fear but from Love. In that vibration, the Universe reflects the same abundance you are offering.

Hiding our gifts is actually the ego afraid of what people will think. When we hold our gifts back, or when we use them only for personal gain, we affirm to the Universe that there is not enough, that we must keep, protect, or control. Because the Universe responds precisely to our vibration, that belief becomes our limitation. We then live in scarcity even if our bank account is full, because scarcity is not about numbers but about the energy we hold inside.

Abundance is not measured by wealth alone. Abundance is wholeness, it is having exactly what you need, when you need it. It is the synchronicity that brings the right person to help you at the right time, the opportunity that arrives like a miracle, the love that embraces you when you thought you were alone. Abundance is joy flowing through your heart. It fulfils your purpose. It is the embrace of a Soul family, the inspiration of creativity, the safety of having what sustains you, and the freedom to serve without fear.

Money is simply one form abundance takes. It is a tool. True abundance is the flow of Life itself moving through you when you align with your heart and share your gifts. The more you share them from Love, the more the Universe multiplies them, for you cannot outgive God. What you give in Love returns to you tenfold, because abundance is the natural state of Oneness.

Question: Why is serving others so important?

Aiyahla: Beloved, as we serve others, we are also empowering ourselves. Service is what truly fulfils us because it aligns us with our Soul's purpose. When we give from the heart, we step out of the small story of *me* and into the vast reality of *we*. Christ revealed that service is part of our freedom journey, because through it, we dissolve separation. You can only be fully empowered and free when you feel you have so much within you that you also have enough to give. When you serve, you are affirming to the Universe: *I am abundant, I am overflowing, I am Love in action.* This vibration draws even more Light, Love, and abundance into your life.

Service is also one of the greatest medicines for the illusion of scarcity and unworthiness. Those who carry scarcity wounds often withhold their gifts, fearing there will not be enough left for themselves. But the paradox is that the more we hold back, the emptier we feel. True abundance comes not from holding back but from circulating Love. The more we give, the more we receive, not because we are seeking a reward but because giving opens our hearts to the endless flow of the unified field.

Serving others also reflects to us the truth of our significance. When you lift someone, when you ease their suffering, when you share your gifts and see another being light up because of your presence, you remember your true essence. You are not here to survive; you are here to co-create, to love, to heal, to nurture. Service frees you from the prison of the ego, because it takes you beyond your own fears and places you in the field of Love where Oneness lives.

The miracle is that as you serve, you are also served. As you heal others, you heal yourself. As you forgive others, you forgive yourself. As you give Love, you discover the infinite Love within you that never runs out. This is why Christ and all masters of Light taught service as the highest path. It is not sacrifice; it is liberation. It is the bridge between the human and the Divine.

Most importantly, service is the very doorway to purpose. Every Soul has received gifts before coming into this lifetime, not to remain hidden but to be shared with the world. You discover more gifts as you start serving. Your true purpose is always linked to service, because your gifts are not only for you but for the healing, growth, and liberation of others. When you share them in Love, you embody why you came to Earth. You become the vessel through which God's infinite creativity flows into the world. In that, you discover the greatest abundance of all: the joy of living in alignment with your divine purpose.

A CLOSING LETTER

Beloved Reader,

What an honour it has been to walk this journey with you to its close. Together, we have touched upon some of the most sensitive territories of the human experience, and I am deeply grateful for your trust, your courage, and your openness.

As you integrate what you have read, I invite you not to receive these words at face value, but to honour your own relationship with your Soul and to follow the guidance of your heart. Different parts of this book may meet you at different moments along your path. Each time you return to them, you may receive something new—layer by layer, in alignment with what you are ready to hold.

The Sixteen Truths of Freedom you have encountered are living codes understood by the Soul, not the ego, and they can be embodied through daily life if you feel guided to do so. One way to ground them is to practise a single truth each week, observing how it mirrors itself in your thoughts, choices, and experiences. When challenges arise, you may find it helpful to return to the truth of the week and allow it to reveal a more conscious, loving, or liberating way of responding.

Another way to work with the Sixteen Truths is simply to return to them when life unfolds unexpectedly. Read them gently, and allow a different perspective to emerge—one rooted in compassion, awareness, and freedom.

These truths are not here to instruct you, but to awaken you.

Your life, beloved reader, is the new temple. We are living an era of self-leadership. Trust yourself. Trust your heart. You are a profoundly beautiful being.

If you feel called to share how this journey has met you, you are welcome to write to us. Your reflections and lived wisdom are part of how this work continues to unfold.

I look forward to meeting you soon.

With all my love,
Aiyahla Lo'Qtus

This book was finished in August 2025, but Free Free is always evolving and to know more about our projects and programs please check out our websites.

www.freefreworld.org for institutional updates
www.freefreworld.com for direct programs